HITLER'S HITMEN

GUIDO KNOPP

TRANSLATED BY ANGUS MCGEOCH

SUTTON PUBLISHING

This book was first published in 1998 by C. Bertelsmann Verlag GmbH, Munich, under the title *Hitler's Helfer: Täter und Vollstrecker*.

This English translation first published in 2002 by
Sutton Publishing Limited
This paperback edition first published in 2006
Reprinted in 2007 by Sutton Publishing,
an imprint of NPI Media Group Limited
Cirencester Road · Chalford · Stroud · Gloucestershire · GL6 8PE

Research: Silke Schläfer, Jutta Dornbusch, Annette von der Heyde
Translation: Angus McGeoch

British Library Cataloguing in Publication Data
A catalogue record for this book is available from the British Library.

ISBN 978 0 7509 4288 1

Typeset in 10/12.5pt Galliard.
Typesetting and origination by
Sutton Publishing.
Printed and bound in England

CONTENTS

Picture Credits

LIST OF ILLUSTRATIONS

INTRODUCTION

CRIMINALS OF A VERY PARTICULAR KIND?

Bormann, Schirach, Freisler, Eichmann, Ribbentrop and Mengele – these six men who all assisted Hitler by executing his orders and committing his crimes – are of very varying significance. But one thing unites them: all were in thrall to Hitler or to his manic vision. They believed that wrong was right. And they became criminals without possessing the awareness that they were doing wrong.

How was this possible? Were they the Devil's Disciples who, once awoken by the kiss of their satanic master, found all their evil energy from their own resources? In other words, were they criminals of a very particular kind? Or were they perfectly normal Germans who by pure chance turned into the men we know as synonymous with a criminal dictatorship?

*

Let us start with Martin Bormann, Hitler's secretary, who, particularly in the latter years, followed his master like a shadow. At the end, the dictator called him his 'most loyal party colleague'. He remained permanently in the background, the 'grey eminence' of the Third Reich. It is easy to overlook men like him. Yet it was his very unobtrusiveness that enabled him to manipulate the levers of power almost undisturbed. For power was all Bormann was interested in. True, it was borrowed power. In order to hold and exercise this power, Bormann subordinated himself to one whose power was greater. Yet in this way the shadow was for a time the most powerful man in Europe.

He was a man with just the qualities needed by a careerist in a despotic regime: outwardly servile, brutal underneath. He was sober and calculating, brusque and domineering, tenacious, hard-working, cunning – and an intriguer. Above all he was indispensable. The dictator found it useful to take a devoted aide with him everywhere, since he liked to pepper his monologues with assignments that had to be carried out quickly and reliably. Hitler was, as we know, a lazy ruler. He found desk-work burdensome: 'A single good idea is worth a whole life spent behind a pile of papers.'

It was Bormann who handled the paperwork. He always carried a notepad and pencil in his pocket. Every task, every question, every throwaway remark was hastily noted down. This is why we also have the bustling secretary to thank for the transcription of Hitler's table talk. Bormann always intended to keep a surety in his hands. And in the Third Reich none was offered by the courts, still less by enacted legislation. The only surety was Hitler's word – even if it was dropped in between the pearl barley soup and the camomile tea.

To attempt to predict future developments and intentions from the secretly jotted-down words of the dictator, in order to follow them even before he ordains them – can there be a higher form of subordination under the absolute rule of a tyrant? If it happened that Hitler suddenly wanted to know something about an event or an individual, Bormann's staff, alerted by a brief note, if necessary in the middle of the night, had to provide what was requested. And no task was so unimportant that Bormann would not deal with it immediately and with assiduous determination. One night at 2.30, when Hitler wanted to know the market price of a hen's egg in 1901, Bormann provided him with the answer within half an hour.

'I know Bormann's a rough diamond', said Hitler, ' but everything he puts his hand to makes sense.' Bit by bit Hitler's secretary took over the dictator's financial affairs. He administered the 'German Industry Donation Fund'. Whenever Hitler needed money, he went to Bormann, be it for the building of tea-house on the Obersalzberg or to buy a new gold chain for Eva Braun.

Bormann cared nothing for honour or fame. He did not even care whether people loved him or hated him, as long his Führer went on saying: 'To win the war, I need Bormann.' For just as Bormann needed Hitler, Hitler needed him, the zealous aide, whose broad back hid anything that the 'aesthetic' Hitler no longer wanted to see. Bormann suspiciously monitored Hitler's contacts with the outside world: 'No-one gets to see the Führer except through me!' In this way Bormann was able to wield power over Hitler himself.

In all this, politics and indeed ideology were essentially foreign to him. His sombre and stolid manner allowed no feeling for any matter that had its roots in ideology. The fervour of someone like Himmler he simply found disconcerting. His strength lay in carrying out instructions, not in 'intellectual design'. National Socialism for Bormann was not a religion, merely a concept.

He nonetheless exploited Nazi ideology for his amorous adventures. The notorious womaniser dressed up his escapades in the unconvincing philosophy that in future as many German men as possible should take and gratify several wives, in order to make good the losses of war.

Hitler's shadow was, in his own way, a participant in the murder of the Jews – as the Führer's envoy to the willing executioners; as informer on them to Hitler; and as a data bank ensuring that the murderers forgot nothing and no-one.

In the last two years of the war Bormann was at the fulcrum of power. He granted and withheld his favour, praised or removed people at his whim – though always with the Führer's utterances as a Bible in his hand. His opponents were meant to realise it was dangerous to cross swords with him; wiser to cultivate his friendship.

At the very end, the secretary was in the position that he had for so long yearned: alone, of all the paladins, at his Führer's side. Beneath the concrete roof of the bunker he was closer to Hitler than ever before and closer than anyone else had been. When Hitler only held sway over a few city blocks to either side of the Reich Chancellery, his shadow had finally reached his goal. But it was no longer any good to him.

None of Hitler's henchmen was born to be a war criminal, though many turned themselves into such. Joachim Ribbentrop was aged seventeen when he went to Canada on a short visit – and stayed four years. Had he settled there, and he was close to doing so, then he would have died a respected businessman and not on the gallows at Nuremberg.

What makes a human being inhuman?

Here is a young man, considered sophisticated and charming,

with a reputation as a ladies' man who broke the heart of many a daughter of good family. Here is a successful wine-merchant, whose circle of friends included the statesman Gustav Stresemann, the white hope of German democracy.

And here also is a bigoted, arrogant jerk; the willing lackey of a diabolical tyrant, to whom he has dedicated himself, body and soul. How does one make sense of this?

Once more we are faced with that almost stereotypical experience of awakening, which Hitler liked to bestow on his paladins. Against his powerful dynamism and his pent-up hatred, there was apparently no remedy within Germany, and certainly no ambitious careerist would oppose him. Ribbentrop succumbed to the demagogue. And his thraldom lasted until 1945.

He quickly made himself useful. It was at the wine-merchant's house that, early in 1933, the critical discussions took place, which ended with Hitler's backdoor filching of power. Soon Hitler made his new man a foreign policy adviser, then his special envoy. He needed an acceptable personality from the upper reaches of society in order to convince sceptics abroad; a willing accomplice of a kind he did not yet have among the recalcitrant diplomats of the Foreign Ministry; someone from the Nazi Party who was unquestioningly committed to him.

True, Ribbentrop was certainly not without political ideas of his own, but he always subordinated them to Hitler's wishes. He never dared to contradict him, a fact which earned him Hitler's favour and protection, especially against his enemies in the Nazi Party, who accused the interloper of toadying and arrogance. 'He married his money, bought his name and swindled his way into office.'

Yet Ribbentrop was not just a lackey, he was also a skilful tactician in power politics. As early as May 1933 he joined the SS and thus linked his political destiny with that of Heinrich Himmler. This set the rules of the game: anyone who acted against Ribbentrop found he had Himmler to deal with. In return, Ribbentrop later filled key posts in the Foreign Ministry with SS people. Without these accomplices Himmler would never have been able to organise the Holocaust so methodically.

Hitler saw Ribbentrop as the great expert on Britain – a misjudgement: 'Ribbentrop, bring Britain into the Anti-

Comintern Pact for me; that would be my greatest wish!' However, as ambassador to London, Hitler's disciple did just about everything wrong that could be done wrong. He greeted King George VI with the Nazi salute and upset even those well-disposed to him with his bigoted attitudes. But not even a diplomatic genius could have made the 'Aryan brother' into an ally. The British would never have dreamed of sacrificing the tried and tested 'balance of power' for a shaky pact with a repugnant dictator.

In that case, Ribbentrop opined, it would have to be 'without Britain or against her'. After all, the important thing was 'changing the status quo in the east'. In this the lackey was less radical than his master. Revising the Versailles frontiers and adding a bit more, ideally as far as the river Bug*, would have been enough for Ribbentrop. This was a minimalist position compared to Hitler's swastika crusade for the conquest of 'living space' in the east. Nevertheless Ribbentrop only distanced himself very mildly from this mania: 'In Moscow, tell them I didn't want this war', he whispered to his Russian interpreter Bereshkov on the night of the invasion of the Soviet Union.

We know how it ended. In between, however, came the climax of a glittering career which took Ribbentrop from champagne salesman to world politician. With the Hitler–Stalin Pact, which he concluded with Molotov, the lackey pulled off a coup which banished the last fears of the Austrian gambler: 'We have always gone for broke and we will continue to go for broke.'

Yet when the first salvo of World War Two was fired by the warship *Schleswig-Holstein* into the Westerplatte fortress in Danzig, Ribbentrop's assistance was effectively no longer required. For the warlord it was now the generals who counted, not the diplomats. Ribbentrop was only needed now when conquests had to be secured by treaty, or disputes between satellite states settled with the arrogance of the mighty.

What remained, in order to prove his indispensability to his hero Hitler and patron Himmler, was the role of the willing accomplice in the Holocaust. Ribbentrop, now a general in the SS,

---

* The river Bug forms part of the frontier between Poland and the Soviet Union (now Belarus).

provided spurious diplomatic cover for the murder of the Jews in the occupied countries where this took place.

It is for this that he was to be hanged at Nuremberg. But he did not feel that he was personally guilty. Had he not simply done what his hero had instructed him to do? Had he not given warnings from time to time? Was it his fault that Hitler had not listened to him? *Vae victis*, woe to the defeated, said Ribbentrop who, to the last, never saw the light. Without Hitler, to whom he was in thrall as few others were, his existence lacked its mystical point of reference. Without Hitler, his henchman Ribbentrop was lost.

Hitler's youth leader, Baldur von Schirach, submitted a confession of guilt at Nuremberg: 'I am guilty of having educated the young for a man who was a murderer millions of times over. I believed in this man. That is all I can say in my defence.' He nonetheless received a 20-year sentence.

Schirach was never a fanatical Nazi. He possessed neither the diabolical gifts of a Goebbels, the cruelty of a Mengele, nor the book-keeping meticulousness of an Eichmann. Yet when it came to gaining Hitler's favour he was certainly assiduous, vain and ingratiating. The cosmopolitan intellectual from Weimar spoke of Hitler in the same breath as Goethe and thus acquired the role of a 'Sorcerer's Apprentice', who could not rid himself of the spirits he himself had conjured up.

But like Ribbentrop, Schirach could have taken a different route. His mother was American and in the late 1920s her brother, a wealthy Wall Street banker, invited the young Baldur to join his firm. Schirach turned him down. He had long since succumbed to other temptations. Shirach gave his soul to Hitler, in order to serve him by capturing the souls of others: '*Mein Führer*, I will build you the greatest youth organisation that Germany has ever seen.' And he did. Before the war six million *Hitlerjungen* obeyed his command. 'Our flag means more than death'; 'War has preserved us for war'; these lines from Schirach's poetry soon gained a tragic significance. All the same, the leader of youth was never a part of it, Hitler's *Hitler-Junge* was never really popular with the *Hitlerjugend*. More aesthetic than ascetic, he preferred luxury hotels and restaurant menus to tents and pea soup.

Schirach was not the back-slapping type, more of a dreamy loner. Lacking the skills to be a seducer of youth, Schirach used Hitler to seduce the young. In this his commitment was total. Schirach celebrated Goebbels' Führer-worship with even less inhibition than its inventor: 'Thou art Germany's future, thou alone.' He passed on to the young that wonderfully thrilling feeling of being part of a secret brotherhood. He persuaded the young that they were quite simply unique and destined to be the future leaders of 'Germany, the world power'. To him Hitler Youth leaders were 'priests of the National Socialist faith'. Anyone who voiced a criticism of their orders was a criminal: 'That is why the *Hitlerjunge* submits silently to the orders of his leaders, even if they are directed against him personally.'

No-one can claim that Schirach made a secret of the aims of the Hitler Youth. 'We are marching to the Führer. If he so wishes, we will also march *for* him.' That was for the boys. To the girls he said: 'You are the mothers of the new generation.' What this really meant was that they had to produce cannon-fodder for the Führer.

The invasion of Poland was to prove that Schirach's educational methods had borne fruit. For years he had preached to the Hitler Youth about patriotism and willingness to fight, obedience to orders and the spirit of self-sacrifice. Now the moment had come. 'We were afraid we would arrive too late', one of the volunteers remembers. What was there left for the *Reichsjugendführer* to do but volunteer himself? For six months he played at being a soldier, then Hitler appointed him Gauleiter of Vienna, where the euphoria of the *Anschluss* with Germany had already evaporated and the tense atmosphere led to occasional clashes between the 'Ostmarkers' (Austrians) and the 'Prussians'. Schirach's task there was to do what he did best: reconciling differences and putting on a good display.

In this he was certainly successful. While all over the rest of Europe people were fighting, murdering and dying, Schirach put on poetry-readings, opera premières and drama festivals. In Vienna the war was a long way away. Only the Holocaust was close at hand. Schirach did not have a fanatical hatred of Jews, but saw himself nonetheless as 'consciously anti-Semitic'. 'I considered the removal of the Jews from government positions as an absolute necessity.' As this 'removal' progressed and took on barbaric forms, the aesthete found it painful. 'I believed one could be anti-Semitic in a decent way.' However, Schirach never felt the urge to protest about maltreatment or worse. On the contrary; as Gauleiter of Vienna he played an early and prominent part in the deportations: 'I still have Jews in Vienna, who just have to be taken away.' Vienna had to be 'cleansed of Jews'; that meant transports to Poland, supposedly for 'resettlement in small towns'. In fact they were going to the gas-chambers.

Throughout his life Schirach maintained that he first learned of the murder of the Jews from Himmler's Poznan speech to the Gauleiters in October 1943. Up till then he had believed Hitler's assurances. 'The Jews are being deported. They are being taken from Vienna to new settlement areas.'

We do not believe this. No later than May 1942 the Gauleiter of Vienna must have found out from Gauleiter Greiser of Poznan what was being done to the Jews in the *Gerneralgouvernment*, German-administered Poland.

Did Hitler see Schirach as his 'crown prince'? Unlikely. Even the repeatedly cited congratulatory telegram to Schirach on his 35th birthday in 1942 is no proof of that. In it Hitler stated that Schirach was 'the best horse in his stable'. But he had said the same thing to Ribbentrop, word for word. Hitler was surrounded by 'best horses'. Things came to a sudden end when Schirach's wife Henriette complained, in front of the assembled company at Hitler's mountain retreat, about the treatment of Jewish women in Holland. 'He can't want that', she had said to Baldur. You bet he wanted it! 'What business is it of yours?' Hitler, who had been a witness at her wedding, shouted at her. 'You must learn to hate!'

The shamefaced Schirach had to suffer for his wife's unprecedented protest. 'The Führer has a very low opinion of Schirach,' Goebbels noted with satisfaction in his diary. 'Viennese life has made the man soft.'

In the last two years of the war the mood of the *Hitler-Junge* swung between the gloomy acceptance that the war was lost anyway, and fanatical efforts to attract, through occasional acts of toughness, the glow of Hitler's grace. Schirach was not a monster, only an opportunist.

As the end approached, the Gauleiter made every effort, so he claimed, to keep the Hitler Youth out of the war. Yet he himself had summoned them to the *Volkssturm*, that last desperate contingent made up of old men and mere boys. Until the day he died Schirach never admitted his responsibility for the countless young lives lost fighting for Vienna, Breslau and Berlin, in that sacrifice that he had celebrated in his verses.

History is nothing if not ironic. At Nuremberg Schirach was condemned for something that he never accepted as a personal crime: the deporting of Jews from Vienna. He was not condemned for indoctrinating an entire generation. He died a broken man.

Roland Freisler, President of the *Volksgerichtshof*, the People's Court, never had the opportunity to plead guilty. He would not have done so anyway. Hitler's executioner died before the end of the violent regime which he supported with judicial terror. Justice was whatever served the ends of Hitler's rule. In the virtuoso manipulation of injustice he was a master. Freisler, the Grand Inquisitor of the Third Reich, wanted not only to annihilate any man who stood before him, he wanted to destroy his dignity as well.

He never succeeded in winning the goodwill of his adored Führer. But because Hitler granted him absolutely limitless power over life and death, Freisler thought the dictator had selected him for some very special purpose. Yet the Führer exploited Freisler as nothing more than a compliant tool. The warlord needed quiet on the home front – the quiet of the grave – and Freisler provided that. His 'tragedy' was that he never received the praise from Hitler that he so fervently longed for – though he trampled over corpses to get it. When his close friend Goebbels proposed his appointment as Minister of Justice in 1942, a curt refusal came back from Hitler: 'That old Bolshevik? No!'

Freisler had, however, never really been a 'Bolshevik' and suffered all his life from the latent mistrust of the 'old campaigners'. It is true that, as a prisoner-of-war of the Soviets after the First World War, he had been a 'camp commissar'. That was not 'Bolshevism', but it was nonetheless a stigma that the hanging judge had to struggle against to the end. Freisler wanted to prove that despite this he was Hitler's most loyal retainer.

To him the defeat of 1918 was 'betrayal' – such a thing must never be allowed to happen again in Germany. Thus he always saw himself in the judicial front line against all those who harmed the 'national community'; it mattered not whether they were criminals or political opponents, they were all 'traitors'. And traitors, 'a pest on the nation', had to be exterminated.

Thus he became the prototypical 'terror of the courts': precipitate, loud-mouthed, moody, abrupt, conceited, arrogant and unpredictably brilliant. 'Raving Roland', they called him. 'Freisler could switch on his fanaticism just as you or I switch on an electric light', said a lawyer who knew him well.

In the struggle towards final victory on the home front the executioner wielded his scythe like the Grim Reaper: death by judicial verdict, 'justice' of the most barbaric kind. It was sufficient for someone to express doubts about ultimate victory. That was known as 'undermining the military effort'. It was not a question of dispensing justice but of destroying 'traitors'. Yet what use was that if the Führer he idolised was scarcely aware of his activities?

Things only changed in 1944 with the trials of the men and women involved in the 20 July plot to assassinate Hitler. While the German fronts were collapsing everywhere, the unholy executioner launched a final emotionally charged assault against the righteous. He not only howled the defendants down, he insulted them in the most vile manner. His aim was to ridicule them. But in the event it was not the defendants (the 'dishonoured traitors') who lost their honour, it was Freisler himself. The bellowing mountebank sat in front of a swastika flag and raged himself into exhaustion. And what did he achieve? Most likely embarrassed dismay, not to say sympathy for his victims. Even the ruthless Gestapo chief, Ernst Kaltenbrunner, said at the time: 'That cheap play-actor can single-handedly turn incompetents into revolutionaries and even make martyrs of failed assassins – just by the absurd way he runs his trials.'

Freisler's real enemy was not the defendant but the truth. With his inhumane verdicts he was actually battling against his own fears before the end inevitably came. It descended on him out of a clear sky. A bomb fragment killed the executioner as he was attempting to get to an air-raid shelter. Freisler bled to death on the pavement in front of the People's Court. The day after he had passed his last death sentence and the day before he pronounced his next, the terror of the courts was himself brought low by providential justice.

This same justice did not strike down Adolf Eichmann until decades after the war which he had waged – the war against the Jews.

'I was never an anti-Semite', he insisted when interrogated by the Israeli police. Yet, like an unstoppable motor, Eichmann obsessively pursued Hitler's goal of destroying Europe's Jews, as though it were his life's work. As late as the summer of 1944, when the war had long been lost for Germany, he was still fighting for each train that would carry his victims to be murdered. Eichmann was a perpetrator who seldom left his office, who relied not on violence but on collaboration. He made accomplices of his victims. Blindly obedient and fanatical he would, on his own admission, have killed his own father had he been ordered to do so.

Banally evil, this bureaucrat of death was no genius – yet had power over millions of human beings. His 'department of Jewish affairs' was initially a clearing-house for deportation, then, as night follows day, for extermination. Eichmann's job was organising the transport, and this he did soberly, efficiently and mercilessly. In 1945 he told a friend: 'Having five million Jews on my conscience gives me a feeling of great satisfaction.' Yet before the court in Jerusalem he claimed he had had nothing to do with the murders: 'I never killed a Jew.' But had he not delivered them to their death? 'I was given orders to evacuate them. However, not every one that I evacuated was killed.' Eichmann's defence might have been conducted under the slogan: 'I was only the ticket-collector.' Yet, above all he was the man who planned and put into effect the Holocaust.

At the so-called 'Wannsee Conference', at which the genocide was organised, Eichmann took the minutes: 'There it was the "Popes" who gave the orders. I just had to obey them.' These 'Popes' – eight ministerial permanent secretaries, six police and security experts and one departmental head – spoke in plain language: 'There was talk of killing and eliminating and exterminating.'

'I was free of any guilt', Eichmann said. 'Who was I to sit in judgement?' From then on his death-trains rumbled by day and by night into the extermination camps. In this timetabled mass murder the Reichsbahn, Germany's state railways, and their major customer worked closely together. The fare worked out at 4 pfennigs per passenger-kilometre. That was for a third-class ticket, one way only. With painstaking attention to detail, Eichmann, the department head, monitored the departure and arrival of the death-trains. If there was a threat of delay, the bureaucrat flew into a rage: 'I could handle anything', he said in his Argentinian exile, 'except a hold-up in the schedule. Because then I would have been blamed for other hold-ups in the railway network.'

Even though the Wehrmacht needed every available train to take supplies to the Front, Eichmann was always given preferential treatment by the Reichsbahn. Only once did he see the results of his handiwork at Auschwitz. His reaction: 'I felt sick.'

When Hitler sent his troops into Hungary in 1944, it was irrelevant to the course of the war, in fact it weakened Germany by fragmenting its forces. But Hitler had his reasons: he wanted to get at the 750,000 Hungarian Jews who, up to that point, had been successfully protected by the head of state, Miklos Horthy, from being shipped off to the death-camps.

In this way the Holocaust reached its horrific climax in the summer of 1944. The chimneys of Auschwitz smoked day and night. They could not keep up with the burning of those hundreds of thousands of Jews who had been driven into the gas-chambers by SS thugs – in the final days before the camp was closed down. The last victims could already hear the rumble from the Front as the Russians approached.

It was in Hungary that the exterminator completed his 'life's work'. Eye-witnesses who saw him in the last year of the war tell us that he appeared to have no remorse but was certainly frightened. Anyone attempting to photograph or film him received clear evidence of his nervousness. He smashed cameras and tore the film from them. Eichmann knew that one day he would be hunted as a war criminal. 'How many of them, *Obersturmbannführer?*' a young SS man asked him in mid-1944. 'Over five million', said Eichmann. 'What will happen when the world starts asking about those millions?' Eichmann's reply: 'A hundred dead are a disaster, a million are a statistic.'

In late August 1944, when Himmler banned all further deportation of Hungarian Jews, Eichmann was furious. He wanted to bring his assignment to completion. Even if Germany's war was lost – he wanted to win his own war against the Jews. 'The greatest thing he wanted', a 'colleague' remembers, 'was to be received just once by Hitler and thanked by him for the extermination. That was his dream. He never made it and he never got over that.' Instead he heard a final word of praise from his boss, 'Gestapo' Müller. 'If we'd had fifty Eichmanns, we'd have won the war.'

In his self-imposed exile in Argentina the exterminator worked as a 'hydrologist' – which meant he read off water-levels. 'He was certainly no organiser', his ex-boss remembers about the employee who called himself 'Klement'. Questions about his past were taboo. 'Just don't ask him', Frau Eichmann ordered. 'He has been through terrible experiences.'

The rest is criminal history: a team from Mossad, the Israeli secret service, abducted Eichmann to Jerusalem. At the trial he of course acted the innocent: military discipline, only following orders. Eichmann even apologised to the Jewish people: 'I had the misfortune to be involved in those horrors. But the atrocities were committed through no intent of mine. I had no wish to kill people.'

Six years previously in Argentina he had spoken the truth when he said: 'If I had been given orders to gas Jews or to shoot them, then I would have carried out those orders.'

Shortly before his execution, he looked coolly at the Jewish agent who had brought him back to Israel, and said: 'I hope that all of you will soon follow me.' Then he walked calmly to the gallows. The perpetrator met the same end as his victims. His body was burned, and the ashes scattered over the Mediterranean. Nothing was to be left to show that he had ever existed. But the memory of Adolf Eichmann – the exterminator – is something that can never be extinguished.

The same is true of Dr Josef Mengele, the death-doctor of Auschwitz, whose mortal remains, unlike Eichmann's, are still physically present: his skeleton lies, packed in two cardboard boxes, in an institution in São Paulo, Brazil.

He was another who had never shaken Hitler's hand. We may

assume that Hitler never even knew about this man's activities. Nevertheless, the doctor of death symbolises Auschwitz, the scene of possibly the greatest crime in history. And although the prime mover of the crime never once set foot there, Mengele, who stands for Auschwitz, was still an accomplice of Hitler.

Mengele was not the only Nazi doctor who daily betrayed the Hippocratic Oath. Nonetheless, he stands out from the others through the way he behaved, the objects of his experiments, and his mysterious disappearance after the collapse of the barbaric Nazi regime.

As a child, Mengele was ingratiating and obedient. But the atmosphere surrounding his childhood was devoid of emotion. His parents quarrelled constantly. His mother, a corpulent, domineering giant of a woman, had an effect on the boy that was both intimidating and demanding. Her son was ambitious. He wanted to impress: 'My name is going to be in the encyclopaedias.' His goal was a career in research, and he studied medicine.

When he first encountered racial obsession it was clad in an academic gown. The fashionable subjects he chose, anthropology and genetics, were, in the Nazi period, intended to prove the racial inferiority of non-Aryan races – the basic dogma of brownshirt ideology. The perverted notion of the 'valueless life' was given 'scientific' credentials. Mengele was a quick study. In 1935, the year of the anti-Semitic Nuremberg Laws, he graduated in anthropology with a thesis which stressed the 'differences between primitive and advanced races'. Mengele struck the right note. The work was awarded a *summa cum laude*. The young doctor became a research assistant with Otmar von Verschuer, the doyen of German research into twins. This genetics guru wanted his pupil to build up a central collection of genetic material – with the ultimate objective of breeding a superman.

It was Professor von Verschuer who sent Mengele, the SS doctor, to Auschwitz, with the encouragement that he would there be given an incomparable scientific opportunity: many different races, no shortage of people to act as test subjects, a 'researchers' paradise' that was unique in the world. On 30 May 1943 Mengele duly reported for duty at Auschwitz-Birkenau.

From then on, when the death-trains arrived, there would

frequently be a tall young doctor standing at the unloading ramp. Wearing white gloves, the 'elegant and slimly built' man looked 'like a host welcoming guests into his house', as eye-witnesses remember: 'Madam, you are tired and unwell after the long journey; give your toddler to this lady, and you can collect it again later from the crèche.'

When Mengele was making his selection from the new arrivals, they sometimes heard a tune on his lips, whistled nonchalantly, and the image was captured of a white-gloved hand gently beating time, to the right – life, to the left – death, to the tune of Schumann's *Träumerei*. The inmates called him 'The Angel of Death'.

He was never crude. And to one female prisoner-doctor it seemed as though his domineering mother was always present. 'He looked as if his mother had warned him not to get any stains on his best Sunday jacket.' As the senior doctor in the women's camp he was feared and hated – yet also admired. Quite a few women admitted, ashamed and with reluctance, that they had found Josef Mengele rather attractive.

Mengele collected human beings. He wanted his research into twins to earn him a professorship, like Verschuer. The twin children that he fished out from stream of those going from the trains to their death, he called his 'guinea-pigs'. He would often drive the young twins around the camp in his car and give them sweets. The very next day they were lying on Mengele's dissection-table, child-corpses for him to gloat over. The representative of the 'master race' possessed a human zoo with which he could do as he pleased.

Mengele sent the results of his 'research' to Verschuer's institute. First the questionnaires, then the blood-samples, a little later the skeletons – carefully wrapped in brown paper and marked 'URGENT! War material!'

By the summer of 1944 any remaining inhibitions had fallen away. Mengele killed twins with chloroform injections, removed organs from living bodies, transplanted bone-marrow, and sewed twins together, back to back. At the same time, this young man was not a murderous sadist who derived pleasure from the pain of his victims. Rather, Mengele was coolly cynical, not particularly interested in the suffering of his guinea-pigs. As he saw it, he was not in Auschwitz as a murderer but as a researcher. And as such, he killed 'in the interests of science'. Verschuer's intention was to make use of Mengele, but Mengele was determined, with his own physiological study of twins, to write his name in the annals of genetics.

In January 1945, when the Red Army liberated the Auschwitz camp, only 180 of Mengele's 3,000 twins were still alive. As he fled, Mengele dropped his research notes off at his home in Bavaria. He actually hoped that one day he would be able to make use of them.

For several years he remained hidden, working as a labourer for a Bavarian farmer. Then in 1949 he escaped through Austria and Italy to Argentina and later Paraguay. The man who had sent him to Auschwitz was never called to account: in 1952 Professor Otmar von Verschuer took over the presidency of the German Anthropological Society.

As an ageing emigrant, Mengele had no feelings of guilt. In the 1970s, when the world press began to describe his atrocities, he was outraged: 'It is unbelievable what filth the German magazines are allowed to put out. Behind all this there is only one thing, and that is the Old Testament hatred of everything to do with being German, everything that is heroic and on a higher human plane.'

His punishment was not discovery, but the fear of it. 'I dream of a double-bladed guillotine.' The death-camp doctor who had once dissected children, complained of headache, earache, insomnia and poor digestion. It was the fear of death.

For thirty-four years he lived with this fear, from his flight from Auschwitz until his death in the sea near São Paulo. It was the punishment of a mass murderer who killed for the purposes of research.

And what is the moral of all these stories? It is that anyone could have become one of Hitler's accomplices. Everyone runs this risk, when a criminal state tears down the barriers between right and wrong. On its own, human nature is too weak. For within all of us there lurks an Eichmann, a Mengele, a Bormann, a Ribbentrop, a Schirach or a Freisler. In other times and under other circumstances, these men would have had quite normal careers, would have been citizens of no particular note. In the case of

Ribbentrop and Schirach, they could even have lived at that time – if only they had decided to go in another direction.

The Eichmann within us is always there. At least we have the choice to let him lie. And it often takes more courage to say no, before it is too late.

Yet it would be irresponsible to rely on the humanity of man, fragile and delicate as it is. Only a strong body politic with clear standards based on a humane society can effectively prevent right from becoming wrong. The emergence of another criminal state must never be permitted.

CHAPTER ONE

THE EXTERMINATOR

ADOLF EICHMANN

Remorse is for children.

I did my job according to the iron imperative that was imposed upon me.

I refuse to grovel in any way whatsoever. I cannot do so because my innermost nature rebels against saying that we had done anything wrong.

Had I been ordered to gas Jews or to shoot them, then I would have carried out the orders.

The Jews deported by me did not interest me. If people were carted off, they were carted off.

The words of the Führer have the force of law.

I was never an anti-Semite, I was a nationalist.

We fought a decent fight.

I lived believing in God, and I die believing in God.

My guilt is my obedience.

A hundred deaths are a catastrophe, a million are a statistic.

If I have to, I will go to my grave with a smile, for the knowledge of having five million Jews on my conscience gives me a feeling of great satisfaction.

Adolf Eichmann

He was a book-keeper of death.

Simon Wiesenthal, Nazi-hunter

The banality of evil.

Hannah Arendt

The greatest thing he wanted was to be received just once by Hitler and to be thanked by him. He never made it, and that was something he never got over.

Wilhelm Höttl, former SS Sturmbannführer

He was a conceited popinjay, in other words a vain man, who was aware that his dapper appearance was meant to create a big impression.

Willi Stern, errand-boy for the Israelite Cultural Community in Vienna

Eichmann is synonymous with severe physical persecution, with murder and with terror.

Teddy Kollek, former Mayor of Jerusalem

He was a man who in his insolence was lord over life and death, a man who was crude and ranted at us.

Franz Meyer, German Zionist

Eichmann had an inferiority complex. He was determined to show people: all right, I'm no academic but I can still deliver, and I'll prove it to you. And that dogged him throughout his life.

Wilhelm Höttl, former SS Sturmbannführer

Eichmann liked to give the impression of being a forceful, intrepid officer, a daredevil who knew what he was about.

One of the things he used to say was: 'We German soldiers aren't afraid. Where would we be if we were scared of death? My comrades are fighting in Russia, and I'm fighting in this job'.

Carl Lutz, former Swiss Vice-consul in Budapest

The 'Eichmann Problem' is not yesterday's problem: we are all sons of Eichmann, or at least sons of Eichmann's world. It is the world of machines of destruction whose effects surpass our powers of imagination. This creates the risk that we may function without resistance and without conscience like cog-wheels in those machines, that our moral strength is insufficient to stand up against the machine and that anyone can become an Eichmann.

Günther Anders, Austrian philosopher and author

If we'd had fifty Eichmanns, we'd have won the war.

Gestapo chief Heinrich Müller

He had a pronounced aptitude for list-making, organisation, and other forms of painstaking and systematic work.

Dieter Wisliceny, a colleague of Eichmann in the Central Office of Reich Security

To his crudeness and obscene way of talking he added a new characteristic, which was to play a major part in his activities from now on, namely treachery and deception.

Gideon Hausner, chief prosecutor at Eichmann's trial

Had he been more human, his humanity would have restrained him from his evil work; had he been a lesser person, he would have lacked the ability for the job. But as he was, he embodied the banality of the individual who, when ordered to do so, would press the button and whose only concern would be to press the button correctly, without regard to who dies in the process.

Bruno Bettelheim, American psychoanalyst

The essential thing about him was his inferiority complex. In the Security Service, all the top jobs were held by academics. He didn't even have a school-leaving certificate and that irked him terribly. Added to that were his colleagues' nasty remarks about his 'Jewish appearance'. They called him 'Ziggy' Eichmann and that was hugely insulting to him.

Wilhelm Höttl, former SS Sturmbannführer

I don't know if I would have paid much attention to him if I had met him on a bus. Yet sometimes, if he was displeased by something, there was a look in his eyes which could strike fear into you – a tigerish look.

Gabriel Bach, prosecutor at Eichmann's trial

*

The man made no particular impression; boringly respectable, around fifty years old, of average build, with a high forehead and cheap glasses. He wore a tie with a suit that had seen better days. He looked like a salesman who was not doing much business. Or a criminal who wanted to avoid attracting attention.

The man was walking at a leisurely pace towards a single-storey house that was little more than a shack – plain and shabby. He stopped beside a small boy, stroked his hair affectionately, chatted to him for a moment or two and tidied up the lad's clothes. Then he disappeared into the little house. The door had been opened to him by a plump woman. The boy, the woman, the little house – it looked like any family man coming home. It was Sunday 20 March 1960.

The man had not noticed that only a few hundred yards away binoculars were focused on him. His every movement was being closely observed. Zvi Aharoni, an agent of the Israeli secret service, Mossad, crouched in the back of a pick-up truck, where he could not be seen. Looking through a crack between the planks, he could see exactly what was going on at No. 14 Garibaldi Street, San Fernando, Buenos Aires. 'He suddenly came out of the house again', Aharoni remembers. 'He was wearing blue-and-white striped pyjamas. It was obvious that this was no visitor. The man lived there.'

The longer Aharoni observed the suspect, the more certain he became. 'The age, the height, the shape of the face, the whole impression he made on me told me: this is the man you are looking for.' That same evening the agent contacted Mossad's headquarters in Tel Aviv: 'I think we have enough information to plan the next step . . . I await further instructions.'

Zvi Aharoni, born Hermann Aronheim in Frankfurt-an-der-Oder, had fled from Germany to Palestine in 1938. Now, for the past three weeks, he had been travelling through Argentina on a secret mission, under a false name and with a diplomatic passport – on the trail of a man who during the war had sent millions of people to their death. Aharoni was convinced he had found his quarry. But he also knew that his superiors would only act when all doubt as to the target's true identity had been removed. What he lacked, as final proof, was a photograph, preferably one taken in profile.

The risk was enormous, almost incalculable. The slightest mistake could put the entire operation at risk. 'We could not let him find out that foreigners were trying to get in touch with him. So I instructed a local assistant on how to use a brief-case camera.' The assistant, an Argentinian named Rendi, was to engage the target in conversation and at the same time secretly press the shutter-release. As Aharoni tells it: 'One Sunday morning we drove to the house and stopped 300 metres away from it, until I saw *him* leaving the house.'

Rendi went up to the man and held him in a brief conversation at his front gate. Moments later the trick had gone off perfectly: 'Four fantastic shots', as Aharoni describes them, showed *his* face from every direction – including profile. These pictures cleared away any remaining doubts. The man in Garibaldi Street was one of the most wanted war criminals, Adolf Eichmann, 'expert on Jewish affairs' in the Central office of Reich Security, a bureaucrat of death – fanatical and blindly obedient. A desk-bound perpetrator whose signature sealed the fate of millions of human beings, who at his trial before Jewish judges in Jerusalem admitted that he would even have killed his own father if ordered to do so. The Nazi-hunter Simon Wiesenthal, who had never given up the search for Eichmann, said about this man: 'If he had been given orders to kill all red-haired people, or everyone whose name began with K, he would have done it.'

As for Eichmann, he saw himself as an obedient SS man who, loyal to his SS oath, had done his duty, nothing more. In fact he had done more than he was ordered to do. Obsessively, like a motor that could no longer be stopped, he followed through Hitler's plan to murder the Jews of Europe, as though it were his life's work. Until just before Germany's collapse, long after the war had been lost, the lord of the death-trains to Auschwitz and Treblinka did everything he could to go on waging his personal war against Europe's Jews to its end, and fought for each individual train, so that he could go on deporting his victims. Not the sort of man who could build anything up, Eichmann wanted to destroy – mercilessly and completely. 'I have absolutely no regrets.' That is what he told the former Dutch SS man, Willem Sassen, in a tape-recorded conversation in what he presumed to be the security of his Argentine hideout. 'I refuse to grovel in any way whatsoever. I cannot do so because my innermost nature rebels against saying that we had done anything wrong. I have to tell you in all honesty: if, out of the 10.3 million Jews that Korherr had identified [referring to Richard Korherr, chief statistician with the SS], we had killed all 10.3 million, then I would be satisfied and would say: "Fine, we've destroyed one enemy!"'

> I was always a conventional SS officer who was willing to obey, and did obey.
>
> *Eichmann in conversation with Willem Sassen, 1955*

Several of the more than seventy tapes have been preserved. They document how Eichmann 'in full possession of my physical and mental freedom' accounts for his life. What we hear is a man with a snarl in his voice, who pronounces the verb '*vernichten*' – destroy – with the same rolled 'r' as Hitler did, almost relishing it on his tongue. Eichmann was proud of his murderous work. In 1945, among the ruins of Berlin, he boasted to Dieter Wisliceny, then a friend, colleague and godfather to his son: 'If I have to, I will go to my grave with a smile, for the knowledge of having five million Jews on my conscience gives me a feeling of great satisfaction.' In Argentina Eichmann had revoked this statement. The question was not about Jews, he said, but about 'enemies of the Reich'. In the same conversation he declared: 'If I had had to occupy the post of concentration camp commandant, I would have done just the same [referring to Rudolf Höss, commandant of Auschwitz]. And had I been ordered to gas Jews or to shoot them, then I would have carried out those orders.' Can we really accept Eichmann as a perfectly ordinary man acting on orders?

I am a man who cannot lie.

Eichmann on trial in Israel

What turns a man like Eichmann into a criminal? Wherein lie the roots of his fanaticism? The trail leads back to his childhood. Adolf Eichmann was born on 19 March 1906, the oldest of five children, in the industrial town of Solingen in Westphalia, and even at an early age he was a worry to his parents. The family moved to Austria, and he was a failure at the Kaiser Franz Secondary School in Linz – the same school that Adolf Hitler had attended fifteen years earlier, and where the future Führer had been equally unimpressive. Eichmann went on to a polytechnic and flunked out of there as well. Nevertheless he found a job as a travelling salesman for the Vacuum Oil Company, which, as the advertisement in the *Linzer Tageblatt* stated, was seeking a 'first-class executive'. For the first time Eichmann was earning money, but his career ended abruptly when he was fired during the Slump. He had anyway been bored with delivering petrol and oil door-to-door in the rural Mühlviertel district of northern Austria. Eichmann was looking for a new challenge that would give meaning to his life. Though not politically minded, out of curiosity he attended a meeting of the NSDAP, the growing Nazi Party, in Linz's Märzenkeller beer-hall. In the interval a heavily built man with duelling scars approached him. Eichmann knew him by sight; he was a young lawyer and business acquaintance of his father. Ten years later this man would be Eichmann's superior in the Central Office of Reich Security, the principal organ for the persecution of Jews. As Eichmann recalled, the man, whose name was Ernst Kaltenbrunner, told him 'categorically': ' "You're joining us!" So I said: "Yeah, all right!" And that's how I joined the SS.'

> Kaltenbrunner had suggested to him: 'Why don't you join the SS?' And he had replied: 'Well, why not?' That's how it happened; there was no more to it than that.
>
> *Hannah Arendt, Jewish author*

It was not out of any political conviction that Eichmann became a member of the Nazi Party and the SS. Ideology had never interested him particularly. It was just that he was fed up with his sterile existence. By marching in step with Hitler's brownshirt battalions, which by now were gaining support in Austria as well, Eichmann hoped for personal advancement. It was the longing for social acceptance, for companionship and a career that brought him into the SS and the NSDAP. To opportunists like himself, a salesman with no qualifications, Hitler's party promised the chance to make a completely fresh start, to rise in spite of everything and achieve 'great things'. Following the banning of the NSDAP in Austria, Eichmann was ordered to Germany by his local party officials on 1 August 1933, and in the Bavarian towns of Lechfeld and Passau he was drilled to become an SS man in the 'Austrian Legion'. In Germany, which until 1914 had been his family's country, there lived 503,000 Jews, making up just 0.76 per cent of the total population. Later Eichmann of the SS would send them to their death.

His new life started out disappointingly. Just as he had done as a commercial traveller, Eichmann was soon complaining of boredom in the SS training camps: 'I found the monotony of military service abhorrent. Every day the same thing, always the same thing.' In order to get out of the rut, he successfully applied in 1934 for the 'SS intelligence service', known as the *Sicherheitsdienst* (Security Service) or SD. However, the architectural magnificence of the Hohenzollern palace which served as the SD's headquarters in Berlin was in stark contrast to the dreary job that was assigned to him. As an assistant in the 'Freemasonry' section, Eichmann typed index-cards about such organisations as the *Schlaraffia*, a quasi-masonic society that he himself had nearly joined in Linz. Even at that early stage, Dieter Wisliceny reported after the war, Eichmann had 'a pronounced aptitude for list-making, organisation and other forms of painstaking and systematic work'. For five months Eichmann languished in the Freemasonry Section, and then his career took a decisive turn.

> Eichmann was an enthusiastic SS man. He was proud of his uniform and keen on decorations.
>
> *Wilhelm Höttl, former SS Sturmbannführer*

The young SS *Scharführer* was transferred to the 'Jewry' department, where he rapidly worked his way into the new field of activity. His superior, Leopold von Mildenstein, recommended that he read the book *The Jewish State* by Theodor Herzl, the founder of political Zionism. The new arrival in the department studied it in detail – and was a changed man: 'Up till then I knew nothing about these things. Somehow that book struck a chord with me and I absorbed it all . . . .' Henceforth, he saw himself as a 'Zionist' and an 'idealist', whose ideas followed a circular pattern: the 'political solution of the Jewish problem' meant the expulsion of Jews from Germany. Eichmann gave lectures on the subject and even acquired a smattering of modern Hebrew, which he boasted about to colleagues and later to his victims. He would like to have gained perfect mastery of the language of his opponents, and actually wanted to take lessons with a rabbi for 3 marks an hour. But his request was turned down. If an SS man insisted on learning Hebrew, then would he kindly do so with a 'non-Jewish' teacher.

But Eichmann did not let put-downs like this deter him. He had realised how he could get ahead in the SD – as a specialist in Jewish questions. With fanatical zeal Eichmann strove, as a personnel report states, 'to improve his education and perfect his practical knowledge'. It was not long before the autodidact with his half-digested theories became known in Party circles as an 'expert' who was credited with 'a comprehensive knowledge of the forms of organisation and of the ideology of our Jewish opponents.' Within the SD Eichmann was seen as the coming man, since he had experience which was rare for an SS man: Eichmann had once actually been to Palestine – into the very Lion's Den.

His official trip to the Holy Land in the summer of 1937 was personally approved by his mentor, the SD chief Reinhard Heydrich. In the guise of a journalist with the once renowned *Berliner Tageblatt*, the 31-year old *Hauptscharführer* Eichmann, with his new commanding officer, Herbert Hagen, was to explore the possibility of deporting Jews to Palestine. Eichmann visited a kibbutz, looked down on Haifa from Mount Carmel and paid a call on a community of Knights Templar. Appealing as this tourism was, the four-week trip ended without any result to speak of. Palestine was then a territory under British mandate; the bogus SS tourists were unmasked by the British authorities and expelled. For Eichmann the Palestine mission ended in a military hospital with a paratyphoid infection.

Nonetheless, Eichmann's superiors recognised his relentless industry and promoted him. Yet colleagues joked about the ambitious upstart, who had few friends. One of those who did befriend him at the time is former SS man Wilhelm Höttl, who knew Eichmann better than almost anyone. 'The essential thing about him', says Höttl, 'was his inferiority complex. In the Security Service all the top jobs were held by academics. He didn't even have a school leaving certificate and that irked him terribly. Added to that were his colleagues' nasty remarks about his "Jewish appearance". They called him "Ziggy" Eichmann, which was hugely insulting to him.' Eichmann was also derided by his colleagues for having a Czech wife. 'That was very much held against him', Höttl remembers. 'Officially there was no objection, but his colleagues ribbed him about it and said: "That's all we need; you going with a Czech woman!"' Eichmann had always been an outsider. The feeling that he was not being taken seriously had fatal consequences. Eichmann was determined to use every means to prove to his mockers what he was made of.

He found himself repeatedly exposed to attacks and viewed as an outsider, and then he would drown his sorrows in alcohol.
Wilhelm Höttl, former SS Sturmbannführer

His first opportunity to do this came in March 1938. Hitler's seizure of his former homeland, Austria, gave a decisive boost to Eichmann's career. The 'specialist' was despatched to Vienna in order to 'force the pace' of Jewish emigration. What this actually meant was to expel all Jews as rapidly as possible. In Vienna Eichmann took up residence in the palatial town-house expropriated from Baron Philip de Rothschild. Under police interrogation in Israel, he himself described his new working environment as modest. 'I was allotted a small room in which there was nothing but a desk, and I was informed that here I had to deal with Jewish affairs.' What that meant in reality became very clear on 18 March 1938, when police and SS stormed the premises of the Israelite Cultural Association in Seitenstettengasse. Featuring prominently on that occasion was Adolf Eichmann, head of department II–112, SS Over-Sector Austria. Photographs show the 32-year-old at the scene, rummaging through papers in the office of the president of the Cultural Association. Documents were confiscated, and senior Jewish officials arrested. Instead of sorting through card-indexes, his word now decided who would be sent to a concentration camp. For the first time in his career the fast-rising Eichmann had power over others.

Thousands of Jews had got the message and fled in fear of their lives from the terror of the '*Anschluss* pogroms' to foreign countries which, at the time, still offered a safe haven. But the exodus was too slow for Eichmann. In order to expel more Jews more quickly he had the 'Clearing-house for Jewish Emigration' set up in Prinz-Eugen-Strasse. Anyone who wanted to flee the country could get all the necessary papers here within eight days. But the price was a fortune. Owners had their property sequestrated. Emigrants were forced to buy foreign currency, indispensable as proof of 'economic viability', at dizzyingly high and totally fictitious exchange rates. It was Eichmann who first turned expulsion into a business worth millions. A Jewish official from Berlin, summoned to Vienna to visit the clearing-house, noted how it operated like a conveyor belt. 'In at one side comes a Jew who still has some assets, a shop, a factory, a bank-account. Then he goes right through the building from counter to counter, from office to office, and when he comes out the other side he has been robbed of all rights, doesn't have a pfennig to his name, but in return he has a passport on which it says: "You have to leave the country within 14 days, otherwise you'll go to a concentration camp." '

The idea for the clearing-house may have come from others, but Eichmann was the driving force that actually made the thing work efficiently. Yet it was not SS men that he had carrying out the organised robbery. Behind the long tables, where the continuous banging of rubber stamps on forms could be heard, sat Jewish employees of the Cultural Association. Eichmann made his victims assist him. From time to time he would go in person to make sure that *his* robbery-and-expulsion machinery was running really smoothly. Willi Stern, then a messenger-boy at the Israelite Cultural Association, remembers how an arrogant Eichmann 'slapping a riding-crop against his jackboot, strode hurriedly like a *deus ex machina*,' through the ornately decorated rooms, 'so that he would not have to put up for too long with the Jew-infested air'. When being interrogated by the Israeli police Eichmann insisted: 'I have never been anti-Semitic, and I have always made that clear. I'm not trying to praise myself by saying this. All I mean is that the work we did at the clearing-house was, from an objective point of view, carried out correctly.'

It is true that to begin with, in Vienna, Eichmann was distinguishable from other brutal SS thugs. Apart from one slap on the face, for which he apologised to Josef Löwenherz, the head of the Cultural Association, Eichmann was known as a cold bureaucrat who relied on collaboration rather than violence. In conversation he tried to appear 'courteous'. He was always ready to listen to any suggestions which would serve to accelerate emigration. This was something experienced by Teddy Kollek, later to become Mayor of Jerusalem, who at that time was organising rescue operations for Jews from a base in London.

Kollek wanted to secure the freedom of 3,000 Jewish youngsters in his home city of Vienna. Only one man could decide on this: Adolf Eichmann.

Kollek succeeded in getting an appointment with Eichmann at the Palais Rothschild. After a brief wait he was ushered into Eichmann's presence. 'He was sitting at his desk in a large panelled room – a smartly dressed, smooth-shaven young man in a black uniform with a swastika armband. He had the manner of a minor official and was neither aggressive, loud nor impolite.' Twenty minutes later Eichmann had granted freedom to the 3,000 young people. 'I had imagined it would be more complicated than that', Kollek says today. 'It was only later that I realised why it went so smoothly. Eichmann had simply got rid of 3,000 Jews and for him that was a success.'

With pride Eichmann reported to Berlin on his Viennese 'success'. He wrote on 21 October to the headquarters of the SD to say that up to the end of September 'an estimated 50,000 Jews' had been expelled from Austria. In Germany the figure for the same period had been only 19,000. Eichmann's 'success' had spelled misery for tens of thousands. To this day there are still visible traces of his manhunt. On the tombstone of a rabbi in Vienna's Central Cemetery, still clearly legible, are cries for help scribbled in pencil – shattering documents of despair: 'Pray for us, good Rabbi. The good Lord must help us and cause a miracle to happen.'

Pleased with himself, Eichmann wrote at the same time to his superior in Berlin, Herbert Hagen: 'Anyway, I've got these fine folk on the run, as you can imagine.' Eichmann was satisfied with his work. Looking back, he would describe his time in Vienna as the highlight of his career. The whole atmosphere in Vienna had been 'uplifting', he averred. Eichmann enjoyed the trappings of power; he had himself driven through the city in the Rothschilds' luxurious limousine. Everyone was meant to see how far he had come. He graciously served his colleagues with vintage 1875 from the Rothschild wine-cellars. Eichmann was fond of alcohol and often drank more than he could handle – first wine, then spirits. He usually carried a hip-flask with him. When he and his SD colleagues sat until late at night, knocking back the local Heuriger wine, Eichmann, the family man, seldom had his wife with him at the table but, as Wilhelm Höttl puts it, 'some female who was a complete stranger to us. He always had a floozie – what the Viennese call a *pantscherl*, a "bit on the side".'

> He was very fond of his children, though his wife had become indifferent towards him.
>
> *Dieter Wisliceny, Eichmann's colleague in the*
> *Central Office of Reich Security*

Eichmann's superiors in Berlin studiously ignored these peccadilloes. Eichmann was an effective and relentless worker and that was what mattered. In a confidential personnel report of June 1938 we read that 'his particular abilities lie in negotiation, public speaking and organisation'. The overall assessment was 'Very good'. Eichmann, it said, was an 'energetic and hard-driving person, who has great abilities in the independent management of his area.' He was a 'recognised specialist' in the expulsion of Jews. Promotion was not long in coming, and Eichmann rose to the rank of *Obersturmführer*. In the regular army this was equivalent to an *Oberleutnant* (Lieutenant or US First Lieutenant).

Among his superior officers it was Reinhard Heydrich who was the most satisfied with his model pupil. Two days after the *Kristallnacht* pogroms of 9 November 1938, at a conference on the 'Jewish Question' held at the Reich Aviation Ministry, Heydrich let Hermann Göring into the secret of the Jewish expulsions from Vienna: 'The way we did it was by making wealthy Jews hand over a certain sum at the Cultural Association. We then used this money and foreign currency payments to get a number of poor Jews out of the country. The problem wasn't getting the rich Jews out but getting rid of the Jewish rabble.'

Heydrich recommended that this model be applied 'throughout the Reich'. Shortly afterwards, in January 1939, a 'Reich Central Office for Jewish Emigration' was set up in the Ministry of the Interior in Berlin. The Eichmann method was to be put into practice everywhere. Eichmann was now considered not merely as the 'expert on Jewish matters'; within the SS hierarchy he was *the* authority on questions of emigration. With joking respect his colleagues now called him *Meister* – a master of his trade.

Promotion and the praise he received from the highest quarter went to the 'expert's' head. He now adopted a coarser tone towards his victims. Dr Franz Meyer, a German Zionist, described him in his trial in Jerusalem as 'a man who in his insolence was lord over life and death, a man who was crude and ranted at us'. Even his colleagues noted uneasily how Eichmann had changed. 'There were a lot of complaints about it', says Wilhelm Höttl. 'He wasn't just proud, he was arrogant. He kept on saying: what they're doing in Berlin, I've known how to do for a long time. I gave *them* a demonstration of how it's done.' Eichmann wanted to command respect, to be known – Höttl says – as 'big, bad Eichmann'. Yet his SD colleagues continued to make fun of the pedantic paper-pusher, who insisted that even the most trivial memo should bear the heavy, black 'Eichmann' signature – as though he had to prove his importance to everyone.

Eichmann would have liked to stay longer in Vienna, but men with his talents were needed in other theatres of action. In April 1939, after Hitler had marched into Czechoslovakia, Eichmann received orders to proceed against the Jewish inhabitants of the newly created 'Protectorate of Bohemia and Moravia'. Eichmann the expeller, who by now had risen to the rank of *Hauptsturmführer*, did not merely want to repeat his 'tried and tested' practices in Prague, but to put them into effect with greater efficiency. Yet the success of Vienna would not prove so easy to reproduce. Scarcely a country in the world was still willing to accept persecuted Jews. As the would-be emigrants were told in travel agencies, 'the only country currently issuing entry visas is the Dominican Republic'. Even Berlin was only moderately interested in 'forced emigration' from Bohemia and Moravia. Precedence had to be given to the Jewish exodus from the 'old Reich'. Heydrich would only agree to the setting up of a 'clearing-house' in Prague on condition that it did not hinder the expulsion of Jews from Germany.

Heydrich actually wanted to get rid of Jews by other means. They were to be deported to Poland, where a 'Jewish state under German administration' was to be created near Cracow. The job of organising the mass deportations to Poland, Heydrich assigned to his 'specialist', Eichmann. He, in turn, immediately swung into frantic activity, visited the actual site of the proposed 'state territory', hurried from Cracow via Ostrava in Moravia, to Vienna, where he instructed the Israelite Cultural Community to assemble two transports per week, each made up of 1,000 Jews. On 18 October 1939 Eichmann began the 'despatching' to eastern Poland. His aim was to get all Jews concentrated in the area around Lublin. In order to calm the fears of those being 'resettled', Eichmann, the practised deceiver, spun a tissue of disgraceful lies. Any Jew was 'free to settle' in the 'Lublin Reserve', he assured them. In fact as soon as the newcomers arrived, they were packed off further east, beaten up and killed. Only a few trains reached their destination. Eichmann had failed in his task.

This setback did him no harm – on the contrary. His superiors had seen that this man was capable, in a short time, of shipping off thousands of people in trains to any chosen destination. Eichmann was clearly destined for greater things. In the newly founded Central Office of Reich Security he was assigned to Department IV B 4, 'Evacuation matters and Reich central office for Jewish emigration'. Eichmann was to develop 'clearance plans', co-ordinate the expulsions, agree timetables with the Reichsbahn (state railways) and monitor all 'clearing-houses'. In October 1940 Eichmann personally took charge of the first deportation from German territory. A total of 7,500 Jews from the regions of Baden, Palatinate and Saarland were 'offloaded' in an unoccupied zone of southern France.

Eichmann appeared to have climbed a step further up the career ladder, but he found his hands were increasingly tied. The machinery of expulsion had almost ground to a halt. In his Berlin headquarters, the former premises of the Jewish Friendship Society at 115 Kurfürstenstrasse, Eichmann searched with growing anxiety for places to which Jews could still be sent: 'On both sides there was a lot of shuffling of feet, a distinct lack of enthusiasm, I might say. On the Jewish side because it was really hard to find any worthwhile opportunities for emigration. And on our side because we had no manpower and no assistance from the Party. It was a vast building and virtually deserted.'

Where were the Jews to go? No other question occupied Eichmann so intensively. In June 1940 there were as many as 3.25

million Jews living in the Reich and countries under German occupation. And the number was rising. Heydrich was pushing for a 'final territorial solution'. But in what part of the world? After the defeat of France it seemed that the answer had been found. In the German Foreign Office an old 'idea' came back into fashion, one which Eichmann immediately subscribed to enthusiastically: Europe's Jews should be deported to the large tropical island of Madagascar, a French colony. There they would establish a kind of 'Jewish state'. With the 'Madagascar Project' Eichmann believed he would be able to realise one of Theodor Herzl's dreams, although Herzl had considered Uganda rather than Madagascar as a possible national homeland for the Jews. Until the invasion of the Soviet Union Eichmann chiefly devoted himself to the 'Madagascar Project', but six months later none of his superiors wanted to know about it. To ship millions of people to an island off the African coast in the middle of a war was unthinkable, since Germany lacked the ships for one thing, and for another Britain and the USA controlled the sea routes to Madagascar. The plan was finally shelved when preparations for the Russian campaign opened up new possibilities for solving the 'Jewish problem'. On his own admission Eichmann was 'embittered and disappointed.' His only comfort was a further promotion – to *Obersturmbannführer*. He was now one of 1,159 men holding that rank, and although in the years that followed he wielded enormous power as Europe's 'Commissioner for Jews', he was not to ascend any further rungs on the promotion ladder. In the hierarchy of the 'Final Solution' no higher rank was foreseen for Eichmann's activities. He was 'only' a departmental head, in charge of the 'Jewish department' in the Central Office of Reich Security. In the designation 'IV B 4', 'IV' stood for Gestapo, and 'B' for 'sects'. There were four such departments: 1. Catholics; 2. Protestants; 3. Freemasons; 4. Jews. Not for much longer would IV B 4 be the control centre for expulsion. It would soon be the control centre for annihilation.

Until 1940 Eichmann's department regulated the planned emigration of Jews. From 1940 until the beginning of 1942 the operative policy was the concentration of all Jews in Polish ghettos. The Jews were herded together so as to be deported more easily. Tens of thousands died from disease and hunger in the wretchedly confined space. The ghettos were the antechamber to the hell of the concentration camps. The conditions in the Lodz ghetto were described by SS *Sturmbannführer* Heinz Höppner in a letter to 'My dear friend Eichmann'. It would, he said, be 'seriously worth considering whether the most humane solution is not . . . to get rid of the Jews by the use of some fast-acting agent. At all events that would be less unpleasant than letting them starve to death.'

After the assault on the Soviet Union on 2 June 1941 the first 'fast-acting agent' came into use: behind the lines mass shootings took place everywhere. In one of the biggest single operations, on a November day in the Rumbuli forest near the Latvian capital, Riga, Heydrich's death-squads slaughtered 15,000 men, women and children.

It was Eichmann's initiation into mass murder. In the late summer of 1941 Heydrich had summoned him to Berlin. Eichmann's superior officer seemed unusually restless, ill at ease. 'The Führer . . . um . . . well, you see . . . this emigration . . . ', Heydrich began haltingly. As Eichmann recalled: 'He then said: "The Führer has ordered the physical destruction of the Jews." And as if wanting to judge the impact of his words, he paused for what was, for him, an unusually long time. I can still remember it today. At first I was incapable of assessing the enormous consequences of this statement, why he was choosing his words so carefully. But then I realised what it meant and said nothing in reply, because there was nothing more I *could* say.'

Eichmann was put in the picture because he was to organise the transport. Hitler's henchman was always told just enough for him to know exactly what he had to do. On Heydrich's orders he set off for Poland. It was presumably in Treblinka that a *Hauptmann* in the civil police told Eichmann in autumn 1941 how Jews were being gassed – with the exhaust-fumes from the engine of a Soviet submarine. Shortly afterwards, at Chelmno in the Warthegau district of Poland, Eichmann saw for the first time how the murders were carried out. He told Israeli police interrogators: 'What I saw was this: a room which, if I remember correctly, was perhaps five times as large as this one. In it were Jews. They had to undress; then a truck, completely sealed, drove up to where the doors had been opened, and then more or less right up to a ramp. The Jews, naked as they were, had to walk into it. Then the doors of the truck were closed and it drove off.'

Obersturmbannfuhrer Eichmann followed the truck in a car. 'There I saw the most appalling thing I had ever seen in my life up to that time. The truck drove up to a rectangular pit. The doors were opened and out were thrown corpses. The limbs were so supple, it was as if they were still alive . . . And then I got the hell out. Got in my car and drove off, without saying a word . . . I'd had enough. That finished me.'

But the bureaucrat of death was to see more. He received an order from the Gestapo chief, *Gruppenführer* Heinrich Müller: 'Jews are being shot in Minsk. I'd like a report on how that's progressing.' In 1956 Eichmann described the event to the former SS man, Willem Sassen: 'I once saw Jews being shot. I arrived at the very last minute. But I did see a woman, a Jewess, holding up a little child. For me that was a terrible moment.'

Eichmann travelled on to Lvov where he reported to the SS commanding officer on the dreadful things he had seen in the Byelorussian city of Minsk. But he found that shootings were taking place in Lvov as well. 'There I saw another terrible thing. There was a pit but it had been filled in. A stream of blood was bubbling out from it like a geyser . . . I'd had enough of my assignment; I drove back to Berlin and reported it all to *Gruppenführer* Müller'. As Eichmann told the SS man Sassen in 1956: 'I said to Müller: "*Gruppenführer*, This is no good. This is not how to solve the Jewish problem. This way we're just teaching our own men to be sadists."'

Yet such impressions were swiftly suppressed. At his desk in Berlin Eichmann went on signing instructions as if nothing had happened, and co-ordinated the timetables of the special trains which carried the victims from the Baltic countries directly to the firing-squads. On 18 October 1941 the first transport left Berlin. On 25 November, in the Ninth Fort in Kaunas, Lithuania, an old Tsarist fortress, the victims were murdered by Unit 3 of *Einsatzgruppe* (Action Squad) A. Before the court in Jerusalem Eichmann would claim that he had nothing to do with the killing: 'I have never killed a Jew. I have never killed anyone at all. I have not even given an order for the killing of a person, either a Jew or a non-Jew.' But, insisted police captain Avner Less at the trial in Israel, he *had* 'delivered people up for killing'.

Eichmann: 'Well, yes, that is correct, Captain, to the extent that I received orders for the evacuations. But not everyone I evacuated was killed. It was entirely beyond my knowledge, as to who was killed and who was not.'

To the very end Eichmann was convinced of his own innocence. He did not believe he could be accused of murder. 'I know that no-one can produce documentation that shows I did any such thing.'

The documents tell a different story. On 12 December 1941 the German envoy in Belgrade enquired from the Foreign Office in Berlin about what was to be done with the Serbian Jews, since there were no trains. Counsellor Rademacher picked up the phone and asked to be put through to Eichmann. While he talked to the 'Jewish expert' he made a hand-written note on the telegram: 'Eichmann suggests shooting.' His proposal was followed through.

In the east the murderers soon reached the limits of their capacity. For Eichmann the shooting was not only too brutal but also too inefficient. The departmental head sought new methods of killing. In summer 1941 Eichmann set out on an official trip to Auschwitz, in order to discuss important 'details' with the camp commandant, Rudolf Höss. As a prisoner in Poland after the war, Höss remembered the conversation: 'Eichmann familiarised me with killing by engine exhaust fumes in sealed trucks . . . For the mass transports that were expected at Auschwitz, this was out of the question.' According to Höss, Eichmann explained that destroying Jews with carbon monoxide gas 'required too many special premises, and obtaining enough gas for such large numbers would be very problematic'. The 'specialists', Eichmann and Höss, talked for a while longer about organisational 'problems' of the 'Final Solution', but came to no conclusion. As he left, Eichmann assured the camp commandant that he would make enquiries about a gas that was 'easy to obtain' and which required 'no special installations'. Eichmann was not merely the deporter – he was also the planner and executioner. But as a defendant in court he would of course always say that he co-ordinated the train timetables, and nothing more.

By September 1941 the gas that Eichmann had promised Höss had been discovered. In the basement of Block 11, one of the original buildings of the Auschwitz complex, Russian prisoners-of-war were gassed with Zyklon B – an anti-infestation agent that was now turned against human beings. As Höss recalled, shortly before his execution in 1947: 'Eichmann was an active man, constantly on the go, full of energy. He always had new plans and was always seeking innovations and improvements. The Jewish question and the Final Solution which had been ordered were an obsession with him.'

Only seldom was Eichmann at a loss about the right thing to do in his field of expertise. In September 1941 when his boss Reinhard Heydrich, newly appointed 'Reich Protector of Bohemia and Moravia', grandly announced at a press conference that the 'Protectorate' would be 'cleansed of Jews' in eight weeks, Eichmann immediately had a proposal at the ready: 'There is only one possibility, if this announcement is to be made good', he told Heydrich. 'Release enough land to accommodate all the Jews living in the Protectorate of Bohemia and Moravia, so they can all be in one place. That is the only way.' A ministerial permanent secretary, Karl Hermann Frank, immediately proposed Theresienstadt. Heydrich agreed, and sent Eichmann to inspect the small fortified town on the river Ohre (now Terezìn). The trip proved disappointing, as Eichmann wrote in his report: 'This is hopeless. Theresienstadt is too small; it can only provide a temporary answer for a small proportion of the Jews resident in the Protectorate.'

Theresienstadt was indeed only to be a stopgap. For tens of thousands, this concentration camp was merely a staging-post on the way to Auschwitz, an anteroom to the extermination camp. The idea of converting the old garrison town into a special ghetto for prominent Jews and those over sixty-five years old in fact came from Heydrich, not from Eichmann, who nonetheless liked to brag about his 'paternity' of this apparently 'privileged ghetto' with parks, family accommodation, a Jewish management and even its own orchestra.

Theresienstadt played a special part in Eichmann's career. It was the only concentration camp over which he had control. His own staff provided the commandants. He made the camp into a notorious 'human showcase', a propaganda weapon designed to deceive the world and blind it to the horrors of the extermination camps. The disquiet of inspectors from the International Red Cross was allayed when Eichmann showed the camp off to them as a 'model Jewish settlement'. For these visits, houses were specially painted, parks tidied up, and concerts and theatre productions put on. The inspectors allowed themselves to be bamboozled by Eichmann – music and dancing in place of murder and beatings. As Eichmann strode through the camp, the inmates scarcely dared to look up at him for fear of catching his eye. They knew what it meant when he turned up. Rudolf Gelbard, then a prisoner in Theresienstadt, recalls: 'Everyone tried to avoid being noticed. Because whenever Eichmann came to Theresienstadt, it had to do with deportations to the east.'

In the constantly overcrowded camp, transports were regularly assembled – destination Auschwitz. On about a dozen occasions Eichmann visited his Theresienstadt 'baby', to interrogate prisoners and issue instructions on the running of the camp. Scarcely a detail escaped his obsession for regulation. On 19 January 1942, while on an inspection of Theresienstadt, he approved a new type of 'two-tiered, four-person bunk'.

The following day, 20 January 1942, Eichmann was back on duty in Berlin. In the villa at 56/58 Am Grossen Wannsee, outside the capital, a number of senior officials convened under Heydrich's chairmanship. The topic for discussion: how the mass murder was to be organised. It was Eichmann who took the minutes. It was also he who provided the facts and figures for Heydrich's opening address, in which the security chief confirmed the task which Hermann Göring, as 'Commissioner for the Four-year Plan' had, in black and white, on 31 July 1941, instructed him to carry out. Heydrich, the authorisation stated, was to 'make all necessary preparations for a complete solution of the Jewish question in the German sphere of influence in Europe'. This also meant an enormous boost to Eichmann's position of power. As his colleague Dieter Wisliceny observed: 'He could simply override any objections and influences from other ministries and authorities.'

Six months after Göring had put his signature on the document, Heydrich was explaining to his Wannsee audience: 'In the scope of this final solution of the European Jewish problem, around 11 million Jews come into consideration.' They would 'be sent for forced labour in the east', in the course of which 'doubtless the majority would drop out through natural wastage'.

'What was meant by "natural wastage"?' Captain Avner Less asked Eichmann in the police interrogation twenty years later.

'It was people dying from completely normal causes. Things like a heart attack or pneumonia. If I were to die at this moment, that would be natural wastage.'

'The residue we will inevitably be left with at the end', Heydrich explained to the gentlemen around the table, 'will no doubt be the hardiest element, and will have to be given appropriate treatment, since it must be assumed that these people, representing a naturally selected group, would if liberated form the nucleus of a new Jewish revival.'

Avner Less: 'What was meant by "appropriate treatment"?'

Eichmann stuttered: 'It . . . it was . . . something that came from Himmler. Natural selection – that was his . . . his hobby-horse.'

'Yes, but what did it mean here?'

'It meant killed, killed! Certainly!'

'At the Wannsee Conference', Eichmann said in court, 'the leading figures of the then Reich were speaking. It was like the Pope giving orders. I had to obey.' After the conference, the meaning of this became clear. Heydrich's 'Jewish expert' was more than a mere minute-taker. He 'translated' what had been said around the conference-table into the coded language of the murderers. In the transcript we find no suggestion that the participants had in fact, as Eichmann confirmed to the court, 'discussed the business in very blunt terms . . . There was talk of killing and eliminating and exterminating.'

'The Popes of the Third Reich', as Eichmann called them, were the eight ministerial permanent secretaries, the six police and security experts and one departmental head, sitting round the Wannsee table. They spoke in plain language about procedures which Eichmann had seen with his own eyes. Yet he experienced no doubts or even scruples. 'At that moment', he told the court, 'I felt like Pontius Pilate, since I was free of all guilt . . . Who was

I to sit in judgement? Who was I to have an opinion of my own in this matter?' If the 'Popes' ordered it, then he clearly had to obey. For Eichmann it was as simple as that.

After the meeting Eichmann, Heydrich and Heinrich Müller, the Gestapo chief, withdrew to a room with a large open fire. For the planners of murder it was a job well done. Stewards handed round glasses of cognac. The atmosphere rapidly mellowed. 'I had never seen Heydrich so relaxed', Eichmann remembered.

Only after the Wannsee Conference do we find the term 'Final Solution of the Jewish problem' in Eichmann's decrees. In late January he informed all police stations in the 'Old Reich' (i.e. Germany) and all 'clearing-houses', that the latest deportations were the 'beginning of the Final Solution of the Jewish problem in the Old Reich, the eastern territories and the Protectorate of Bohemia and Moravia'. The course towards mass murder had finally been set. From March 1942 onward transports arrived in the extermination camps from all over Europe. The man responsible for the central direction of the deportations was the 'Jewish expert', Eichmann. On 22 June 1942 he wrote by express letter to the German Foreign Office: 'Our plans are, from mid-July or early August this year, to convey in special trains departing daily, each carrying 1,000 persons, initially some 40,000 Jews from the occupied zone of France, 40,000 Jews from the Netherlands and 10,000 Jews from Belgium, to forced labour in Auschwitz camp.' Day and night Eichmann's death-trains rumbled into the extermination camps. In timetabling the mass murder the German State Railways and their major client, Eichmann, worked closely together. The transport costs were 4 pfennigs per 'passenger' per kilometre. Third-class tickets were issued – one-way tickets, of course. Despite occasional 'transport problems' due to a shortage of railway wagons, Eichmann assumed he could 'carry the Final Solution through to completion' by June 1943. But all too often Eichmann's timetables fell foul of the war – for instance in June 1942 when the Wehrmacht needed every available wagon for the Don Offensive, just at the time when Eichmann was anxious to deport all the Jews from France to the east as rapidly as possible. Despite the pressure being placed on the German front line Eichmann wanted to raise the rate of deportations to three transports a week, each of 1,000 Jews. After several meetings with the Reich Ministry of Transport Eichmann got what he wanted: trains.

With painstaking precision Eichmann, the departmental head, saw to it that the death-trains departed and arrived on schedule. If any delay was threatened the bureaucrat flew into a rage. On 14 July 1942 the transport supremo received news of a monstrous occurrence in Paris: a train bound for Auschwitz was to be cancelled. Eichmann immediately grabbed the phone and spoke to the 'case officer' in Paris. At the other end of the line, *Obersturmbannführer* Heinz Röthke made a note of what his superior in Berlin bellowed at him: it was a 'matter of prestige', the whole business was 'very embarassing'. He, Eichmann, was considering whether to drop France as a country for deportation. Röthke implored Eichmann not to go to such lengths.

A week later, on 20 July 1942, Eichmann decreed that even children were to be sent to the death-camps. From France alone by June 1944, 15,000 children had been sent to the gas chambers. The commandant of Auschwitz, Rudolf Höss, declared to Eichmann that the children of the Jews had to be killed first, because they were the 'nucleus of the Jewish race', the generation of potential avengers. To Eichmann, people of the Jewish faith were simply 'material' to be freighted off to the extermination camps – for 'special treatment'.

Auschwitz-Birkenau, the scene of the greatest crime of the twentieth century, was a place that Eichmann knew only too well. In the summer of 1942 the man who 'supplied' victims for the gas-chambers paid another visit to the death-centre. Eichmann wanted to see convincing on-the-spot evidence of how many transports the extermination camp was capable of 'processing'. 'I could cope with anything,' he told Sassen in one of their conversations after the war, 'anything except a hold-up in the timetable. Because then I would have been held responsible for other hold-ups in the Reich railway network.'

With anxieties of this kind at the back of his mind, Eichmann, together with the camp commandant, Rudolf Höss, took a close look at Auschwitz (as Eichmann later noted: 'That man had an understanding of people's difficulties'). 'As I was driving through', Eichmann recounted during his interrogation, 'I saw a big building.

It was almost the size of a factory, with a huge chimney, and Höss said to me: "There's your capacity! Ten thousand!" . . . I didn't watch the gassing business. Couldn't do it. I'd probably have keeled over. And I thought: well, I've got away with it again! And then he drove me to a big pit, it was very big . . . And there was a huge grid, an iron grid. And on it corpses were burning. That made me sick. I felt sick.' He confided to Sassen, the SS man, that at that moment he recited the Creed: 'I believe in God, the Father Almighty, maker of heaven and earth . . .'

A desk-bound perpetrator at the scene of the crime, he felt a lot of self-pity, but offered no word about the suffering of his victims. 'When I saw dead Jews for the first time', Eichmann said in court, 'I was shattered. And from that time on this nervous reaction never ceased. It continued to affect me.' Is there any truth in Eichmann's statement? Did the sight actually move him? Wilhelm Höttl describes Eichmann as being 'inwardly not all that strong'. It was seeing the cremation-pits in Birkenau that particularly shook him. 'He didn't admit it, but his nerves were all to pieces and he took a quick swig of slivovitz from an army water-bottle.'

The scenes he witnessed may have momentarily shocked Eichmann, but his conscience remained silent. He was unaware of any personal guilt and continued as usual, co-ordinating death-trains and signing sentences of death. However, he placed the hideous images from the extermination camps in the bottom drawer of his memory. 'The Jews I deported didn't . . . interest me', he told Willem Sassen in Argentina. 'It was of no interest to me whether they were alive or dead. If people were carted off, they were carted off. I wasn't interested in them!'

We stood like sardines in a can, with scarcely enough air to breathe. It was as if we were travelling down a long black tunnel from which there was no escape. We didn't know where our journey was taking us, or when and how it would end.

Valéria Wache, death-camp survivor

Posing as the remorseful penitent, Eichmann declared at his trial: 'Even at that time I regarded the violent solution as unjustifiable, as a dreadful act in which regrettably, being bound by my oath to the flag, I was obliged to participate in my field of transportation matters; and I could not be released from this oath.'

Five years earlier, in 1956, it was a different Eichmann that Willem Sassen saw in their conversations together: 'I did my job according to the iron imperative that was imposed upon me . . . If I'd been put in the post of commandant of a concentration camp, I would have acted no differently. And if I'd been ordered to gas Jews or to shoot Jews, then I would have carried out the orders.'

By the spring of 1944 five million Jews had already been murdered. On 19 March the Holocaust finally reached Hungary, the country which, at that time, had the largest Jewish community in Europe. Eleven divisions descended on Hungary from every direction, including from the air. Hungary's defence force, the Honved, put up no resistance. Eichmann had made detailed preparations for his new 'mission'. A week before the invasion he had assembled a small band of extermination 'specialists' for a conference at the Mauthausen concentration camp, on the Danube in Austria. The first item on the agenda was: what is the quickest way to deport 750,000 Hungarian Jews to Auschwitz? On the day the Germans marched in, Eichmann's 38th birthday, the *Sonderkommando* went straight into action. Throughout the country raids were mounted in search of Jews. On the first day of the occupation 200 Jewish lawyers and doctors were arrested in Budapest and dragged off to Mauthausen. Their names had been picked at random from the telephone directory. Terror became a daily experience for the Jews of Hungary: robbed of their homes and their possessions they were no longer allowed to travel, nor to practise their professions, not even to own a telephone or radio set. They were crammed together in 'transit ghettos', maltreated, humiliated and beaten up. It is true that a Hungarian government nominally remained in power, but the country was actually ruled by one Dr Edmund Veesenmayer, Hitler's 'viceroy'. However, the man who made the decisions about the destruction of the Hungarian Jews was Adolf Eichmann. It was there that he intended to bring to completion what he considered his 'life's work': the annihilation of every Jew in Europe.

He was the typical sadistic bureaucrat. In Hungary he was capable of sitting down together with the leaders of the Jewish community, although he knew that the next day he would be sending them to their death. He made them promises and he issued threats. This game of cat-and-mouse gave him real satisfaction.

Gabriel Bach, prosecutor at Eichmann's trial

Eichmann set up the headquarters for the Hungarian mass murder in the Hotel Majestic, on a hill high above the city. Things were working in his favour, though with a deadly outcome. The Hungarian authorities were only too willing to help the executioner in his hunt for Jews. The new prime minister, Döme Szotay, assisted Eichmann with enthusiasm, as did two permanent secretaries in the Ministry of the Interior, who were notable for their particular fanaticism: Laszlo Endre, officially responsible for the 'Liquidation of the Jewish Problem', and Laszlo Baky, the chief of police. Eichmann could rely on these accomplices. Hungarian police beat up and mistreated Jews under German supervision.

At the end of March 1944 Hitler's henchman, Eichmann, made it clear to his lackeys that the hour had struck for Hungary's Jews: 'At an informal gathering over a glass of Hungarian wine, I informed them that Himmler had given an order to the German police, and that he would very much like to see the Jews evacuated from the east of Hungary to the west and then taken to Auschwitz.' The details were discussed at a conference on 7 April 1944, attended by Eichmann and his team, Wehrmacht officers and representatives of the Hungarian government and police. Hungary was to be divided into six zones and 'cleansed of Jews', step by step. It was decided that the extermination campaign should begin in the eastern region of Siebenbürgen and end in Budapest. The estimated time allowed for the murder of Hungary's Jews was three months, preferably less. At the start of the German occupation, the Swiss Vice-Consul, Carl Lutz, had paid a call at the Hotel Majestic, to intercede on behalf of Jewish families who had been detained.

The impression Eichmann made on him was of 'a forceful, intrepid officer, a daredevil who knew what he was about. One of the things he used to say was: "We German soldiers aren't afraid. Where would we be if we were scared of death? My comrades are fighting in Russia, and I'm fighting in this job.'

> Without the help of the Hungarian authorities, Eichmann could not have taken one step in Hungary. He himself said it would have been impossible without the help of the Hungarian gendarmerie, the local authorities and the railway management. We could not have deported the provincial Jewish communities the way we did.
>
> *Istvan Domonkos, Hungarian Jew*

Eichmann's principal weapons in this battle were lies. He engineered the deportations with a diabolical guile. He could foresee that his mission of destruction could only succeed if his victims did not stage a revolt. The comparatively weak German forces occupying Hungary would have great difficulty quelling an uprising like the one in the Warsaw ghetto. So for his deportations to run according to schedule Eichmann needed calm to reign among his victims – a funereal calm. To achieve this end, he resorted to treachery and deceit. He sent men to Budapest synagogues in military uniforms without insignia of rank, who announced themselves as 'Jewish labour' from the Wehrmacht and gave glowing reports of the 'good work to be found in German armaments factories'. Women and children received the best of care in family camps, they claimed – a lie which was subsequently reinforced by mail. In those fateful days many Jews received mysterious postcards. Valéria Wache from the provincial Hungarian town of Bonyhad received a card purporting to be from relatives. Under a postmark reading 'Black Forest', the 'relatives' wrote: 'We're doing fine. Don't worry about us.' Hundreds, if not thousands, of such cards were sent to victims at that time. The tone was always the same: 'We are in a beautiful spa town. Come and join us soon, so that you can still find accommodation. Don't forget to bring good, strong shoes for country excursions.'

Eichmann had thought of everything. All along the battlefronts the German army was short of good footwear.

Eichmann's lies spread like a cancerous growth, which propagated as quickly as it did because the victims themselves had been inveigled into helping with the deception. Eichmann had established a Central Jewish Council – an assembly of prominent Jews, whose task was to convey his instructions to the Jewish communities. Thus the lies were lent a fatal credibility. It was announced that the Jewish population had to be removed from the battle area for safety reasons, and transferred to a labour camp. This lie, coming from the mouths of respected Jewish councillors, sounded to many like a promise of better things, rather than a sentence of death. In Hungary, just as he had done in Vienna, Eichmann made accomplices of his victims and lulled them into believing that their collaboration could prevent worse from happening. Trapped in this illusion, the Jewish Council organised ghettos and provided Eichmann's *Sonderkommando* with lists of names.

In Budapest Eichmann regularly received Jewish functionaries in his office, calmed their anxieties, and spoke to them with feigned sympathy about the agonising situation of the Hungarian Jews – for which he himself, of course, was largely responsible. One of these meetings, on 5 April 1944, produced the impetus for a fiendish scheme. Rudolf Kasztner, head of the Jewish-Zionist Rescue Committee, asked Eichmann what price he would exact for abandoning all deportations of Jews from Hungary. There was nothing new about such 'business practices': the freedom of several hundred Jews had already been bought from the SS. On Himmler's instructions Eichmann played along with this approach. On 16 or 25 April 1944 Hungary's extermination chief proposed a fateful deal to his interlocutor, Joel Brand, who like Kasztner was a member of the Zionist Rescue Committtee. After the war Brand recalled the oppressive atmosphere of the 'negotiations': 'Eichmann said "Do you know who I am? I carried out the operations in the Reich, in Poland, and in Czechoslovakia. Now it's Hungary's turn . . . I'm prepared to sell you a million Jews. I won't sell you all the Jews. You wouldn't be able to raise that much money and goods. But one million is possible. Goods for blood – blood for goods. You can collect this million from any country where there are Jews. You can take them from Hungary, Poland, the Eastern Territories, from Theresienstadt, from Auschwitz, wherever you like. What kind of people do you want to rescue? Fertile males? Women of childbearing age? Old people? Children. Sit down and let's have it!'"

Joel Brand had been carefully observing the man, who spoke in a sharp, staccato manner: 'He looked like an average business executive. It was only his eyes that were unusual. Steel-blue, hard and menacing, they seemed to be boring into the person facing him . . . He wore an elegant uniform and his movements were brisk and somewhat jerky. His way of speaking was unusual, too. He would fire off a few words and then pause. When he was talking, it always reminded me of the chatter of a machine-gun. He didn't speak with a regional accent, but occasionally used a word wrongly. For example he talked about men capable of "production" (*Erzeugung*) instead of "reproduction" (*Zeugung*)'.

Brand flew to Istanbul to make contact with the Allies and persuade them to pay the ransom. He took his leave of Eichmann on 15 May. It was the day that the deportations began in the Carpathian region of Hungary. Forty sealed cattle-trucks left Hungary bound for Auschwitz. Ever deceitful, Eichmann had warned Brand he must be back with an answer within two weeks, 'otherwise I'll set the mills of Auschwitz grinding!' Even as Joel Brand's aircraft took off, Eichmann was on his way to Auschwitz-Birkenau to check that the camp had been made ready for the transports from Hungary.

While Brand was doing everything he could in Istanbul, his wife Hansi and their two children had to remain in Budapest – in Eichmann's power. She had to report to his staff by telephone every day. She repeatedly went to see Eichmann in person as well. 'We wanted to keep in contact', she says today, ' because the lives of the Jews depended on Eichmann.' But Hansi Brand denies emphatically that this was 'a pact with the Devil'. 'It was an attempt to save lives. Of course we had to negotiate with the man who held the power.'

The truth was that Eichmann's 'offer' was a ruse to keep the victims in suspense so that the deportations could proceed calmly. He had engineered the 'blood for goods' deal because he had been ordered to do so. *Reichsführer* SS Heinrich Himmler had hoped in this way to establish contacts with the west, which might pave the way to a separate peace. Seeing himself as Hitler's successor, Himmler wanted to present himself to the world as a 'humane' alternative to the Führer. However, Eichmann was interested in one thing above all: keeping the trains rolling, so that the Jews of Hungary could be transported by the swiftest means possible to the extermination camps. For him the discussions with Jewish officials were no more than an amusing game, played against a background of tragedy. In Jerusalem Gabriel Bach, prosecutor at Eichmann's trial, questioned every witness to Eichmann's activities in Hungary and worked his way through mountains of documents. 'Eichmann was the typical sadistic bureaucrat', he said in his summing-up. 'In Hungary he was capable of sitting down together with the leaders of the Jewish community, although he knew that the next day he would send them to their death. He made them promises and issued threats. This game of cat-and-mouse gave him real satisfaction.'

In the course of these 'negotiations' Eichmann made a forced attempt to appear intimidating, in the manner he imagined an SS man should adopt: emotionally cold, pitiless. But the impression he left with Hansi Brand was rather one of nervous agitation. 'He seemed to be afraid. A steel helmet and revolver lay on his desk and there was a nervous twitch at one corner of his mouth. We were standing two metres away from him and could still smell clearly that he had been drinking.'

What was it that was destroying Eichmann's nerves? The awareness of his shared guilt for the murder of millions? Or fear of assassination, the fate that his mentor and superior Reinhard Heydrich had met in Prague? His worries were not without justification. As Manus Diamant, a member of the Jewish resistance group, Hagana, told us in an interview: 'We wanted to kill Eichmann at the railway station in Debrecen. I had disguised myself as a porter and was carrying a suitcase full of explosives. I watched Eichmann walking up and down the platform, supervising the transports. Things couldn't move fast enough for him.' However, the bomb was not detonated. 'Our HQ in Budapest were against it, because they anticipated reprisals, as there had been when Heydrich was assassinated. Our people believed such an act would only accelerate the deportations.'

Eichmann suspected that his victims would try to kill him. Anyone trying to photograph or film him got a very clear indication of his nervousness. He smashed cameras and tore the film from them. As Simon Wiesenthal reads this behaviour: 'He knew very well that one day he would be hunted as a criminal.'

On 20 July the BBC announced from London that the German offer of 'blood for goods' had been turned down. Brand's mission had failed, not just because of Eichmann's duplicity, but due to the indifference of the Allies. The 'mills of Auschwitz' continued to grind with deadly precision. Every day, between 14,000 and 15,000 Hungarian Jews reached the death-camp; in just two months no less than 450,000 were deported. Death came for some even before the trains arrived in Auschwitz. As many as a hundred people were crammed into each cattle-truck; in the middle stood two pails, one of water, the other for calls of nature. Though it was only May, the temperature had reached midsummer levels, further intensifying the struggle for survival in the agonising confines of the trucks.

On arrival in Auschwitz-Birkenau, the victims, exhausted and close to death, shuffled along the ramp, driven by barked orders from SS men. For most of them, their journey led straight to the gas-chamber. To the end they believed they were being 'resettled' – in a labour-camp. Jehoshua Rosenblum who, as a member of the Jewish *Sonderkommando* or camp labour squad, was forced to work in the crematorium, can never forget the horrifying scenes in the preparation-room outside the gas-chamber: 'The Hungarian Jews didn't know what was going to happen to them. They asked us: "Where are we? Are we in a family camp?"' Eichmann's lies were effective to the last.

Miraculously, on 7 April 1944, two prisoners named Walter Rosenberg and Karl Wetzler managed to escape from that Hell. A few weeks later, the Jewish leaders in Hungary knew where the transports were really going. Wetzler and Rosenberg wrote a terrifying report on the mass murder in the gas-chambers. The so-called 'Auschwitz Protocol' was the first precise and detailed eye-witness account to come from the innermost depths of the murder-machine. 'Currently there are four crematoria operating in Birkenau . . . Next to the furnaces there is a large preparatory hall which is built to look like a bath-house . . . The victims are led into the hall where they are told they are going to have a bath. There they undress and, in order to reinforce their belief, they are given soap and a towel. Then they are pushed into the gas-chambers.'

Tragically, the world did not hear of the Auschwitz Protocol until early July, by which time two-thirds of the Hungarian Jews had been murdered. However, a number of Jewish officials knew of the report some time earlier. Rudolf Kasztner had known of the annihilation since the end of April without informing the Jews in Hungary. What would have happened if he *had* warned the victims? Would he have actually been believed? Kasztner was scarcely known in Hungary. Nevertheless he succeeded in negotiating with Eichmann that a total of 30,000 Jews would not be deported to Auschwitz, but to other concentration camps where the chances of survival were higher. Even before the end of the war, 1,800 Jews were able to travel to the safety of Switzerland with Eichmann's permission – on one condition: that Kasztner must keep to himself the fateful secret of the annihilation, so that Eichmann could complete his deadly assignment without interruption. The few who were warned and who heard about the mass murder from the BBC's Hungarian-language broadcasts, would not and could not believe what hitherto had seemed unthinkable.

By this time the Allies had long known about the mass murder. On 4 April 1944 US reconnaissance aircraft had taken photos of Auschwitz-Birkenau from a height of 27,000 feet. The crematoria could clearly be recognised. Even so, the death-camps remained untouched – photographed but not bombed! In the words of the Allied strategists Birkenau was a 'secondary war target'. In the summer of 1944 world opinion was focused on other events. The landing of Allied troops on the Normandy beaches promised an early end to the war. The tragedy of the Hungarian Jews went almost unnoticed. Events throughout the world seemed to be conspiring against Eichmann's victims.

Until that point, not even Hungary's regent, Miklós Horthy, had dared to protest against the crimes. Not until 8 July 1944, too late for hundreds of thousands, did he speak from his position of authority, announcing an end to the deportations. Protests from neutral countries, a threat by US President Roosevelt to bomb Budapest and not least the 'revolt of conscience' within his own family had moved Horthy to take this step. Eichmann reacted with indignation. 'He was terribly angry', recalls Wilhem Höttl, who was working in Budapest for the foreign intelligence service of the SD. 'He called Horthy "an old *depp*", an Austrian word for nitwit. Horthy's got no say in this. *We* decide what happens in Hungary.'

Eichmann's henchmen went on rounding up Jews in the outer suburbs of Budapest, and carting them off. Paul Lendvai, today a leading journalist, author and director of Radio Austria International, was forced to watch as one of his female cousins, despite the decree by Hungary's Crown Council, 'was deported to Auschwitz, just because Eichmann insisted on it'. Eichmann used every trick to bypass Horthy's authority. With no intention of giving in meekly, he gave orders for 1,500 Jews from the Kistarcza assembly-camp near Budapest to be despatched to Auschwitz. But Horthy, alerted by the Jewish Council in Kistarcza, had the train halted just short of the frontier. Two days later – when the train was back in Kistarcza – Eichmann issued new orders for the transport. This time he was successful. He had the Jewish Council put under arrest for the whole day, so that Horthy could not be informed. The train reached Auschwitz.

In late August 1944 Eichmann called, as he often did, at the Budapest apartment of his friend Wilhelm Höttl. Eichmann was in a bad mood, he looked exhausted and depressed. The military situation was getting worse by the day. In Italy the Americans had advanced as far as Florence, and in the east Minsk, Vilnius and Warsaw had fallen; the Red Army was pushing forward relentlessly, and on 23 August even Roumania had changed sides. Eichmann knew the war would soon be over and that he would then be hunted as a criminal. Höttl took this opportunity of putting to Eichmann the all-important question: how many Jews were murdered? Eichmann knew the exact number of victims. As Höttl remembers: 'He talked of six million dead. Four million had died in the extermination camps and two million at the hands of the *Einsatzkommandos* or from hunger and disease.' Eichmann's estimate has today been confirmed by historical research.

It was not the first time this question had been put to him in

Hungary. Once before, a young *Untersturmführer* had wanted to know: 'How many, *Obersturmbannführer*?' 'Over five million,' was Eichmann's reply.

'What will happen after the war, *Obersturmanbannführer*, when the world asks about those millions?'

Eichmann answered: 'A hundred dead are a catastrophe, a million are a statistic.'

Eichmann's project, the deportation of all Jews to extermination camps, was under increasing threat from resistance activities. Eichmann's opponents were chiefly among the staff of neutral embassies. Diplomats and businessmen from Portugal, Spain, Italy, the Vatican, Sweden and Switzerland faced up to Eichmann because they wanted to retain their humanity in inhuman times. The chief actors in this drama were the Swiss vice-consul Carl Lutz and the Swede Raoul Wallenberg. 'When Wallenberg came to Hungary', recalls Alexander Grossman, Lutz' closest colleague in Budapest, 'he asked Lutz for advice and Lutz told him: "Wallenberg, if you want to save lives, do what I do and issue letters of safe-conduct."' Some hope remained for Jews who possessed such a document or who were named in a 'group passport', since they were under the protection of Switzerland or Sweden. The bureaucratic Eichmann could be defeated with his own weapons: an obsession with papers, documents and rubber stamps. Lutz was prepared to allow the forgery of Swiss protective passports and soon tens of thousands of these documents were circulating in the Hungarian capital. Eichmann was incensed. He complained about the flood of protective passports to Rudolf Kasztner, with whom he was still playing the negotiating game. 'Lutz and Wallenberg will pay for this damned mess', Eichmann ranted.

He even described as 'intolerable' the so-called safe houses which, like islands in the ocean, offered a refuge to persecuted Jews. In Budapest, 72 buildings enjoyed Swiss sovereign status and over 30 were under the protection of the Swedish crown. In the houses marked with the yellow star desperate people could hope to escape the Eichmann terror, albeit in very cramped accommodation. One of them was Paul Lendvai, who had fled with his parents to a Swiss house of safety. 'There were 50 or 60 people living in a two-room apartment. Everywhere was packed out, even the staircase. The conditions were inhuman, and death was lurking outside.' Protective passports and houses of safety saved the lives of over 100,000 Jews. They sent Eichmann into such a rage that he threatened to shoot the 'Jew-loving wretch'. However, an attack on the Swede's car misfired.

On 25 August Himmler himself forbade any further deportations of Jews to any part of the Reich, which included Auschwitz. Yet Eichmann no longer understood the meaning of the word 'stop'. He wanted to bring his task to total completion. Even if the war against the Allies was lost, he wanted to win his personal war against the Jews – just to please Hitler. 'The greatest thing he wanted,' says Wilhelm Höttl, 'was to be received just once by Hitler, for Hitler to thank him for the extermination. That was his dream. He never made it, and that was something he never got over.'

On 15 October Hungary's fascists, the Arrow Cross, seized power. Miklós Horthy was overthrown, and with him went any official resistance to the deportations. Once again the way was clear for Eichmann. After the coup d'état the Hungarian Jews were threatened on two sides: by the new government and by Eichmann's thugs. 'It was a unique kind of reign of terror, rule by the mob', recalls Paul Lendvai. 'The Arrow Cross people were accomplices of the Germans. They went on killing people to the very end and we realised that now we really *were* in for it.' Immediately after the fascists had seized power Eichmann set about carrying out his last assignment in Hungary: 50,000 Budapest Jews were sent to the Austrian frontier, to build defensive installations there. It all had to be done very quickly. The Red Army had already reached Kecskemet, 50 miles south-east of Budapest. On 6 November Soviet units had advanced as far as the outer ring of defences around the Hungarian capital. Eichmann knew how the fronts stood. He listened to the BBC. He only had a little time left. Yet the problems were piling up. Allied bombers had destroyed the railway line between Budapest and Vienna; and he was short of trains. So Eichmann sent 40,000 Budapest Jews on foot towards Austria. It was on 10 November that the death-marches began. Thousands died on the highway from Budapest to the Austrian border and Vienna. 'Even when we were only a little way out of Budapest,' says Paul Lendvai, who succeeded in escaping from the death-column, 'people who were tired or couldn't walk fast enough, were shot. It was a race against death.'

In the first week of December 1944 the Red Army captured the outer suburbs of Budapest. At 3 p.m. on Christmas Eve Eichmann left Budapest for Berlin. There was an apocalyptic atmosphere in the Central Office of Reich Security. Documents were being destroyed, and the guilty men were concocting their stories for after the war. For the last time Eichmann was praised by his superior officer. The Gestapo boss, Heinrich Müller, said, 'If we'd had fifty Eichmanns, we'd have won the war.'

In March and April 1945 Eichmann returned three times to take a look at Theresianstadt, *his* concentration camp. What drew him back there? On 6 April he gave a presentation to a delegation of the International Red Cross, about how 'humane' the conditions in the camp were. This falsification of the facts was successful, as we can see from IRC reports. But Eichmann had yet another task to deal with: on Himmler's instructions he was to select between 100 and 200 prominent Jews and take them safely to the Austrian Tirol – as hostages in Himmler's fantasy of peace negotiations with the Western Allies, who were advancing on all sides.

Eichmann now began a journey of escape which was to last a year: 28 April, departure from Prague; 29 April, stopover in Budejovice; 1 May, arrival in Ebensee, northern Austria. On 2 May Eichmann found himself in the Salzkammergut lakeland of Austria, the last refuge of many leading Nazis. There in the mountains of his homeland, Eichmann planned to fight to the last, at the head of a partisan resistance group. Yet he was exhausted and downcast. His boss, Ernst Kaltenbrunner, who had originally brought him into the SS and was now awaiting the end of the war playing games of 'patience', would not even receive him. In the shadow of the Loser mountain, overlooking Lake Altaussee, Eichmann met an old friend from his Vienna and Budapest days: Wilhelm Höttl. 'He was a nervous wreck and was supporting himself with a stick. He complained that Kaltenbrunner refused to see him and had simply asked his adjutant to hand over a wad of British banknotes to him. He was furious. "To hell with that. I don't need money. I've got my own. I want orders! I want to know what we do now!"'

Without orders Eichmann seemed to have no orientation. He had always been an outsider. Now he was proving to his accomplices that he was also a security risk. 'They'll be searching for *you* as a war criminal, not us', the commandant of Theresienstadt, Anton Burger, told him in no uncertain terms. 'You'll be doing your colleagues a great service if you make yourself scarce.' Eichmann counted out 5,000 reichsmarks to each of his henchmen, who all had to sign receipts. Then, together with a room-mate from his SD days in Berlin, Rudolf Jänisch, he set off for Salzburg. After all, there might still be an SS unit there that he could join. As Jänisch recalls: 'We were in scruffy civilian clothes. No sooner were we back on German soil than we ran straight into an American patrol. The blood-group tattoos underneath our arms gave us away as SS men.' But the GIs still did not know exactly who it was they had caught in their net. In the guise of 'SS *Untersturmbannführer* Otto Eckmann' Eichmann disappeared among the vast horde of German prisoners-of-war. One among millions – unrecognised, and yet plagued with the fear of being discovered. He thought about suicide. 'It wouldn't have mattered a damn', Eichmann confessed to Willem Sassen in Argentina, with the usual pathos in his voice. Eichmann planned to take his life with an injection of morphine – but 'I didn't have a hypodermic'.

> The Americans had really no idea of the importance of Eichmann's role; they only fished him out, so to speak, when they had no-one else left.
>
> *Wilhelm Höttl, former SS Sturmbannführer*

As a prisoner he had only one thought in his mind: escape. In December 1945, when he was being tried *in absentia* at the Nuremberg war crime tribunal, he was able to escape from the Oberdachstetten camp with false papers in the name of Otto Henninger. He now remained for five years in Germany –

unmolested, a criminal on the run from terrestrial justice. Eichmann kept his head above water financially by taking on casual work. In Lower Saxony he became known as a lumberjack, then in a village near Celle, under the noses of the British army of occupation, he began keeping chickens. No-one suspected anything.

Meanwhile, Eichmann's wife and their children were living at Fischerndorf 8, a house beside the Altaussee lake in Austria. It was anticipated that her husband might attempt to re-establish contact with her. American officials of the Counter-Intelligence Corps (CIC), alerted by Simon Wiesenthal, went to see Vera Liebl. She assured them, however, that she had been divorced from Eichmann since March 1945 and had heard nothing from him. No, she did not have a photograph of him. As far as she knew, he was no longer alive.

In 1947 Vera Liebl tried to have her husband declared dead, so that his name could be removed from the 'wanted' list. But this did not fool Simon Wiesenthal: the supposed eye-witness to the shooting of Eichmann in Prague turned out to be Vera Liebl's brother-in-law. With some justification Wiesenthal says: 'This unspectacular step was probably my most important contribution to the Eichmann case.' No-one hunts for dead criminals.

'Otto Henninger' now saw himself in ever increasing danger. With all the incriminating documents that were coming to light in war crime trials, he had to face the fact that any day his cover could be blown. Eichmann planned his escape from Germany. Churchmen in Rome, including the Austrian bishop Alois Hudal, obtained a passport for the bureaucrat of death. A little later, in June 1950, thanks to this help from the corridors of the Vatican, Eichmann left Europe by ship. A photograph published later shows him on deck, wearing sun-glasses and a bow tie – flanked by two men helping him in his escape. It was on 14 July 1950 that Adolf Eichmann, an ordinary man in a hat and bow tie, first set foot on Argentinian soil. His passport declared him to be Ricardo Klement, Catholic, unmarried, stateless. False papers, a work-permit and an alias made him confident that he would finally be able to leave his murky past behind him. His family was soon to follow him.

Back in Europe, however, survivors of Eichmann's death industry had no intention of giving up the search for him. Simon Wiesenthal, whose office in Linz was right opposite 'Adolf Eichmann & Sons', electrical retailers, was especially tenacious. Rumours were going round that Eichmann was living in Syria, or perhaps in Kuwait or Brazil. He had probably had his appearance altered. Wiesenthal received the first concrete evidence of Eichmann's whereabouts early in 1952, when an Austrian baron showed him a letter he had received from a friend in Buenos Aires. In it was one sentence which electrified Wiesenthal: 'I've seen that swine Eichmann, who bossed the Jews about. He lives near Buenos Aires and works for a water company.'

Eichmann's employer was in fact CAPRI, a dubious firm in which high-ranking Nazis and Wehrmacht officers earned a living as advisers to the Argentinian army. Officially, however, CAPRI was responsible for the water supply in the provinces of Tucuman and Santiago del Estero. As a 'hydrologist' Eichmann had the job of checking the water-levels – hardly a demanding occupation. His former boss in CAPRI, Heinz Lühr, remembers an unreliable, taciturn employee named Klement: 'He wasn't accurate enough. He was sloppy and reported water-levels which, given the weather conditions, were simply not possible. I challenged him about it but he just shoved the blame on to his Argentinian assistants. You certainly couldn't call him a good organiser.' Lühr had once even been a guest at Eichmann's house in Tucuman. Frau Eichmann served roast wild boar, which her spouse had personally bagged with a rifle in the forest.

Their family life had impressed Heinz Lühr as 'harmonious'. But any questions relating to Eichmann's past were taboo at table. 'He was very suspicious; perhaps he already had an idea that bloodhounds had been put on his trail.' Lühr did as he was advised: 'Don't ask him about it; he has been through terrible experiences.'

In 1955 Eichmann's fourth son came into the world. He was christened Ricardo Francisco – 'Ricardo' being his own alias, and 'Francisco' after the priest in Rome who had helped him escape. A year later he confessed to his confidant Willem Sassen: 'I'm slowly getting tired of living as an anonymous wanderer between two worlds . . . I'd be more than willing to give myself up to the German authorities, if I wasn't concerned about the fact that the interest in the politics of the affair might still be too great for a clear, objective outcome to be achieved . . . I was nothing other than a loyal, conscientious, correct and proper member of the SS and the Central Officer of Reich Security – and only inspired by idealism towards the Fatherland to which I had the honour to belong. Deep down I was never a *schweinehund* [bastard], nor was I a traitor. Despite rigorous self-examination I am convinced in myself that I am not a murderer, still less a mass murderer.' With not a word of remorse, Eichmann sought refuge in concepts like 'oath to the flag' and 'performance of duty'.

Since Eichmann had proved to be incompetent, he was dismissed by CAPRI. The firm bought him a steam laundry, but the business of washing dirty linen did not appeal to him. He was soon forced to sell the laundry at a loss. He moved with his wife and children to Buenos Aires, survived for a while as a car mechanic and preparer with the Argentina branch of Mercedes-Benz, then tried his hand at breeding rabbits. Precisely where he lived was for a long time a mystery to his pursuers until, of all people, a blind Jew tracked him down.

> Eichmann had made many attempts to break out from his anonymity, and it is quite remarkable that it took the Israeli secret service several years – until August 1959 – to establish that Adolf Eichmann was living in Argentina under the name of Ricardo Klement.
>
> *Hannah Arendt*

In 1957 a Jewish pensioner in Buenos Aires, Lothar Hermann, wrote to Fritz Bauer, the Attorney-General of the state of Hessen, in Frankfurt, to say that Eichmann was living in Olivos, a suburb of Buenos Aires, at 4261 Chacabuco Street. Bauer passed on the information to Isser Harel, the head of Israel's secret service, Mossad. An agent immediately put the house in Chacabuco Street under observation but reported to Tel Aviv that it was unlikely that

Eichmann would be living in such a shabby building. In 1958, when Hermann's story became a tangle of contradictions, Harel lost interest in the trail. The Hermann file disappeared into a bottom drawer and Eichmann was able to survive another year at liberty.

Even today Harel will not admit that he missed a trick here. However, more than a quarter of a century later, one of his agents, Zvi Aharoni, is all the more critical of his boss: 'If I were Harel, I couldn't bring myself to speak the name of Eichmann. For over two years he knew the exact address of the Eichmann family and did nothing, absolutely nothing.' Isser Harel makes no reply to these reproaches: 'I prefer not to get into a debate in the German media with one of my people.'

Meanwhile, Attorney-General Bauer had not given up. In late 1959 he went to see his colleague Chaim Cohen in Tel Aviv. The German jurist was furious that Mossad had not continued to follow the Hermann trail. Bauer presented new evidence which shed a different light on Hermann's information that the name 'Klement' was among those listed on the electricity meter of 4261 Chacabuco Street. For he now knew that Eichmann had left Europe nine years before under the name of Ricardo Klement. Now Harel had to act. He promised Bauer he would put an agent on to Eichmann. On 1 May 1960, two and a half years after Mossad had first found out Adolf Eichmann's exact address, secret agent Zvi Aharoni landed in Buenos Aires.

Aharoni's first move was to locate the house at 4261 Chacabuco Street. He had an unpleasant surprise. It was empty. Inside, decorators were painting the walls. If Eichmann had indeed lived there, he had now disappeared. Aharoni summarised his investigations over the next few days in a coded telex to his boss, Isser Harel: 'The beater has gone. He moved out of the copse three weeks ago and I am trying to find out the new address.'

From a householder in Chacabuco Street Aharoni found out that Klement had moved to a single-storey, bare brick shack in the San Fernando district. The address was 14 Garibaldi Street, and Aharoni watched the house. 'Suddenly I saw a man who fitted our profile in age and height.' Aharoni's next step was to find out who owned the house. The information was obtained for him by a Jewish architect: No. 14 was registered in the name of 'Veronica

Catarina Liebel de Fichmann'. Liebel was Vera Eichmann's maiden name and 'F' in place of 'E' in the surname was a deliberate falsification by Eichmann when registering the property. 'When I saw that', Aharoni remembers, 'I knew I'd cracked it.' Now the next stage of 'Operation Eichmann' could be planned. In April 1960 an eleven-strong Mossad team began the final preparations in Buenos Aires, organised plane tickets, false passports and a house where Eichmann could be hidden after his abduction. In various Buenos Aires cafés they sat and discussed it: there was Rafi Eitan, the slightly built leader of 'Operation Eichmann', Zvika Malkin, the team's strong-man, who with another agent was to overpower Eichmann, the head of the secret service, Isser Harel, who pulled the strings in the background, and Zvi Aharoni. They debated how, where and when Eichmann could best be picked up. 'We happened to notice that at a quarter to eight in the evenings he would walk home from the bus stop', Zvi Aharoni tells us. 'Then we watched him every evening and he always came back on the same bus. So we then decided that it would be best to grab him outside his house.' The date for the pick-up: 11 May 1960, just before 8 p.m., in Garibaldi Street.

At 19.40 Aharoni parked the getaway vehicle in a side-street along which Eichmann walked home from the bus stop every evening. The bus came along as usual, but did not stop. 'In the past seven days,' Aharoni recalls, 'Eichmann had always been punctual. We waited for a quarter of an hour; according to our original plan we should have driven away.'

'My men were becoming uneasy', Rafi Eitan, leader of 'Operation Eichmann' confirms. 'Aharoni said nervously, "Maybe we've been seen; maybe we should come back tomorrow." I said: "No, wait! At eight o'clock he asked again: "What should we do?" I said once again: "We wait!"'

Aharoni: 'We stayed another few minutes then along came the bus and in it sat Eichmann.'

Eitan: 'Aharoni was the first to spot him. He noticed that Eichmann had his hand in his pocket and was afraid that he might be armed.'

Aharoni: 'He came straight towards us and I could see his left hand in his pocket. I hissed to Rafi: "Maybe he's got a gun!" Then I pointed it out to Zvika Malkin.'

Eitan: 'It was incredibly tense. Eichmann came closer and closer and as he passed our car Zvika stood in his path and said: "*Momentito, Señor!*"'

Aharoni: 'Eichmann tries to make a run for it. Zvika's after him. They're both rolling in the gutter. Eichmann fought back. He shouted and I revved up our engine so that no-one would hear him. Then I bawled at Rafi, who was still sitting in the car: "Go on, help them! You needn't stay out of sight any longer!"'

Eitan: 'I jumped out of the car and helped my men. The three of us got Eichmann into the car.'

Aharoni: 'Once he was in the car, he immediately went quiet and stopped struggling.'

Eitan: 'Eichmann's head lay on my lap. He was breathing heavily. He didn't say a word, but he was extremely angry.'

Aharoni: 'I drove off and immediately said to him in German: "Keep quiet and nothing will happen to you. If you struggle, you'll be shot!" No reaction. I yelled at him: "Can you hear me? What language do you speak? *Que lengua habla?*" Nothing, not a word. I thought perhaps he was unconscious, maybe dead even. Then after we had driven 400 metres, he suddenly said quite calmly, as though talking to himself: "I am already resigned to my fate."'

Eitan and Aharoni gained the impression that Eichmann was relieved. Eitan is convinced of it: 'He had been waiting for us. He had feared all the time that something like that would happen.' Towards midnight the agents reported to their chief, Isser Harel, on what had happened. Harel had been waiting impatiently in a café. 'Suddenly, two men from my team turned up. They were tired and dirty, but their faces were beaming with happiness. Then I knew that the operation had been successful.'

The Mossad agents took their prisoner, huddled on the back seat with a blanket over him, to the 'safe house' where he would be hidden. There a doctor who was a member of the Mossad team examined Eichmann for poison capsules. He found none. Eichmann was handcuffed to a bed. Then the first interrogation began. It was of supreme importance that 'Ricardo Klement' told them who he really was. Aharoni put the first question: 'What's your name?'

'Ricardo Klement.'

'What was your name before that?'

'Otto Henninger.'

'That's what he had in fact called himself, but we didn't know that. Than I asked him a hundred questions that only he could answer: shoe-size, collar-size, clothing sizes, SS number, membership number in the Nazi Party . . . All his answers were correct. Finally I asked him: "What was your name at birth?" And he said without hesitation: "Adolf Eichmann." That was the greatest moment in the whole operation.'

Eichmann's behaviour was co-operative, he answered all questions and never complained. Isser Harel: 'During the ten days and nights that he was in our custody, I made sure he was always well treated, that no-one physically molested him or insulted him. It was my job to ensure that he felt at ease, so that he would co-operate, and the operation succeeded.' However, to start with Eichmann still believed that his abductors intended to kill him. As Harel recalls: 'Every time we gave him something to eat, he thought we were about to poison him; if we took him out to walk in the courtyard, he was afraid we would shoot him. Later, when he realised that no-one was going to bump him off, he co-operated. I have never come across anyone with Eichmann's status who had sold his soul like that. We thought we were dealing with a man of particular intellectual qualities. But before us stood a nobody, a coward who co-operated all down the line, who never gave us any problems and sometimes even offered to help us.'

Only on one point did the prisoner dig his heels in. He would not, he said, answer for his crimes before any Israeli court. Aharoni guaranteed him a fair trial with his own defence counsel, and held under the eyes of the world's media. The agent believed it would only be a matter of time before Eichmann gave in. The prisoner did not know that his abductors were waiting for a plane to arrive from Israel; he had no idea what his kidnappers had in mind for him. Eichmann could see and hear nothing. He lay on a bed in a darkened, sound-proof room, being watched round the clock. As far as he could tell it was probable that he would have to spend months like that. 'He thought it over for two whole nights', Aharoni tells us. 'On the third morning he announced: "I am prepared to come to Israel." For the past days he had been under great mental strain. Now he appeared to be at ease with the idea that it was finally all over.'

After this the Mossad team agreed that they should get Eichmann out of the country, not by ship, but disguised as a crew member in an aircraft of El Al, the Israeli national airline. Circumstances were favourable. Argentina was celebrating the 150th anniversary of its independence and as part of the festivities was expecting a delegation from Israel. On 19 May 1960 an El Al turbo-prop landed in Buenos Aires. It was this aircraft that was to spirit Eichmann away to Israel.

Dressed in airline uniforms the Mossad agents and their prisoner got through the Argentinian passport control undetected. Only semi-conscious, Eichmann was aware that his warders were leading him towards a gangway. 'He had a needle in his arm the whole time', says Aharoni. 'Our doctor had assured me that he could be kept anaesthetised in such a way that he could walk and keep his eyes open, but not speak.' The El Al aircraft touched down at Ezeiza airport the same day. Four days later, on 23 May, Israel's prime minister David Ben-Gurion stepped up to the rostrum in the Knesset and announced: 'I have to inform you that a short time ago Israel's security forces located one of the biggest Nazi criminals, Adolf Eichmann . . . He is already in detention in this country and will shortly be brought before the court here under the law of 1950 on the punishment of Nazis and their accomplices.'

On 29 May Adolf Eichmann found himself for the first time face to face with Berlin-born police superintendent Avner W. Less, who recalls: 'Suddenly there stood before me a very ordinary-looking man, not much taller than me, skinny rather than slim, certainly no Frankenstein monster, nor a devil with cloven hooves and horns.' For 275 long hours Less interrogated the bureaucrat of death. Before each session Eichmann would stand to attention behind his chair until Less invited him to sit down. Eichmann expressed great willingness 'to pass on everything I know'. Throughout the interviews he spoke German in an awkwardly formal style. In court in Jerusalem he said: 'Official language is the only language I know.' To the very end Eichmann had no concept of guilt. When Avner Less asked him if there was anything he regretted, 'he looked at me in astonishment and said that remorse was just something for little children'.

After eight months of preliminary investigations the trial of Adolf Eichmann began in Jerusalem, as 'criminal case 40/61'. Sitting in a bullet-proof glass box, the gaunt defendant with thinning hair and a dark grey suit looked like a complete nonentity. 'Anyone could see that this man was no monster', wrote the German-Jewish philosopher and sociologist Hannah Arendt, who was reporting on the trial for the US *New Yorker* magazine. Gabriel Bach, deputy chief prosecutor, gained a similar impression: 'I don't know that I would have paid much attention to him if I had met him on a bus. Yet sometimes, if he was displeased by something, there was a look in his eyes which could strike fear into you – a tigerish look.'

Despite the efforts of the Public Prosecutor, anyone could see that this man was no monster. In fact it was very difficult not to suspect that we were dealing with a buffoon.

The longer one listened to him, the clearer it became that this inability to express himself was very closely connected with an inability to *think*. That is to say, he was incapable of imagining anything for himself from the point of view of another person.

Hannah Arendt

Through the lenses of his horn-rimmed glasses Eichmann looked without visible emotion at the president of the court, Moshe Landau, as he read out in Hebrew the fifteen counts of the indictment. Eichmann remained dispassionate as Landau listed the names of the extermination camps. Even when a film about the mass murders was shown to him, he showed no reaction – except at one point. 'As the film was running', Gabriel Bach recalls, 'he suddenly spoke very angrily to his guards. Later I asked one of them: "What did he want? Why was he suddenly so annoyed?" He said he'd been promised that for the public proceedings he would be taken into court in a blue suit. And now he was wearing a grey suit. People shouldn't make these promises if they couldn't keep them. He wanted to protest vehemently.

This was the only thing that moved him during the showing of that horrifying film. That doesn't say much, but at the same time says everything about him.'

> He had absolutely no motivation, other than a perfectly normal eagerness to do anything that could serve his own advancement; and this eagerness was in no way criminal in itself; he certainly would not have killed his superior officer in order to take his place. He simply never figured, to remain in the vernacular, what he was actually about.
>
> *Hannah Arendt*

What was going on in the defendant's mind? What findings did the psychologists come up with? The Israeli psychiatrist, I.S. Kulcsar, of the Jerusalem district court, was given the task of establishing whether Eichmann was mentally fit to stand trial, whether he could be brought before the court at all. Eichmann had to produce some psychological test drawings which would reflect the characteristics of his subconscious. Five American psychologists analysed the drawings without knowing who had done them. Eichmann drew a tree, a house, a woman, a hand, and the face of a Red Indian in war-paint. Their findings gave a clear message: 'A very aggressive man'; 'In his hostility he is sadistic and violent'; 'A strongly sadomasochistic person'; 'He is an aggressor, capable of naked cruelty.'

In court scarcely anything of this aggression was noticeable. It seemed that the wolf had been tamed. His defence strategy was that he had never done more than obey orders. He found his fulfilment in obedience. He called the murder of millions one of the 'most capital crimes in the course of human history'. Eichmann even apologised to the Jewish people and declared: 'I had the misfortune to be involved in that horror. But those atrocities were committed through no intent of mine. I had no wish to kill people.'

And supposing he had been ordered to do so . . . ?

In Argentina in 1956, six years before the trial, Eichmann said to Willem Sassen, with a snarl in his voice: 'If I'd been given the post of commandant of a concentration camp, I wouldn't have acted any differently. And if I'd been given orders to gas Jews or to shoot them, I would have carried out those orders.'

On Friday 11 December 1961 at 8.21 a.m., Judge Moshe Landau pronounced the verdict in Hebrew: '*Beit din seh dan otcha limita.* The court condemns you to death.' Ramrod straight, his face immobile, but maintaining his composure with difficulty, the former SS *Obersturmbannführer* stood in the large bullet-proof glass box. Landau lowered his voice and continued: 'You will he hanged by the neck until death ensues.' Eichmann was found guilty on all fifteen counts.

> Naturally he hoped he would be given life imprisonment and that after a certain time he would go free. Look, I have always been against the death penalty. But I'm in favour of imprisonment that really *is* 'for life' in all such cases.
>
> *Simon Wiesenthal, Nazi-hunter*

In a handwritten letter Eichmann appealed to President Ben Zwi of Israel for clemency – but to no avail: 'There can be no pardon for what this man has done!' Eichmann spent his last hours in Ramleh prison, near Tel Aviv. Once more Rafi Eitan had a chance to see the man he had abducted from Argentina to Israel. 'Shortly before he had to go, he looked at me and said a few words in German, which were translated for me by the representative of the prison governor: "I hope you will all soon follow me." Then he walked to the gallows, with extraordinary calmness.'

On 1 June 1962 three executioners carried out the first, and to date the last, death sentence in the history of Israel. In the death-cell of the Ramleh prison ended a career which had been directed against the lives of millions of people. No-one other than the official witnesses to the execution would ever know who actually released the trap-door beneath the gallows. Eichmann's last words were: 'Long live Germany. Long live Argentina. Long live Austria. Those are the three countries I have the closest ties with. I will not forget them. I send greetings to my wife, my family and my friends. I had to obey the laws of war and of my flag. I am ready.'

Eichmann's body remained hanging from the gallows for an hour, until the doctor of the court confirmed his death. His corpse was cremated, and his ashes scattered in the Mediterranean. Nothing was to be left to remind the world that he had ever existed.

CHAPTER TWO

THE HITLER-YOUTH

BALDUR VON SCHIRACH

We were children of an age whose general attitude was anti-Semitic.

Everyone has their destiny. I have mine.

To avoid any mistaken impression arising: I was at that time a convinced anti-Semite and remained so for a long time to come.

There were moments when one's conscience was awakened, but then everything was submerged under a great feeling of national resurgence.

The youth of Germany is innocent of that which Hitler did to the German and the Jewish peoples.

The young knew nothing about the destruction of the Jews and they did not intend this crime to happen.

Power makes people evil. There is no-one, be he ever so saintly, who can withstand having unlimited power.

I believed in Hitler.

There are many cases in which the measure of our guilt cannot be encompassed by the law.

Baldur von Schirach

You shall study under me!

Hitler to the student Schirach

Mass murder is not something one automatically connects with the name of my grandfather.

Eva von Schirach, granddaughter, in 1997

Schirach was an artistic and, I might almost say, an unworldly person and he was basically not up to handling that organisational task.

Renate Ross-Rahte, daughter of Colin Ross

Baldur von Schirach had a reputation for being rather too much of a grandee. The aristocratic prefix 'von' and his American relatives – it was really a bit much for us.

Hartmann Lauterbacher, Schirach's deputy chief-of-staff

For twelve years Schirach reared the youth of Germany. He instructed young people on how to jump like police-dogs on to a man if he was wearing a red shirt or had a Polish mother or a hooked nose – or quite simply if a shout of 'Go get 'im' came from above.

Peter von Zahn, former war-reporter

I never personally came face to face with him. You saw his picture in the papers, you occasionally heard him making a speech. I couldn't tell you whether he exerted . . . any special fascination or whether he impressed us. He was just the Number One and pretty close to the centre of things; that's why he was important.

Hans-Jochen Vogel, SPD politician and former member of the Hitler Youth

He was a bit podgy, not at all athletic. But it was his ideas which did somehow get us enthused.

Karl-Heinz Müller, former member of the Hitler Youth

Baldur von Schirach was our model. We told ourselves: that's the man we're striving to emulate.

Klaus Mauelshagen, former member of the Hitler Youth

Adolf Hitler once said in a speech, that we had to be as fast as greyhounds, as hard as Krupp steel, as tough as leather. Baldur von Schirach wasn't any of those things.

Walter Goergen, former member of the Hitler Youth

Schirach imparted things to us that were more on an intellectual plane. It was ideology that he emphasised, rather than anything athletic or physical. We sometimes found that boring.

Klaus Mauelshagen

Schirach lived in a world where laws were broken, which they had imposed on themselves. It is one of the most central factors of a Fascist regime that they lay down laws which they then do not abide by, and they act according to an ideology, but mostly in a way that benefits themselves. In that sense Herr Schirach was an extraordinarily successful man. In everything he was and did, things went well for him, and for his family too. And I do not believe he ever gave a single thought, not even in the remotest way, to one or ten or a hundred or a hundred thousand of his Jewish victims.

Paul Grosz, leader of Vienna's Jewish community

He was certainly a cog in the machine; I am sure he was thoroughly influenced by the ethos of those in power at the time. He was a – hanger-on is perhaps the wrong word – but he was imprisoned, along with the rest, in this state philosophy and was probably also shaped by a fear of what would come after.

Dr Gerhard Kastelic, Vienna

Schirach was not in the top category. He was one of those who stood in the second rank of that whole ruling team. Goebbels was always ahead of Schirach and Göring certainly was. Even some of the Gauleiters, who were old campaigners, often took precedence over Schirach.

Walter Goergen

The Führer doesn't want to hear another word about Schirach. Schirach is a weakling, a waffler and, in deeper political questions, a nitwit. I would have him recalled from Vienna today rather than tomorrow, if only he had a successor.

Goebbels, diary, 21 August 1942

Note: The words of Schirach himself, quoted in the following pages, are either taken from an interview with Jochen von Lang (1966) or from his memoirs *I Believed in Hitler* (1967).

DEM FÜHRER

Das ist die Wahrheit, die mich Dir verband:
Ich suchte Dich und fand mein Vaterland.

Ich war ein Blatt im unbegrenzten Raum,
nun bist Du Heimat mir und bist mein Baum.

Wie weit verweht, verginge ich im Wind,
wärst Du nicht Kraft, die von der Wurzel rinnt.

Ich glaub an Dich, denn Du bist die Nation
Ich glaub an Deutschland
weil Du Deutschlands Sohn.

Baldur von Schirach

TO THE FÜHRER

This is the truth which bound me to thee:
I looked for thee and found my Fatherland.
I was a leaf floating in limitless space,
Now thou art my homeland and my tree.

How far would I be carried by the wind,
Wert thou not the strength that flows up from the roots.

I believe in thee, for thou art the nation.
I believe in Germany
For thou art Germany's son.

*

The lights go down in the great hall of the Palace of Justice in Nuremberg. Suddenly all the muttering and whispering is hushed. The only sound to be heard is the monotonous whirr of the film-projector as it throws horrifying pictures on to the screen on the courtroom wall. The flickering images on the screen are like nothing ever seen before: mountains of corpses, starving figures, children staring with empty eyes. The pictures of horror and misery are reflected in the dark glasses of the defendant, whose face appears frozen in the pale spotlight. On the floor in front of him, court psychologists are crouched, noting down his every twitch.

Baldur von Schirach, once the youth leader of the German Reich, Gauleiter and Reich Defence Commissioner of Vienna, and now one of the principal defendants at Nuremberg, is deeply and unmistakably aghast. His horror appears genuine. What he is being shown here is a shock to him.

Only a few days before, in a shower-room conversation with Hitler's one-time second-in-command, *Reichsmarschall* Göring, he had casually boasted: 'This whole thing is just a show-trial. The really clever thing would be for the whole lot of us to reject the jurisdiction of the court.' Yet now he was being assailed by the first doubts.

On the 108th day of the proceedings Rudolf Höss, the former commandant of Auschwitz concentration camp, is called as a witness for the prosecution. With the matter-of-factness of an accountant, the camp chief describes down to the smallest detail the industrial precision with which millions of men, women and children were murdered. In the nights that follow, Schirach lies on the bunk in his cell, unable to sleep. He finally comes to a decision which will have far-reaching consequences. As the defendant steps up for his cross-examination, he declares to the Allied judges, whose jurisdiction he had so recently denied, that he could not hold it against them if they demanded: 'Off with all their heads!' Then the man who was one of Hitler's most devout acolytes, makes a sensational confession:

'I brought up that generation in a belief in Hitler and in loyalty to him. The youth movement which I built up bore his name. I thought I was serving a Führer who would make our nation and its youth great, free and happy. Millions of young people believed that with me and saw National Socialism as their ideal. Many died for it. I am guilty of having educated the young for a man who was a murderer millions of times over. I believed in that man; that is all I can say in my defence.'

The confession of guilt drew a final line under a career which had seemed to fly on the wings of success. The youngest of Hitler's paladins was for a long time treated like the dictator's heir-apparent. More than any other man, he shaped the young generation of the Reich into his master's most loyal retinue. To Hitler he promised to build Germany's greatest youth movement. In his name he enlisted a vast organisation whose number of members ended by breaking world records. To an entire generation he praised as a saviour the man whom, when it was far too late, he recognised to be a criminal. He was a masterly educator and knew how young people could become swept up with an idea: 'The young are, of course, always rather self-absorbed and in love with themselves', Schirach said later. 'And if one applauds them, honours them and puts them on display, they are grateful for it.'

With his watchword 'You are the future of Germany', the youth leader recruited even the very youngest. Like the children of Hamelin following the Pied Piper, they were seduced by his promises – and were led to their ruin. 'We were held up as the elite, the race of leaders, the people who were ready and able to dominate the world. If you tell that to fourteen-year-olds, they will believe it', recalls Ingeborg Seldte, who at that time found herself at home in the *Bund Deutscher Mädel*, the 'League of German Lasses'. 'A whole young generation were cheated – of their youth and, in a great many cases, of their lives as well.'

Was this the consequence that Schirach accepted? Was he dedicated to delivering cannon-fodder for his Führer's planned wars of conquest? Or was he a misguided idealist, over-enthusiastically chasing after a mirage? Baldur von Schirach does not readily fit the role of a fanatical executive in the ranks of Hitler's henchmen. He possessed neither the diabolical talents of a Goebbels, the cold cruelty of a Mengele, nor the number-crunching meticulousness of an Eichmann. The cosmopolitan and cultivated intellectual, who spoke of Goethe and Hitler in the same breath, found himself cast as a Goethean 'sorcerer's apprentice'. Convinced of his master's genius he summoned up spirits from which even he could not escape until it was too late.

> Baldur's parents came from the USA, his mother was born in New York and his father's mother in Baltimore; a Schirach had been an American major and had stood guard with a shining sword beside George Washington's coffin. One of his ancestors was the navigator Sir Francis Drake.
> *Schirach's wife, Henriette, in* The Price of Splendour, *1975*

The career of harbinger to a demagogue was not one that Schirach was born to. The creatively gifted youngster came from a well-connected, cosmopolitan, upper-class family, a fact which opened up for him horizons that were unusually wide for those times. His mother, born Emma Middleton, was a wealthy American from Philadelphia. His father, Karl Baily Norris von Schirach, also had American ancestry. At home the Schirachs spoke only English; not until the age of five did Baldur become acquainted with the German language. The family's aristocratic title went back to the eighteenth-century Habsburgs. An ancestor of the Schirachs had been granted it by the Austrian empress Maria Theresa for services to literature and had thus gained access to the highest reaches of society.

Baldur von Schirach was born in Berlin in 1907. He was not quite two when the family moved to Weimar, where his father – a former officer in the Royal Prussian Regiment of Cuirassier

Guards – had been given the post of *Intendant* of the Court Theatre there. Under the influence of cultured parents, and in the birthplace of Germany's classical literature, the young Baldur soon developed into something of an aesthete: even as a child he began writing poetry and learning the violin. For a time he considered becoming a musician.

The Schirach household placed no great emphasis on an authoritarian, Prussian-style upbringing. *Laissez-faire* was more the motto. But the parents made sure that the boy received a solid, all-round education. At the age of ten he attended the *Waldpädagogium*, a private school in the Thuringian spa town of Bad Berka, where the children were taught according to the ideas of the progressive educationist Hermann Lietz. In the tradition of the early *Wandervogel* movement, the aim of the school was to teach the boys independence and self-confidence, far removed from the pernicious influences of the big city. According to Lietz, 'the training of the body and character should be given equal status with the imparting of knowledge'. In this community, pupils and teachers called each other by their first names and the older children were made to take responsibility for the younger ones. 'Youth is led by youth': this notion from his idyllic rural boarding-school won Schirach over, and he was later to make it part of his repertoire.

Baldur's carefree childhood days came to an abrupt end in 1919. Not even the Schirach family were left untouched by the aftershock of the lost war. Baldur's brother Karl, seven years older than himself, committed suicide. Since the beginning of the First World War it had been his dream, as a Prussian officer, to perpetuate the myth of the front-line fighter. With the Kaiser's abdication and the acceptance of the Treaty of Versailles by the National Assembly in Weimar, all of that was over. 'I do not want to live to see Germany's misfortune', Karl wrote in a farewell letter. The death of his beloved brother strengthened Schirach's antipathy towards a republic which was already pretty unloved in a household loyal to the Kaiser. The shaming removal of his father from the post of *Intendant* by the new government had the effect of confirming him in his bitterness.

However, political events did not plunge the family into poverty – the Schirachs were very well off. Baldur returned to Weimar from his boarding-school in Bad Berka and received private tuition at home. Despite his father's dismissal their house in Gartenstrasse remained a focus of artistic life in Weimar. Painters, singers, actors, poets and musicians were frequent guests in his parents' elegant drawing-room.

A stark contrast to these aesthetic distractions was provided by the birth-pangs of the young republic. Looking back, Schirach had no doubt as to where his sympathies lay in the battles between rebellious workers and the nationalistic *Freikorps* militias: 'In Thuringia we all felt we had a knife at our throats. If we didn't fight back we would be slaughtered by the communists.'

Spurred on by this kind of combative spirit, the seventeen-year-old joined a nationalist militia, the *Knappenschaft* or 'Brotherhood of Squires', which was led by officers of the illegal 'Black Reichswehr'. In his search for a role-model Baldur seems at first to have found one in the war hero Erich Ludendorff. Yet this rather old-fashioned icon was soon overshadowed by an itinerant orator who appeared like a shaft of light in the life of the aspiring schoolboy.

When Adolf Hitler relaunched his recruitment campaign in Weimar in March 1925, soon after his release from imprisonment in Landsberg castle, Baldur was one of the 'squires' given the job of keeping order in the hall. Merely the voice of this back-room demagogue was enough to entrance him. 'It was deep and husky, as resonant as a cello. The accent sounded strange and for that reason compelled one to listen', Schirach later recalled. He listened enthralled to Hitler's tirades of hatred against the Treaty of Versailles. Baldur transformed him into his idealised image of the unknown soldier of the First World War, upright and selfless. Here at last was a man who did not just make speeches, but entered actively into politics in order to give the Fatherland a future again – a revolutionary who had put his life on the line in the march on the Feldherrnhalle. This was the form which the young Schirach gave to his hero. So it seemed to him like a stroke of fortune when he was personally introduced to the party leader after the meeting. Hitler squeezed the young man's hand for a long moment and looked him straight in the eye. Back home in his attic room the young admirer penned an emotional tribute in verse:

Du gabst uns Deine Hand und einen Blick,
Von dem noch jetzt die jungen Herzen beben:
Es wird unser dieser Stunde mächtig Leben
Begleiten stets als wunderbares Glück.

Thou gavest us thy hand and such a gaze
As caused e'en now our youthful hearts to quake:
The mighty life-force of that hour doth take
Us by the hand through Fortune's wondrous days.

Im Herzen blieb der heisse Schwur zurück:
Du hast uns nicht umsonst die Hand gegeben!
Wir werden unser hohes Ziel erstreben,
Verkettet durch des Vaterlands Geschick.

Th'impassioned vow remains deep in our soul:
And not in vain didst thou thy hand extend!
We strive towards our high, exalted goal,
Bound by our Fatherland, aye, to the end.

His boundless admiration for Hitler, his almost religious faith in a man whom he repeatedly compared with God, were things which Schirach was to retain almost to the bitter end. Later he was to explain it like this: 'Just as Shintoism requires veneration of the emperor, of one's ancestors and of the nation, in the same way the faith in National Socialism could demand firstly veneration of the Führer; secondly veneration of one's nation and ancestors.' The citizen was free to belong to various religious communities, 'as long as devotion to the Führer was paramount for him'. Shirach offered up his soul to Hitler, later to serve him as a catcher of other souls.

The enthusiast could hardly wait for his eighteenth birthday when he could at last join the Party and the SA (the paramilitary *Sturmabteilung* or storm-troopers). After taking his school-leaving certificate at a high school in Weimar he was free to embark on a career. In this his parents allowed him a free hand. 'Come and see me in Munich; we need men like you', Hitler had urged him during his visit to Weimar. Baldur decided to take up the invitation: wherever Hitler was, he wanted to be as well.

> In those days I devoured everything that Hitler wrote about
> international politics and economics, about parliamentarianism
> and revolution, about Aryans and Jews. Hitler's book [*Mein
> Kampf*] was my creed. Today I know that it was a catastrophic
> programme for Germany.
> *Schirach in his autobiography,* I Believed in Hitler, *1967*

He had already long been familiar with the conceptual world of
his mentor: he had studied *Mein Kampf* line by line. 'To us that
book was like a bible which we learned almost by heart', he
confessed later. The plans for world conquest, which Hitler openly
expounded in his polemic, and the all-consuming hatred of the
Jews, were things which Schirach did not take particularly
seriously, or so he claimed in retrospect. Years later, he said, he
challenged Hitler on these points and received the reply that it was
just a book after all and was not binding, once one found oneself
in a position of responsibility.

'That was precisely what so fascinated me about Hitler',
Schirach declared, looking back. 'The fact that even then, when
he was not yet in power, he already had this concept of Germany's
position of supremacy on entirely the same footing as the
great world powers, and in a way he was playing out sand-box
war-games as an exercise in the whole question of ruling the
world. Obviously for me, a man in my early twenties, it
was enormously exciting to be part of that. It was absolutely
clear to me, as it was to Hitler himself, that he would come to
power. And when he was in power he would first of all solve the
domestic problem of unemployment, and then in foreign policy he
would immediately sit at the first violin desk in the great orchestra
of nations.'

Schirach wanted to be in there where the music was playing. He
wanted to be around when they had to 'pull the cart out of the
dirt'. What this dirt was, he admittedly only knew at second hand.
For 'even if we came from families who had it good, very good
even, we had, through belonging to those nationalist militias,

come up against countless young fellows who were unemployed. We knew the poverty and hardship those young people suffered.'

National Socialism – to me that meant Hitler, the comradeship of like-minded people, the community of high and lowly, poor and rich.
Schirach in his autobiography, I Believed in Hitler, *1967*

In 1927 Baldur moved to Munich, took an apartment and very soon – thanks to his father's connections – was being invited to the most influential salons of Munich society. At the university he enrolled for his favourite subjects of English and German literature and the history of art; at the same time he attended lectures in Egyptology, in order, as he put it, to broaden his horizons. He had no ambitions to graduate. What interested him above all was the Party. The first contact he made was through the Führer's secretary, Rudolf Hess, who asked the student to help him out with simple written work in the Party office.

But Schirach had his eye on bigger things. No sooner had he enrolled at the university than he eagerly set about getting its little National Socialist group into shape. In the strife-torn Party scene at that time it had scarcely been making any impact at all. Baldur was convinced that there was only one man in a position to win over the academic population to the brownshirt cause: Hitler himself.

As early as 1929–30 there were universities where the Nazis had a majority among the students. It was a known fact that he [Schirach] had been very active there.
Hans-Jochen Vogel, SPD politician and former Hitler Youth member

One day, when Schirach happened to meet Hitler walking along Maximilianstrasse, he plucked up the courage to speak to him.

Hitler recognised the young admirer from Weimar and invited him back to his apartment. Eagerly Schirach proposed a big student gathering at which Hitler would speak as party leader. But Hitler was sceptical. He did not believe that the Nazi Party would ever succeed in winning over more than one in ten of the academic youth. In any case he hated the idea of having to address a student audience. But finally he gave in: if Schirach could manage to fill the hall of the *Hofbräuhaus*, Hitler promised, he would come and give a speech to the students.

Schirach drummed up support – and passed the test. A full hour before the event was due to start the hall was packed solid. Hitler spoke, and drove the students wild with enthusiasm. Schirach had had a presentiment of the effect the demagogue would have on them: 'The academic youth in those days wanted to be addressed by mass leaders. They were more susceptible than the workers were to the mass hypnosis of those big political meetings. It was something they were lacking in their own student lives.' With that meeting Hitler attracted attention even among the educated classes.

For Schirach it was a breakthrough. He had found a gap in the market for propaganda, a gap for which he would from now on claim a monopoly: the recruitment of the young. And he could immediately count on the approbation of his mentor. Hitler respected the young disciple who, in his eyes, had shown he had a feel for politics. Contact between Hitler and Schirach became frequent, they called in on one another, and met from time to time in the salon of the publisher, Bruckmann, who had published the anti-Semitic works of Houston Stewart Chamberlain. Schirach even enjoyed the privilege of telephoning his master whenever he wanted to speak to him.

Within a short time the dynamic student had gathered a group of supporters around him and, without meeting much resistance, placed himself at the head of the student body in Munich. In his fight for the top student position he soon came into conflict with the leader of the Nazi Student League, Wilhelm Tempel. However, when Tempel saw that Hitler's support for him was evaporating, he lost his nerve and resigned from his post. Schirach now had a clear run. This would not be the last time that he was to win in a struggle against an unwelcome competitor. To avoid further weakening the faction-riven student federation, Hitler and Hess decided not to appoint a new leader but to arrange for one to be elected. In the election on 20 July 1928 Schirach emerged as the winner. At the age of twenty-one he was now head of the National Socialist student league throughout Germany and became a member of the central party leadership. It was to be the start of a rapidly ascending career path.

At this point, however, Schirach was offered a unique opportunity to steer his life in a completely different direction. In the summer of 1928 he travelled with his mother to the United States to visit relatives in Philadelphia and New York. In a penthouse high above Manhattan his uncle Alfred Norris, a wealthy Wall Street banker, made the tempting offer for him to join the family firm. Schirach's mother encouraged him to accept. She saw a golden future for her son in a country of unlimited opportunities. But Baldur turned the invitation down. Although the Nazi Party had suffered a defeat in the general election that May, Schirach had made up his mind: 'I wanted to go back to Germany, back to Hitler.' He was wallowing in the romanticised dream-world of an impending national rebirth of Germany. He was infected by Hitler's ideas. He 'simply believed'.

Schirach had his next objective clearly in view: the conquest of the universities for Hitler and his party. University politics as such held little interest for him. He campaigned tirelessly, organised processions, printed leaflets and held meetings for which he procured influential Nazi politicians as speakers, men like Alfred Rosenberg, the party's chief ideologue and editor of the Nazi newspaper, the *Völkischer Beobachter* (National Observer).

As a professional organiser he had long since given up his studies. 'You shall study under me', Hitler had said to him, placing a benevolent hand on his shoulder. By now Hitler had recognised the importance of students to his cause and readily accompanied Schirach from one demonstration to another in an effort to recruit new supporters. This propaganda yielded success. More and more students gave their vote to the Nazis; the number of party members soared. The triumphal progress through the universities and colleges had begun. But at the same time there was a growing incidence of wrangling, provocation and violence.

At this time Schirach himself enjoyed playing the ruffian and gave free rein to his antipathy towards the republic and its representatives. Early in July 1931 he made an inflammatory speech against the 'Diktat of Versailles' at the University of Cologne, and because of the rioting which followed it he was arrested by the police and put into solitary confinement for a week. The court then sentenced the troublemaker to three months on probation. Outside the courthouse thousands of his supporters greeted the newly acclaimed 'martyr' with shouts of '*heil*' and sang the Horst Wessel song. As though he had to demonstrate his true fighting spirit by this, in retrospect the 'aesthete' liked to emphasise this episode in which he fetched up in the 'dungeons of the System'.

> Before 1932 a reasonably shrewd republican federal government could already have brought about the break-up of the whole National Socialist movement.
> *Schirach, in an interview with Jochen von Lang, 1966*

Yet Schirach also had opponents in his own ranks. Not all the Nazi student leaders saw it as their task to act as political shock-troops of the National Socialist revolution. They wanted rather to turn the student league into an intellectual spearhead of the party or to debate questions of university policy. The fact that Schirach, in order to increase the size of his following, opened up entry to the Nazi student league to members of the elite *Burschenschaften*, or duelling fraternities, also met with criticism. For Schirach these were all problems of a very minor order and he responded tersely with a quote from Hitler: 'I would prefer the NS student league to have a lower intellectual level, but all the more comrades-in-arms.' On the organisational side things were not going too well either. The reins were threatening to slip from Schirach's hands. He was accused of seldom giving clear instructions, of being disorganised or quite simply 'incompetent'; his leadership style was said to be imperious and to have the stamp of tsarism. Opposition began to form against him.

It was clear that his rapid success had gone to Schirach's head. He displayed signs of megalomania. In the 'Arrangements for Schirach meetings' which he had especially drawn up, we read among other things: 'Care must be taken to see that, after his speech, Party-member von Schirach is not questioned by every party-member who feels the urge;' and 'Party-member von Schirach is always to be provided with hotel accommodation. Lodging in private premises requires express prior approval.' Such presumption might just have been accepted with a shrug of the shoulders. But when he grandly arrived at an assembly of the entire student body of Germany with an SS escort and carrying a riding-crop, in an obvious attempt to emulate Hitler, the enraged student leaders called for his dismissal.

> Conversation with Schirach. I explain socialism to him again and talk him out of his silly excuses about the honour of being a student. He can't build up his league like this, otherwise it will be nothing more than a student club.
>
> *Goebbels, diary, 17 March 1931*

Although in later years Schirach was described by contemporaries as 'detached', 'self-controlled' and a man with 'good manners', in those early 'fighting days' he had apparently developed a taste for the bohemian life. Once, when very drunk at a student gathering, he aimed his pistol at a portrait of Adolf Hitler. However, this led to no further action against him. In one of his escapades he came close to fighting a duel with Hans Donndorf, an old friend from the *Knappenschaft*, who had served with Schirach as a marshal at Hitler's first speech in Weimar. After 'drinking his way through New Year's Eve' Schirach had gone to the room of the girl Donndorf wanted to marry and 'had sexual intercourse with her'. Donndorf was beside himself, but Schirach refused to accept that his behaviour in any way impugned his friend's honour and wrote to him: 'You are obviously incensed to find that the girl whom you worshipped as a madonna, is an extremely normal little kitten. The fact that you unjustly turn your disappointment into resentment against me in this way is just very foolish. After all, it was her business and a matter of conscience whether she was faithful to you or not. You were not engaged to her and so there was no barrier between her and myself. I would not wish to make it appear by this letter that I attribute any kind of deeper significance to this episode. To me the little girl (I have even forgotten her name!) was an amusement of no importance. And in your case, I hope that you will be sufficiently mature one day to be able to laugh about the whole affair as heartily as I can.' Donndorf accused Schirach of acting like a 'Jew-boy' whereupon the latter challenged his friend to a pistol duel. An arbitrator ended the quarrel with a ruling acceptable to both parties.

The extent of Schirach's lack of self-control, at least in the early years of his career, is shown by another incident which took place in 1933. When Schirach heard that the racing-driver, Manfred von Brauchitsch, had apparently been saying insulting things about his wife, he forced his way into von Brauchitsch's apartment and 'thrashed' him with his riding-crop. Schirach was obliged to pay damages.

Although the student league continued its victorious sweep through the universities and soon gained a majority of votes everywhere, Schirach's opponents now attacked him on a broader front. A memorandum addressed to Hitler was loaded with criticisms of Schirach, but Hitler, impressed by the latter's energy and dedication, stood firmly behind his protégé. 'We have no time to raise leaders with a high intellectual education, since we find ourselves in a massive drive forward. Party-member von Schirach has understood what matters: nothing else but the great mass movement. I stand with all my authority behind Schirach. I have no more loyal and intelligent associate than this young comrade. I would rather be torn in pieces than leave Schirach in the lurch', he told a meeting of student leaders. The Führer had spoken. The opposition collapsed.

Borne along by this following wind, Schirach succeeded in making another breakthrough: at a student conference in Graz, Austria, in July 1931, an emissary of Schirach, named Walter Lienau, was elected president of the German Student League. The same night Schirach reported this success to his lord and master in

Munich. Hitler was delighted. 'You have no idea what it will mean to me, if in my forthcoming negotiations I can say that the majority of the young intelligentsia is behind me.'

The universities were now in the hands of the Nazis. There was nothing more for Schirach to do there, and anyway he was 'sick and tired' of university politics. He needed a new field of action in which to shine for Hitler; a new challenge. He already knew clearly where his goal lay – the conquest of the young.

A National Socialist youth organisation already existed. It had been established first in the Saxon town of Plauen, under the leadership of a law student named Kurt Gruber. At the first party congress of the National Socialist party in Weimar in 1936, it was given the name '*Hitler-Jugend* (Hitler Youth), Youth League of German Workers'. Gruber was appointed its national leader. Unlike its rival *Bündische Jugend* (Youth Alliance), which was recruited from the middle class, the HJ initially directed its main appeal to working-class lads and was positively identified as a workers' youth movement. Even after 1933, the coat-of-arms of the HJ was a crossed hammer and sword on a red background.

Most members of the Nazi Party looked on the HJ as nothing more than a hiking club for adolescents. But Schirach had recognised the potential that lay in the mass of young people. It was Goebbels who had said: 'He who has the youth, has the future', and Schirach, too, had proclaimed to the politicians of the Weimar Republic: 'It has always been true that a government is only strong while it has the youth behind it.' Yet Schirach's interest in the young generation did not only grow out of the calculations of power-politics. He himself conceived of the Nazi movement as a revolution, as a fresh wind which would sweep away the old order he so detested. To him youth was not just a question of age, it was a value in itself: 'Faust, Beethoven's Ninth Symphony and the will of Adolf Hitler, are all expressions of eternal youth', he asserted. His unquestioning belief in Hitler, his romanticised idealism and patriotism were things he now wanted to pass on to the young. Even as a student leader he had celebrated them in his poems as the 'new front' and had played an important part in creating the youth-myth of the Nazi Party.

Schirach's verses which, in the words of the Reich Drama

Director, Rainer Schlösser, ushered in the 'new age of National Socialist poetry', in fact sounded flat and full of hollow pathos. But the messages they contained were at the same time a political programme. Later Schirach repeated them like mantras in his speeches and in his political writings such as *Idea and Form of the Hitler Youth* and *Revolution in Education*.

The stereotypical motifs in his poetry were flag, battle, heroism, self-sacrificing death and victory. For the young who, like him, had been born too late for the last war, he conjured up a mystical brotherhood with those who fell in that war and transformed death for the Fatherland into the 'meaning of existence':

> *Als wir noch Kinder, dröhnten die Kanonen,*
> *und manches Kinderlachen brach entzwei,*
> *kam eine meldung von den Todeszonen:*
> *'Dein vater starb, damit die Jugend frei!'*

> When we were still children the cannons roared
> And many a childish laugh was cut off short,
> When from the battle-zone came word:
> 'Your father died to make the young ones free!'

> *Wehe dem Sohn, der das je kann verwinden*
> *Und nach so grossem Preis vom Kampfe schwieg!*
> *Wir wollen unsres Daseins Sinn verkünden:*
> *Uns hat der Krieg behütet für den Krieg!*

> Woe to the son who can ever conquer this
> And after such a price say nought of battle!
> We must proclaim the reason why we live:
> The war has safeguarded us for war!

Schirach built Hitler up into a heroic cult-figure, the leader and saviour of Germany, for whom it was well worth dying. The poems, short and easy to memorise, quickly went into circulation and brought recognition to the young lyricist even in the inner circle of the Nazi Party. But for many young people the idea of death was the dominant theme of their lives. The message of the poems became the keystone of the HJ education programme and 'taught a whole generation to believe, to obey and to die'.

Schirach was confident that he was the only man to unite German youth under the swastika. When he was the Nazi student leader he had already involved himself in the affairs of the HJ and of the NS-*Schülerbund* (Nazi Schoolboy League) which had been established at about the same time by Adrian von Renteln, and this had brought him into conflict with Gruber, the national youth leader. After the success of the Nazi Party in the general elections of 1930 Schirach now did his utmost to show Gruber up as unfit for his post. 'Gruber was unquestionably the right man, as long as the Hitler Youth was a purely provincial affair. But now, at a national level, he is showing clear signs that he lacks vision and organisational ability, and it is only due to Gruber's obstinacy that all nationalist youth movements have not yet been united.'

It was fortunate for Schirach that Ernst Röhm, Hitler's close associate, who had gone into exile after the failed 1923 putsch, now returned from Bolivia to become the new chief-of-staff of the SA and as such was no longer willing to accept the relative independence of the Hitler Youth. On 27 April 1931 Hitler announced his decision to place the HJ under the direct control of the SA. To make supervision easier, the national command of the HJ was moved from Plauen to Munich. Gruber's position began to look shaky, and Schirach and Röhm, who formed an unlikely alliance that was close to friendship, conspired to undermine him. Gruber was forced to resign.

Schirach's moment had now arrived. When Hitler once more invited him to his apartment for supper and a chat, Schirach put forward his idea to his fatherly friend: he, Schirach, wanted to be the leader of all German youth. Again Hitler was sceptical. 'Don't be funny, Schirach. Do you want to waste your time with those children?' Schirach knew how to convince the megalomaniac. 'So I said to him: "I will build you the greatest youth movement that Germany has ever seen."' That did the trick. On 30 October 1931 Hitler appointed Schirach, aged just twenty-four, to be Reich Youth Leader of the National Socialist Party, and simultaneously head of the Nazi Student League, the Hitler Youth and the Nazi Schoolboy League. Schirach had climbed another rung of his career ladder. He wanted to emulate his lord and master in everything: just as Hitler had won over the German people, he had to win over the youth of Germany for the Nazi Party.

Hitler's new man was greeted in the Party with great scepticism. Among the old campaigners, the prototypes of the Hitler Youth, the new *Reichsjugendführer* was not the warhorse they had dreamed of. 'Baldur von Schirach had the reputation for being rather too much of a grandee. The aristocratic prefix 'von' and his American relatives – it was really a bit much for us', remarked his long-serving deputy, Hartmann Lauterbacher.

But Schirach was very close to Hitler – and that was all that mattered. At this time he made an astute move in his private life which would assure him a 'place in the sun' among Hitler's associates. On 31 March 1932 Schirach married Henriette Hoffmann, the daughter of Hitler's personal photographer, Heinrich Hoffmann. Hitler and Röhm were both witnesses at the wedding ceremony, and the reception was held afterwards at Hitler's apartment. Hitler's present to the couple was something he probably valued above anything in the world: an Alsatian dog.

There is no doubt that this was a marriage of love. Schirach's imposing appearance and success impressed the eighteen-year-old photographer's daughter. And for his part he had fallen in love with the attractive Henriette first sight: 'A fashion-conscious kind of girl – she had chestnut-brown hair cut in a pageboy bob, make-up that was unusual for those days, and wore stylish pullovers, short, tight skirts, silk stockings and high-heeled shoes. I thought she was the most beautiful girl in Munich.'

The alliance had considerable advantages for Schirach too. In Munich Hitler treated the Hoffmanns like a substitute family. 'Henny', as she was called, had known Hitler since her early childhood; he was her 'uncle' on whose lap she had often sat as a little girl. What is more, she was friendly with Eva Braun, who had worked as a sales assistant in Hoffmann's photographic shop before becoming Hitler's mistress. Hoffmann himself was one of Hitler's closest confidants and accompanied him wherever he went. This meant that he could always supply Schirach with the very latest news of the Führer's moods and intrigues and could hold a protective hand over his son-in-law. The marriage brought

Schirach into Hitler's innermost circle of friends. He lunched regularly with the Führer; and in later years the Schirachs were welcome guests at the Berghof.

Nevertheless, Schirach's position as the Party's national youth leader did not go unchallenged. 'I don't want anyone telling me my job', Schirach had requested Hitler. Having been given the rank of *Gruppenführer*, Schirach was still subordinate to the senior command of the SA. This did not appeal to him. In May 1932 Hitler granted his protégé's wish and placed the 25-year-old at the head of an autonomous department within the national leadership of the Nazi Party. This put him on an equal footing with Röhm. From that moment on he would tolerate no 'Führers' around him – only the one above him.

His most serious rival was Adrian von Renteln, who commanded 35,000 youngsters as leader of the HJ and the Schoolboy League. However, Schirach wanted to bring the entire youth into a single organisation. As *Reichsleiter* Schirach now reported directly to Hitler and could take the necessary action. From within the HJ he created the *Jungvolk* and the *Bund Deutscher Mädel*, respectively for boys under 14 and girls of all ages, thus removing them from Renteln's sphere of influence, and placed himself at the head of both organisations. Renteln protested against this curtailment of his authority – but in vain. Schirach got his way and on 15 June 1932 Renteln resigned. Once more Schirach had emerged victorious in the struggle for power within the Party.

But Hitler was not yet in power; the country was still ruled by the hated 'Republicans'. In many regions the HJ was even banned for a time as being an offshoot of the SA. Schirach now mobilised the Hitler Youth to campaign in the forthcoming general election. Its members held demonstrations and processions, put up posters and distributed millions of handbills and booklets. Schirach told his young followers: 'The purpose of a procession is to give friend and foe a picture of the size and strength of our movement.' His incitement often led to brawls in the open street and bloody battles in meeting-halls with communists and democrats. Schirach relished these adventures. 'We were never happier than in those days when we lived in constant danger', he later wrote in blissful reminiscence.

With undisguised emotion he repeatedly conjured up the glorious campaigning days: 'And how we were terrorised! Persecuted, forced to disband, reinstated, reviled, embattled – the young fought their way through a thousand tight situations, won the recognition of doubters in their own camp and the respect of their enemies, stormed over all obstacles and planted the white-striped flag in the middle of industrial centres.'

From 1931 up to the end of January 1933, twenty-one *Hitlerjungen* lost their lives in confrontations of this kind. One of them was soon to become a legendary figure familiar to every younger German: on 24 January 1932 Herbert Norkus, a fifteen-year-old working-class boy from Berlin, was attacked by communists while putting up posters, and stabbed to death. Schirach recognised the propaganda-value of this and elevated the youth to martyrdom.

Every year Schirach made a pilgrimage to the grave of Herbert Norkus and in highly emotive speeches invoked the young lad's 'spirit of self-sacrifice': 'What the Hitler Youth has become since January 1932 it owes not least to that sacred symbol of young self-sacrifice and young heroism whose name is Herbert Norkus. We promise him as the youth of Germany to live and to work for the one Führer, for whom he too gave his life. Our youth movement has been created by the selfless death of inspired youth.'

It was from the 'willing self-sacrifice' of children that Schirach drew the justification for his youth movement: 'The more who die for a movement, the more immortal it becomes. To its critics the Hitler Youth can give a historic reply: its dead. This reply cannot be gainsaid, it is symbolic. There can be no argument against a youth movement which, striding forward in unprecedented commitment to a moral idea, takes upon itself death and injury and persecution as the natural consequences of the struggle.'

Norkus provided the Nazi poet Karl Schenzinger with the model for his novel *Der Hitlerjunge Quex* (Quex of the Hitler Youth), which at Schirach's urging was made into a film that was a 'must-see' for every *Hitlerjunge*. The 'blood sacrifice' of young Quex, who joined the Nazis in the face of resistance from his parents and school, invoked the 'steadfastness of the spirit' which 'stands by Führer and Fatherland for better or worse' and has

renounced the 'unworthy democratic past'. Especially for the film
Schirach wrote the words for a 'March of the Hitler Youth':

> *Unsre Fahne flattert uns voran.*
> *In die Zukunft ziehn wir Mann für Mann.*
> *Wir marschieren für Hitler durch Nacht und Not*
> *Mit der Fahne der Jugend für Freiheit und Brot.*

> Bravely flies the banner at our head.
> Into the future side by side we march.
> For Hitler thus we march through night and dread
> With youth's flag, for liberty and bread.

> *Unsre Fahne flattert uns voran.*
> *Unsre Fahne ist die neue Zeit.*
> *Und die Fahne führt uns in die Ewigkeit!*
> *Ja, die fahne ist mehr als der Tod!*

> Bravely flies the banner at our head.
> It is the flag that heralds a new age,
> And leads us onward to eternity.
> The banner is far greater yet than death!

This *Kampfzeit* or 'time of struggle', when HJ units rode through
towns and villages on hired trucks with flags flying, singing battle-
hymns and shouting slogans, attracted the young in search of
adventure. The number of members climbed to 50,000. Yet the
Hitler Youth was still one among many youth groups, leagues and
associations. It was far from being the 'Germany's greatest youth
organisation'.

Schirach needed a success which would show Hitler and the
world that he knew how to mobilise the masses. He gambled
everything on one card and summoned the entire Hitler Youth to a
national youth rally at Potsdam on 1 October 1932. Here, at the
gates of Berlin, he would publicly demonstrate that the future
belonged to National Socialism. He wanted to prove to his Führer
what he was capable of. It was to be the biggest event that the
Party had held up to that date. The risk that it could also be the

Party's greatest failure was enormous. That was something the Nazis could ill afford at this time. It is true that they had emerged as the largest single party in the general election on 31 July; and Hermann Göring had become chairman of the national assembly, the Reichstag. But Hitler was still wrangling with Papen and Schleicher, the leading conservatives, over the chancellorship. The man who could tip the scales either way was the head of state, the aged and respected President Hindenburg. On no account should the Nazis be presented to him as a weak party.

Once again Hitler had doubts about the magical powers of his apprentice: what if only a few young people turned up? He would be made to look foolish in front of the whole world. For Hitler this was too risky. He would wait in Goebbels' apartment for a call from Schirach. When the Potsdam stadium was filled, and only then, would he come and make a speech.

It was no easy undertaking for Schirach. Such a massive demonstration required not only ideas but organisational talent as well. And Schirach was largely lacking in such skills. For these he had to rely on committed associates, while he himself was an experienced publicist. He had posters printed, recruited, made speeches and persuaded – verbally and on paper, in meetings, on the streets, in schools and sports clubs.

He pulled it off; the 'Potsdam March' became a legend in the Party. From every corner of Germany the youngsters arrived in the old royal Prussian city; on foot, on bicycles, on trucks and by train. The procession itself was enough to attract attention. For the young did not just arrive, they came in droves. Schirach had reckoned on 50,000; in the event some 70,000 besieged the city. The tented camps were hopelessly overcrowded. Schirach's propaganda and the magnetic attraction of mass gatherings had lured the youth in.

It was Schirach's first opportunity to address a mass audience as *Reichsjugendführer*. He was not someone who could speak off the cuff. He wrote out his entire speeches – in advance. Schirach never achieved the rabble-rousing skill of a Goebbels. His speeches were too effusive. They lacked fire and were a 'mixture of academic lecture and lyric poetry'. But 'on a good day he could speak extraordinarily well and excitingly, in a manner that was cultivated but at the same time very stirring', as a contemporary put it.

Baldur von Schirach had reported to the Führer: '*Mein Führer*, 30,000 *Hitlerjungen* on parade!' And then he yelled: '*Heil Hitler, Hitlerjungen*!' And we all shouted in unison: '*Heil Hitler, mein Führer*!' It was unbelievably intoxicating to be swept along with the crowd like that.

Klaus Mauelshagen, former member of the Hitler Youth

At Potsdam Schirach was on brilliant form. At last he could deliver to his lord and master the propaganda spectacle he needed for his election victory. 'Vast masses of National Socialist youth are assembled here on the eve of the great march which is to signify a profession of faith in the Führer, to listen to the man in whom the old soldiers, just as the fighters of the future, see their embodiment. I have chosen Potsdam because for us Germans it signifies all that is most sacred to our nation: Frederick the Great and the Prussian army, that is to say, the concept of a Führer, socialism and the performance of duty. If these ideas are relived today by 14 million of our fellow-countrymen, then no credit is due to Herr von Papen or the gentlemen's club of Germany, but it is solely the achievement of that worker for Germany, Adolf Hitler. That is why this movement is called the Hitler Youth. That is why it marches through this proud old city of Potsdam. We will not let our sacred ideas be stolen from us. We do not want a caste at the head of the German state, we want a *man*.'

Baldur von Schirach didn't employ a ghost-writer. He thought up his speeches on long walks and wrote them out at night.

Günter Kaufmann, Schirach's press officer, 1993

Schirach did not even have to lure the Führer out of Goebbels' apartment. Hitler had already noticed the procession of youngsters and was in his place in the stadium for the evening demonstration. Proudly Schirach presented the assembled young to his idol: 'Your youth, *mein Führer*, has paraded to provide you today with a demonstration of love and faith, such as no young generation has ever given to a living man.' 'Incredible cheering broke out', Schirach recalled later. 'Tears came into Hitler's eyes, the sight moved him so much.' The next day the uniformed columns with their flags and banners marched past him in a parade lasting seven hours. The success of Potsdam brought Schirach, the loyal vassal, praise of the highest order from his Führer. 'You achieved something extraordinary there,' he said to Schirach. 'There has been nothing more devastating for the Schleicher government than this procession of a massive youth organisation right outside Berlin.'

It was an honour for us *Hitlerjungen* to take part in the party rally. The ones who weren't allowed to go felt disadvantaged.
Klaus Mauelshagen, former member of the Hitler Youth

Even as the Weimar Republic was in its dying days, Schirach was surprised to find himself as one of its duly elected representatives. In July Hitler had put his protégé's name on the list of candidates. At the age of twenty-five, Schirach entered the Reichstag as the youngest Deputy. Hitler's paladin could see no political mileage in this assignment. Apart from his delight at the privileges of a member of parliament – 'marvellous, now I get free travel' – the impression Schirach had of his first Reichstag session was of 'a kind of mass meeting followed by a punch-up'. He gleefully helped to deliver the final death-blow to democracy and voted in March 1933 for the 'Enabling Law'. The fact that it was passed with the approval of the conservative parties filled him with disgust. 'If those are democratic patriots, then it's a lousy democracy and not worth a damn. You don't abandon your cause like that.'

Schirach had more respect for dictatorship. 'We were certainly no democrats in those days. When Hitler stated publicly that he was standing on democratic ground and that he wanted to come to power legitimately, we realised even then that this was just a tactic. Having learned from the example of the Italian fascists, we ourselves knew that the only possibility of a future for Germany was the elimination of parliamentary democracy.' Schirach felt himself to be a revolutionary. 'What has been termed "the seizure of power" was, for us, revolution.'

> Hitler was a great, demonic personality, a man who will be seen to play the same sort of part in history as Gengis Khan.
> *Schirach, interview with Jochen Lang, 1966*

Schirach had focused his entire future and all his aspirations on a single man: Adolf Hitler. Only when the Führer came to power would Schirach's star also be in the ascendant. On 30 January 1933 it finally happened. 'Hitler in power!' Schirach exulted. He acted with lightning speed. While all the other party departments remained for the time being in Munich, he immediately moved the *Reichsjugend* headquarters to Berlin. It was there that all political decisions would be taken from now on. It was where Hitler was. Since his student days Schirach had never been far from the Führer's side. He maintained offices in the 'Brown House' and later in the Reich Chancellery. His holiday homes – first in Urfeld, then in Kochel – were only an hour's drive from Hitler's Berghof, so that he could be called over at any time. Schirach knew what crucial importance lay in being close to the Führer: Hitler was his creator – without him he was nothing. Hitler's radiance put him in the spotlight as well. His position stood or fell with Hitler's favour. Schirach admittedly tried to convince himself he was unassailable: 'If there had been differences between Hitler and myself in the period from 1933 to 1936, Hitler could not simply have said, "I'm getting rid of him". Even in a totalitarian movement it is not the case that the boss just says, "That man no longer suits me, I'll send him off into the wilderness." Each person brings into movements like that the people he has convinced and won over. They are his private source of power. And I of course had won over the young. That has to be taken into account.' How dangerous it was to be a competitor in the party, Schirach certainly saw in Röhm's case [executed on Hitler's orders in 1934]. He played safe. Only by staying close to Hitler could he talk through decisions with him, anticipate differences of opinion, gain advance knowledge of his opponents' intrigues and fend them off.

The dictator repaid devotion with promotion: on 17 April 1933 he appointed the 26-year-old Baldur von Schirach Youth Leader of the German Reich. Schirach was now a *Reichsleiter* with ministerial rank, and his *Reichsjugendführung* was a department of state. The entire youth of Germany was now under the command of the poetry-writing lady-killer from Weimar.

The Führer had made clear, in an oft-repeated formula, what he expected of his young people: 'In our eyes the young German lad must be lean and lithe, as swift as a greyhound, as tough as leather and as hard as Krupp steel.' Unfortunately, the senior *Hitlerjunge* hardly lived up to the publicised ideal. Schirach was on the podgy side, and in the words of several contemporaries, had a 'soft, almost feminine face', a 'damp, aspic-like handshake', and looked 'fat and unathletic.' Rumours claiming Schirach's homosexual tendencies and describing his 'white, girlishly decorated bedroom' were persistent.

Baldur von Schirach was very tall, imposing. He had a softish face, which was a disappointment, but his voice was powerful. He had the voice for giving orders, as we used to say.
    Klaus Mauelshagen, former member of the Hitler Youth

I never thought of Schirach as a role-model. Perhaps he was too soft for me.
    Hans-Jürgen Habenicht, former member of the Hitler Youth

The leader of the younger generation was never a part of it, he was never one of the boys – and was never even really popular. He was more aesthetic than ascetic, preferring hotel rooms and a cultivated lifestyle to life under canvas and camp-fire stew. Schirach was 'no backslapper', not a fighter 'who you could sweat with'. He was more of a pensive loner who, to the lusty *Hitlerjungen*, always appeared 'a bit remote', as someone who 'floated above everything'. The seducer of youth lacked the art of seduction. The spoilt boy from a good family tried manfully to live up to the ideal of the raw-boned *Hitlerjunge*. However, his public appearances looked studied, awkward, almost agonised. He avoided plunging in amongst the mob, preferring to remain a pace or two behind his Führer. Dressed up as the hearty youth-leader in shorts, he often looked faintly ridiculous; even in his brown Nazi uniform he seemed unsuitably dressed. In fact, Schirach preferred to wear civilian clothes. Yet however much people laughed at him behind his back, thanks to his position in the leadership Schirach's authority remained unchallenged.

> In retrospect, the Schirach of those days was a vain young man, acclaimed certainly, and yet perhaps something more than people thought. An individualist who collected books, loved nature, horses and sport, but somehow, to me when I look back, not a very likeable phenomenon.
> *Schirach, interview with Jochen von Lang, 1966*

His education and background, so untypical for a leading Nazi, even earned the youth leader a certain respect. He was seen as an aesthete, the 'fine gentleman', the academically educated 'man of arts', the poet of National Socialism who, while not a fighter, deployed his gift for language in the cause of his ideals. Schirach himself appears not have been greatly troubled by these contradictions. True, he fancied a future in diplomatic posts with the Foreign Office, perhaps as ambassador to Washington. Yet he felt perfectly at ease in the guise of 'professional youngster', though it hardly suited him. Arrogance and the love of power permit no self-doubt.

In his new post of Youth Leader of the German Reich Schirach finally had the power to enforce the Hitler Youth's 'claim of totality'. 'Just as the NSDAP is Germany's only political party', he proclaimed, 'so is the HJ Germany's only youth organisation.'

Two months before, Schirach had begun the *Gleichschaltung* or root-and-branch Nazification of the country, with an act of violence. On 5 April 1933 he sent fifty *Hitlerjungen* to occupy the offices of the Reich Committee of German Youth Associations. The committee represented more than 5 million organised young people of whom at the most 110,000 belonged to the HJ. Schirach, who placed himself in charge of the committee, did promise to leave 'the independent life of the associations' undisturbed, but at the same time he threatened to suppress, 'rapidly and with no misplaced forbearance', anything that was inconsistent with the 'goals of the national revolution'. Jewish and Marxist organisations were immediately banned. Essentially Schirach had only one thing in mind: to keep the promise he had made to the Führer. 'It seemed ludicrous to me that it should now be so hugely important that any youth association with 150 members and a special little banner of its own should continue to exist and pursue some separate goal. I wanted a single Germany, a great Germany – a Germany in which the whole youth of the country would have a single home.' After his appointment as *Jugendführer des Deutschen Reiches*, he unceremoniously declared the Reich Committee superfluous.

> I was not, in my own conscience at least, responsible to Hitler, but to the young people I had called upon. To them and to no-one else I was answerable for my actions.
>
> *Schirach, interview with Jochen von Lang, 1966*

The tradition-steeped *Bündische Jugend* (Youth Alliance) was also a thorn in Schirach's flesh. Although many of its members had drifted over to the HJ, it still offered strong competition, since it presented itself as pro-Nazi, ethnic and nationalist. Many of the symbols of the Youth Alliance movement, which Schirach knew to have strong appeal to children, he imitated in his Hitler Youth: banners, badges and sheath-knives, as well as excursions, tent camps, marching bands and buglers. But Schirach could not permit the continued existence of the Alliance if he was to build the HJ up to be the only youth movement in Germany. In vicious attacks he branded the Alliance as an elite movement representing a reactionary Germany, and thus contrasted it fatally with the HJ:

'The principal criticism raised against the HJ is that it is a mass movement. Oh, what a monstrous crime! The small associations put the best complexion on their dwindling membership by saying they only select the best. So selective are they that they are left with nothing. But in their eyes we are number-mad agitators, serving the idol of the 'masses'. Yet none of the demonstrations and processions of the Hitler Youth have anything to do with a supposed love of publicity for its own sake; they are the means to an end. And the end is: new power. All for Hitler, for Hitler is Germany. These so-called 'alliances' are the reaction against him. They are all more or less 'nationalistic'. They all, to a greater or lesser extent, support the battle against Marxism. But their nationalism and their fight are limited to oh-so-stimulating camp-fire discussions among the sons of the upper classes. And discussions are all they are. Hitler Youth! You are a mighty movement of the innocent and the maturing, of the clear-sighted and the faithful! You are the revolution and its culmination, you are the living hope. When your marching steps echoed through Potsdam, the whole world paid heed. You are the socialist conscience of the nation. Uncompromising, unwavering. You will shatter the totems of capitalism and wipe the insolent grimace from the face of reaction. At your hands will die the notions of an age past its time: the "right sort of people", the "upper ten thousand".'

In a precipitate move, the *Deutsche Freischar* (German Irregulars), the German Boy Scout Federation, the *Jungsturm* and the *Freischar Junger Nation* all banded together in the Greater German Federation, under the leadership of a retired admiral named von Trotha. When they also received the protective patronage of influential party members such as Heinrich Himmler and the racist ideologue, Walter Darré, Schirach saw that his hard-fought monopoly of power was looking shaky. He immediately declared all federations that did not form part of the HJ to be 'enemies of National Socialism'. In order to get them out of the way he resorted to a ruse: he simply arranged for a report of the dissolution of the Greater German Federation to be published in the press. Von Trotha was taken in by it. Schirach could not have cared less about unscrupulously exceeding his authority in this way. An angry reprimand from the Minister of the Interior, Wilhelm Frick, was ignored.

However, Schirach did come up against limits when he also set about breaking up the Catholic youth associations, thereby seriously upsetting the negotiations over a concordat with the Vatican. It was no use Schirach protesting: 'With promises of a life hereafter they are trying to deter the young from a selfless dedication to the state. Anyone who wants a Germany at all costs is a mortal enemy of any religious element within a state organisation.' The Reich Minister of the Interior prohibited Schirach from making any 'forcible intervention', and the ban on Catholic youth associations that he had already issued had to be revoked.

On the other hand, Schirach's dealings with the Protestant youth were plain sailing. Reich Bishop Müller of the Evangelical Church, an ardent champion of National Socialism, concluded an agreement with Schirach late in 1933, which delivered to the HJ some 700,000 Evangelical young people. 'May God bless this hour for our nation and our Church', Müller cabled to Hitler. 'May God make His holy word mighty in the National Socialist upbringing of the coming generation.' Schirach could be certain of his Führer's praise: 'In connection with the task assigned to me of achieving the unification of German youth, I can report the integration of the Evangelical youth into the Hitler Youth.'

It is true that confessional youth organisations could continue to exist in name, but they were obliged to 'restrict themselves exclusively to their religious, ecclesiastical and charitable activities'. The 'moulding of the young politically, culturally, ideologically and in martial sports' was the preserve of the Hitler Youth. When Schirach made it illegal to belong to more than one youth organisation, the young came over to the HJ in droves.

Schirach's radical measures were successful. In the weeks that followed most of the groups within the Youth Alliance, the para-military youth formations and the youth organisations of the middle-class political parties, either dissolved themselves voluntarily, joined up with the HJ or, like the *Arbeiterjugend* (Workers' Youth), were banned. From now on, members of youth groups who did not toe the line were intimidated and beaten up. 'The Hitler Youth won out through brute force and brawling', a member of the Trade Union Youth recalls. 'There were more and more of them, and when we went hiking, they lay in wait for us and beat us over the head with rubber truncheons.'

Compulsion and beatings were not, however, the only arguments with which Schirach recruited new members. A massive advertising campaign swamped the Reich. 'Come and join us!' were the challenging words on the HJ posters. The pulling-power of a mass movement was cleverly exploited: 'Why aren't you one of us yet?' was the question shouted out from every billboard. 'Yes, why aren't I?' the children asked themselves. When the schools also began putting on pressure, even critical parents were powerless. As one BDM girl remembers: 'One day the head of our school came and asked: "Who here isn't yet in the *Jungmädel* or the *Pimpfen*?" [The junior girls' and boys' wings of the HJ.] Only two little girls put their hands up, Auguste and me. "All right," he said. "Come and see me in two weeks and by then you will have joined." So I went home in triumph and said: "Well, now you can't say anything more, I *have* to join now."'

The Pied Piper knew his business: he enticed with sounds which were music to the ears of many youngsters. Suddenly boys and girls were offered leisure activities which up till then only the few had enjoyed. Trips all over Germany, hiking, cycling tours and camping were suddenly possible for all. The children sang songs together, learned to play instruments, and were given national awards in sports and skills. 'I used to love marching, I was good at sport and liked going into the countryside. We did all those things. We went on exercises, and the comradeship there was terrific', says an enthusiastic ex-HJ boy even today.

For children from the poorest backgrounds the HJ offered undreamed-of opportunities. 'Some of us joined the HJ because people said: "Man, you just turn up and you get a hot meal and a uniform for free", and because there were musical instruments to play, like drums and trumpets', explains a former member of the Youth Alliance. Until the founding of the BDM, there was no comparable youth organisation for girls. Many parents were glad to know their children were not roaming the streets, while most youngsters appreciated a greater degree of independence from their parental home.

They felt at ease in the company of other children, where the 'feeling of comradeship' counted. The principle of 'youth leading youth', which Schirach had put into practice within the HJ, was very popular with the children. Accustomed to accepting and fearing the authority of teachers or parents, they admired and respected leaders who were only a few years older than themselves. Children who were singled out to take charge of a unit, even if it was only a ten-strong group of little boys or girls, were happy at the trust that had been placed in them and matured with the responsibility they had to bear. The fact that at last someone was taking them seriously filled them with pride.

Schirach particularly liked to stress his successes in the 'working world'. A large number of new members joined the HJ from the labouring and small-business classes, who until then had been excluded from the activities of the Youth Alliance. 'Youth is socialism', was one of his favourite slogans. He never meant by this a 'dictatorship of the proletariat', but doubtless intended the integration of all young people, including workers' children, into the homogeneous ranks of the Hitler Youth. 'A single banner flutters at the head of the HJ. The millionaire's son and the worker's son wear one and the same uniform. For it is youth which alone is free of prejudice in that sense, and capable of true community spirit; indeed, youth is socialism.' Schirach preached his gospel to the faceless masses: the truly socialist were all those who suppressed their own ideas and followed one man only: Hitler. 'The will of the Führer is alive in them, the will of him who gave them the word by which they are guided: "Nought is for us, all is for Germany."' Hordes of children walked into his net. By the end of 1933, out of a total population of seven and a half million aged between ten and eighteen, no less than 2.3 million belonged to the HJ and its component bodies – twenty times as many as when the Nazis seized power at the beginning of that year.

Yet this was not enough for Schirach. He wanted them all. The catcher of souls dreamed up a special surprise for his beloved Führer for the year 1936. In that 'Year of German Youth' he wanted to make a birthday gift to Hitler of every ten-year-old youngster. Every single child born in 1926 was to join the *Jungvolk* or the *Jungmädel* on 20 April. Under the slogan 'All youth for the Führer' Schirach launched a massive advertising campaign on radio, in cinemas, on posters, in schools and at sports events. On 19 April he was able to report its completion on radio: 90 per cent of all ten-year-olds had answered his appeal. By the end of 1936 membership had risen to over six million.

In his ambitious efforts to bring the whole field of education under his control, Schirach came into continuous conflict with the Minister of Education, Bernhard Rust, to whom he was subordinate. It came to a crunch when Schirach used every possible means to get a 'Law on the Hitler Youth' past Hitler. The law was intended to extend Schirach's influence considerably and elevate the youth to the 'State Youth'. Rust complained bitterly that the Youth Leader was attempting to steal the show and that he was splitting the whole educational profession – but it was in vain. Hitler signed the law on 1 December 1936. Once again the careerist had got his way. 'The struggle to unite the youth of Germany is over', Schirach exulted. The *Reichsjugendführung* was now a department of state on the highest level, and Schirach was a secretary of state subordinate only to Hitler. True, compulsory membership of the 'State Youth' was not introduced until 1939, but Schirach had already achieved one of his goals: next to school and the parental home the HJ was now the most important channel for the delivery of education, and Schirach was in effect the 'Reich Educator'.

For Schirach, the senior *Hitlerjunge*, the law was above all proof that the young could lead themselves. Gradually he began to turn into reality his notion of a 'state within a state'. By the outbreak of war a total of nineteen departments had been set up, including a social services office, a health office, offices for sport and ideology, a law office, a radio office, a foreign affairs office and a cultural office. It was the last of these which meant most to Schirach, the aesthete with cultural pretensions. With enthusiasm he organised art exhibitions, musical summer schools, concerts, youth film courses and drama festivals for the Hitler Youth in Weimar, and inaugurated a Youth Book Prize. As if to lend his educational ideals a quality of timeless inspiration, Schirach enlisted the services of the great poet Goethe as a model for all the principles of the Hitler Youth. The principle of self-leadership, the wearing of uniform by the young, even sport, games and camping – for all of these he cited Goethe, in order to construct a spiritual affinity with him: 'When reading [Goethe's] *Elective Affinities* I once came upon a remarkable sentence: "From their youth onward, men should wear uniform, because they must become accustomed to acting together, to losing themselves among their peers, to obeying *en masse* and working towards a totality." It instantly became clear to me that, at a time when Germany was made up of three dozen states, Goethe possessed the inner vision of a unified national German education.'

Goethe as the progenitor of the Hitler Youth – this was something the poet in Schirach could not resist. However, that talent for organisation, which was simply indispensable for building up a youth organisation, Schirach almost entirely lacked. 'We saw the greatest obstacle to the building of any revolutionary structure in Schirach's lack of practical experience of work at a low and intermediate level and in the staffing of the headquarters', wrote Schirach's deputy and chief-of-staff, Hartmann Lauterbacher, on the occasion of a conference of HJ leaders. 'All of them lacked the "smell of the stables", which by then we had acquired in hostel evenings, on weekend excursions, in camps and in debates with our political opponents.' Furthermore, Schirach shared with his Führer a distaste for tedious office chores. He loftily dismissed complaints about the sometimes chaotic conditions in the *Reichsjugendführung* and the lack of proper management: 'It is not replying promptly to letters that characterises good management, but its contact with the campaigning community. That is what we have been taught by the Führer, who again and again lectured me on not getting submerged in paper – one of the greatest and wisest lessons I have learned from him.' Schirach seldom began a working day before 10 a.m., but instead liked to dictate late into the night – when stirring ideas for a speech came to him. Schirach freely admitted that he was no organisational genius. But when choosing his colleagues he had the right touch. He restricted himself to developing ideas, making speeches, attending Hitler's court and, above all, acting as the public face of the Hitler Youth. The tiresome daily routine he left to the capable Lauterbacher who, with his staff, occupied the *Reichsjugend-führung* building on Berlin's Kronprinzenufer.

The Hitler Youth spread out its tentacles like a giant octopus and forced its way into the competing jurisdictions of school, church and family. To parents Schirach proclaimed that 'in a higher sense youth is always right'. He presented his ideas on the family: 'Many a well-off father, who perhaps complains that the HJ is taking his children away from family life, forgets that the HJ has called upon his children, in the community of National Socialist youth, to give the poorest sons and daughters of our nation something like a family for the first time in their lives. The fact that all young people in the HJ and the BDM once more believe in an ideal, must defeat every objection.'

Yet Schirach was increasingly coming into conflict with Party leaders and government ministers. It was particularly with the education minister, Rust, whose office he would dearly liked to have held, that Schirach was in a permanent armlock. Rust was incensed by the introduction of the Adolf Hitler Schools in 1938, with which Schirach became involved in school education in a major way. Boys who had 'proved outstanding' in the *Jungvolk* were to be trained as future Party executives in these leadership factories. 'You boys must realise', he shouted to the pupils of the Adolf Hitler School at Sonthofen after the outbreak of war, 'that you are being trained here to be leaders one day of a world power.' After that great war, they would become 'pillars of Adolf Hitler's global empire'. Schirach actually wanted to establish thirty-two such schools, one in each *Gau* of the Reich. But because of the war the expansion of the Schirach school system ground to a halt.

The comprehensive way in which Schirach monopolised youth met the demands of a dictatorship. Schirach wanted the HJ to 'embrace not only the whole youth of Germany but also every sphere of life of the young German'. His 'revolution in education' aimed at subordinating the young to an organisation from childhood onwards, and influencing them continuously. Significantly Schirach, who produced a slogan for every year, nominated 1934 as the 'Year of Moral Schooling and Orientation'. Hitler's Pied Piper demanded of the young people who were being trained on rapid three-week courses to be HJ leaders and thus his accomplices, not only that they should be 'the most capable mentally and physically' and 'leaders in battle'; he also required that each 'youth leader and educator of the future' should be 'a priest of the national Socialist faith and an officer of the National Socialist service'.

> The young generation experienced comradeship, learned to
> fit in and to take orders, were handed responsibility, found
> their thirst for adventure and need for experience satisfied on
> trips and in camps, felt they were being challenged, were
> motivated towards the common good and found security in
> the community.
>
> *Günter Kaufmann, Schirach's former press officer, 1993*

The structure of the HJ in itself ensured that the children were monopolised at an early age: at ten years old, boys and girls joined the *Jungvolk* and *Jungmädel* respectively, while fourteen- to eighteen-year-olds joined the Hitler Youth or *Bund Deutscher Mädel* (BDM or 'League of German Lasses'). In 1938 a division of the BDM called 'Faith and Beauty' was set up for young women up to the age of twenty-one.

Before long the HJ dominated every free moment in young people's lives. Every imaginable leisure pursuit, sport, singing, long excursions and camping, took place in the framework of the HJ. A 'State Youth day' was introduced: those in the HJ did not have to go to school on Saturdays, but had 'service' instead, which in the summer could last as long as twelve hours. The others had to endure 'at least two hours of classroom instruction' in National Socialist doctrine. At *Heimabende*, or hostel evenings, the children were given 'ideological' schooling in questions such as 'maintaining the purity of German blood' or the history of the Nazi Party, and had to learn Hitler's life story by heart. The ideological influence was reinforced by a weekly radio broadcast, 'The Hour of the Nation'. In addition there were nationwide competitions in sports and other skills. 'We had service twice a week, on Wednesdays and Saturdays', recalls the writer Eric Loest, 'and as I was soon made a leader, there was "leader service" on Mondays as well, then on Sundays there was shooting or we cycled somewhere or else had a procession. That meant I was involved with the Hitler Youth four or five days a week. We had no time to think about what we were actually doing. It was one thing after another, non-stop activity.'

'This young generation', proclaimed Hitler in Reichenberg in

1938, with an almost derisive edge to his voice, 'is learning nothing else but to think German and act German; and when these lads come into our organisation aged ten, there, for the first time ever, they feel they are getting some fresh air; then four years later they go from the *Jungvolk* into the Hitler Youth, where we keep them for another four years. After that, we certainly don't hand them back to our old producers of snobbery and class-consciousness; no, we take them straight into the Party, or the Labour front, the SA or the SS, the NSKK and so on. And if, after two or two-and-a-half years there they still have not become complete National Socialists, they are sent into the Labour Service where they get drilled hard for another six or seven months, all with a symbol of the German spade. Then, after those six or seven months, anyone here or there who still has any class-consciousness or social arrogance left in them is taken on by the Wehrmacht for further treatment over two years, and when they come back after two or three or four years, then, to make sure there is absolutely no backsliding, we immediately take them back into the SA, SS and so on, and they will never be free again for the rest of their lives.'

Many people heard this but did not want to accept the bitter corollary. They preferred to listen to the blandishments of Schirach, who called out to the young: 'You are the future of the nation', 'You are the pillars of a new Germany'. Schirach convinced the young that they were unique. Having their own banners, their own hymns and their own martyrs further stirred up this feeling of being special. They were among their peers: 'Youth must be led by youth' was the formula, coined by Hitler himself, which Schirach made his own and ceaselessly propounded as the guiding principle of his policy.

Never has a young generation been so betrayed. For no young generation was ever more deprived of its own voice. Schirach's 'state within a state' was nothing other than a miniature dictatorship. He turned the National Socialist Führer-principle into an iron rule: 'A community of young people can only be successful if it recognises unquestioningly the authority of its leaders. Otherwise there is no point in having leaders. The success of National Socialism is the success of discipline, the house of National Socialist youth is built on the foundations of discipline and obedience.' Criticism of orders was, he claimed, 'criminal, because it begins to undermine authority . . . That is why the Hitler Youth silently submits to the orders of its leaders, even if they are directed against itself.'

Schirach attempted expressly to prohibit independent thought: 'The millions of young do not represent their own interests but the good of the nation. One faith binds us, one creed commits us, one Führer commands.' With ruthless consistency the HJ was exploited for Hitler's political ambitions.

'This Hitler, as I saw him, was a man whom again and again I portrayed to the young in often fervent words', Schirach later wrote in his memoirs. 'In this way, out of honest conviction, I played a part in creating that myth of the Führer, which the German people were so susceptible to.' Schirach celebrated Goebbels' 'cult of the Führer' with greater panache even than Goebbels. The son of a theatre director, he showed a gift for theatrical and pseudo-mystical 'Führer Masses'. Every year on the eve of Hitler's birthday, for the induction of ten-year-olds into the *Jungvolk*, he staged a ceremony in the West Prussian fortress of Marienburg, the symbol of Germanic invincibility. As the steps of hundreds of banner-bearers echoed through the gloomy vaults of the old castle and the hymn 'We vow to Hitler loyalty unto the grave' was sung in the light of flaming torches, the children were filled with the wonderfully thrilling feeling of being part of a 'band of blood-brothers'. On radio Schirach presented the new annual intake to the Führer. Throughout the Reich children murmured the words of their oath: 'I promise to do my duty in the Hitler Youth at all times, in love and loyalty to the Führer and our flag, so help me God.'

A similar function was filled by the 'Adolf Hitler march'. In a vast procession converging from many points – the organisational details were, as always, worked out by Hartmann Lauterbach – some 2,000 *Hitlerjungen* marched from all corners of the Reich to the Reich Party rally in Nuremberg, where they paraded past Hitler in force. In the process, some HJ groups covered nearly 500 miles. Schirach made it clear that the object of this was certainly not just to keep the youngsters fit: 'We are marching to the Führer – and if he wishes it, we will march *for* him as well.' The Youth Leader achieved the crowning glory of the Führer-cult when, from 1938 onward, he terminated the Adolf Hitler March short of Nuremberg, in Landsberg, where Hitler had been imprisoned in 1923. In a mystic ceremony in the very cell where Hitler had dictated *Mein Kampf*, he distributed to every participant on the march a personally signed copy of the book which had become the least-read bestseller in Germany's history.

It soon became apparent what goals Hitler was pursuing in power-politics. He was on course for war. Yet Schirach was unwilling to attribute to his idol any warlike intentions. 'With a grateful heart', the *Reichsjugendführer* greeted the reintroduction of general military conscription 'as a condition for maintaining peace in Europe'. In order to lend strength to Hitler's 'will for peace', Schirach declared 1935 to be the 'Year of Fitness'. Hitler's youth had to be young, strong, handsome and above all combative. Sport was writ large in the HJ. True to Nazi racial ideology, Schirach expected the girls to school themselves in 'body and mind', in order to face their role as 'mothers of new generations'. It was the girls, particularly, who were said to be responsible for 'maintaining the purity of their blood as part of the national bloodstock' and who were obliged 'to develop their physical assets in such a way that the heredity passed on by them enriches the nation'. It was their 'duty to live up to the standards of beauty desired by young males'. In reality, as a one-time BDM girl bitterly acknowledged, they were meant 'to produce cannon-fodder for the Führer'.

The pre-military training of the young proceeded at a forced pace. Schirach could insist as often as he liked, that 'the HJ is not being mobilised for war but for peace' – but by the time Poland was invaded, if not sooner, the scales fell from the youngsters' eyes: 'From the start we were being prepared for war', a former *Hitlerjunge* protests. From 1936 contact sports such as boxing were compulsory; in HJ service, which already consisted largely of military-style exercises and drill, route-marches with full kit were introduced; war-games with crawling, stalking, map-reading and compass-work were the order of the day. According to a statement by Schirach's successor, Artur Axmann, even in peacetime no less than 30,700 HJ shooting instructors were trained, and 1.5 million *Hitlerjungen* had regular rifle practice.

At the same time reason, education and intellect were openly denigrated. 'By the end of this year', Schirach's military fitness officer, Helmut Stellrecht, declared, 'we want to see German boys handling a rifle with as much assurance as a pen. Liberalism has written over the school gate that "Knowledge is Power". But we have learned, in war and postwar times, that the power of the people ultimately resides in their weapons and in those who know how to use them.'

In pre-military training, Schirach, who was unwilling to share his control over the youth, made every effort to keep the Wehrmacht at arm's length. The latter was very keen to bring the youth under its wing. Not that Schirach had any objection to pre-military training, he just wanted to run it himself. In February 1937 the Supreme Command of the Wehrmacht appointed *Oberstleutnant* Erwin Rommel as liaison between the armed forces and the youth leadership. Rommel proposed to put the pre-military training of the young in the hands of serving officers. That meant more influence than Schirach could stomach. He made sure that the highly decorated Great War hero was removed from his post.

Early in 1939 – even before the war had started – a new agreement was reached. The HJ created special units in which young people were specifically prepared for military disciplines: the naval HJ, the motorised HJ, the air HJ and the reconnaissance HJ. Hitler's paladin knew how things stood: war was in the air. On 15 March German troops had occupied Czechoslovakia. Hurriedly Schirach pushed forward with regulations to implement the HJ law. By 25 March they were in place and membership of the HJ became compulsory. Germany, as Schirach admitted to a meeting of HJ officials, was a country 'which was trying to convince the other nations of its love of peace, in order to be able to complete its rearmament'. Since 'Germany was destined for world domination', he would 'educate the young in such a way that they would, in all the years to come, be capable of representing a world power.' The fruits of the seeds which Schirach had sown in peacetime, his successor Axmann was able to harvest during the war. The young were armed and ready: 'As was acknowledged repeatedly on the part of the Wehrmacht', Axmann wrote, 'the early enlistment of those interested in motors, radio, flying and navigation, and their systematic instruction even before their active service during the war, has proved to be of the highest value.'

> I did not educate the young for war, I educated them for military service. This type of training is a perfectly normal thing, which every country that wishes to defend itself does with its youth.
>
> *Schirach, interview with Jochen von Lang, 1966*

Schirach was less concerned about contact with the SS. In August 1938 he concluded an agreement with the *Reichsführer* SS, Heinrich Himmler. In future the HJ patrol service would be reserved as new intake, not only to the general SS but also for the SS combat troops and the 'Death's head' units which ran the concentration camps. This was because the patrol service had 'similar tasks to perform within the Hitler Youth as the SS does within the Movement as a whole'. The HJ patrol service was an internal HJ police force, which had existed since 1934. It was a small force, which supervised the 'orderly' behaviour of the children before and after service, hauled adolescents out of bars and – especially after youth service became compulsory – pounced on unco-operative youth groups, beat them up and reported them. When it came to recruiting youths for the patrol service, those selected were usually bullying types who worked closely with the SS and the Gestapo. Later, in the concentration camps and on the death-marches, this 'elite' force was particularly noted for its cold-blooded brutality.

Schirach's indoctrination bore cruel fruit. For even in the ideological instruction of the Hitler Youth the notion of race was always present. Here the children learned the myth of the 'ugly Jew', and the right of the stronger over the weak was invoked. Schirach himself preached that 'only those nations which have maintained their individuality survive in the struggle for life', and in the weekly radio programme, *Hour of the Nation*, he tried to teach the young to worship 'the heroic' and despise 'weaklings'.

He complained that in the Weimar Republic 'the anti-social and those unfit to pass on their heredity' had been 'pampered at the expense of the healthy'. At hostel evenings, on posters and in propaganda films Schirach outlined the ideal of the New Man: the Germanic race of the future should be healthy, vigorous, strong, if possible, fair-haired – and, needless to say, Aryan. In order to be sure that no 'non-Aryans' sneaked into the command structure of the HJ, Schirach decreed in 1936 that 'every leader in the HJ or BDM must show proof of their Aryan descent.'

The leader of youth was not a fanatical anti-Semite and even when speaking tended to hold back from making malicious attacks on the Jews. Nevertheless, having been heavily influenced by books like Houston Stewart Chamberlain's *Foundations of the 20th Century*, Henry Ford's *The International Jew* and Hitler's *Mein Kampf*, he described himself as 'consciously anti-Semitic'. 'I considered the removal of Jews from government to be an absolute necessity.' When this 'removal' took on crude forms, the sensitive Schirach was acutely embarrassed. True, he was fond of inflammatory rhetoric: 'Burning is generally the preserve of the new youth. It is a simple but heroic philosophy which says: whoever is against our unity must go to the stake.' However, on the so-called *Reichskristallnacht* on 9 November 1938, when synagogues went up in flames and *Hitlerjungen* in Munich shattered shop windows and looted the home of a Jewish art-dealer, Schirach spoke of a 'cultural disgrace'. The next day he prohibited the participation of the HJ in 'criminal acts' of this kind. Anyone who insisted on taking part would be dishonourably discharged.

However, Schirach never felt the necessity to protest against these excesses. He believed in his Führer and regarded acts of terrorism merely as aberrations from the pure ideal, which he pursued unswervingly to the end, dedicated to his youthful concept of loyalty. Admittedly, he felt for the first time that he was 'no longer among decent people'. 'But what was I to do? I was anti-Semitic and believed it was possible to be anti-Semitic in a decent way. He preferred to abide by Göring's motto: '*I* decide who is a Jew.' If he was particularly fond of someone classed as a 'half-Jew', he included the name on a list and obtained Hitler's personal assurance that the named person would be treated on an equal footing with 'Aryan citizens'.

The gullible courtier claimed to have been caught unawares by the outbreak of war. 'Hitler had always concealed his readiness for war. I was firmly convinced that even this time he was only bluffing.' When Hitler announced on the radio that 'since 5.45 a.m. we have been returning fire', Schirach addressed his staff with pessimistic foresight: 'Don't imagine that this will be a short war. It could last five, six or even seven years . . . You will live to see Berlin burning!'

Indeed, the war came at rather an inconvenient time for Schirach. The would-be Foreign Minister had plunged himself with zeal into the overseas activities of the Hitler Youth and declared 1938 the 'Year of Rapprochement'. Mussolini always made the *Hitlerjungen* welcome. There now began intensive youth exchanges with Britain and France. Schirach himself had travelled widely and approached various rulers: Shah Reza Pahlevi of Iran, King Carol of Roumania, the Prince Regent Paul of Yugoslavia, King Ghasie of Iraq, the Hungarian head of state, Miklos von Horthy and the founder of modern Turkey, Kemal Atatürk. Reciprocal youth visits, Schirach maintained, served to improve international understanding and thus promoted peace. The war put an end to these pleasures.

Visibly annoyed by his Führer's thirst for war, Schirach now tried to bring a tentative influence to bear on Hitler's foreign policy. 'Back from my trip to America. Must speak to you urgently!' read a telegram to Schirach from Colin Ross, who was a well-known travel-writer and friend of Schirach's. Excitedly Ross predicted to the *Reichsjugendführer* that in the autumn of 1940 Roosevelt would be re-elected president and that the USA would then inevitably enter the war. 'God help us if the Americans join this life-or-death struggle. You must put this to Hitler without fail', Schirach said, and arranged for Ross to have an audience with the Führer. However, Hitler was unimpressed. In the days that followed Schirach and Ross drafted memorandum after memorandum, which found their way into Ribbentrop's files, there to gather dust. It appears that the two men even toyed with the idea of bursting in on

Hitler and holding pistols to their own heads, in order to persuade the dictator to change his mind. The initiative came to nothing.

With the invasion of Poland it became clear that Schirach's educational methods had been outstandingly successful. For years he had drummed patriotism and pugnacity, obedience and self-sacrifice into the *Hitlerjungen*; and when war broke out more than half the HJ leaders' cadre voluntarily exchanged their brown shirts for the field-grey of the Wehrmacht. The number of HJ leaders killed in Poland had already reached 314. 'We were afraid we would arrive too late', one of those volunteers recalls. 'That would have been frightful. We thought the war might be over beforehand, and that we wouldn't make it in time, so keen were we.' For Schirach, this enthusiasm for war had a big drawback: the leadership of the Hitler Youth had in effect become detached. In a circular he warned HJ leaders not to volunteer for the armed forces unless someone was ready to take their place. But the instruction came too late.

Soon Schirach was the only 'youngster' in the entire Reich who had still not been through weapon-training. Repeatedly he requested permission from his Führer to join the Wehrmacht. At the end of 1939 the message finally came: 'Permission granted.'

He was only in the army for a short while, and as far as I know there is no picture of him in gym-shorts or even swimming-trunks. He never went out except in uniform and always wore gloves. It didn't look very military. We were a lot more athletic.

Walter Goergen, former member of the Hitler Youth

As a soldier I was of course interested in seeing that the young were prepared for military service. Not, however, through pre-military games of soldiers, but through sport and open-air living.

Schirach in his autobiography, I Believed in Hitler, *1967*

Early in 1940 Baldur von Schirach became a soldier. He spent his time as a recruit in Döberitz, near Berlin, where private quarters and a personal trainer were made available to the *Reichsjugendführer*. He was posted to the elite *Grossdeutschland* infantry regiment, in which he took part, first as a messenger then as an NCO commanding a machine-gun platoon, in attacks at Sedan, on the Somme and outside Dunkirk. It is unclear whether the cosseted aesthete was in fact a hero in the field or contrived to stay out of the firing-line. At all events, Schirach was promoted to *Leutnant* and awarded the Close Combat Badge and the Iron Cross. At the end of June 1940, when he was in Lyon, an order from Hitler reached him: 'Report immediately to headquarters!'

'I'm glad you got through it all safe and sound', Hitler greeted him at his HQ at Tannenberg in the Black Forest. 'I need you for a new assignment. You're to go to Vienna as Reich Governor and Gauleiter.' The reason Hitler gave was that Gauleiter Bürckel did not know how to win the Viennese over to the Reich; he lacked tact and psychology. But he, Schirach, was the right man. What Hitler's purpose was in this change of function remains a matter for speculation. Malicious tongues claimed that Hitler no longer trusted the soft and casual Schirach with the disciplined leadership of the HJ in wartime. According to Schirach Hitler was 'in genuine difficulties' because he had found no-one else for the post. But Vienna was not just another city. The Danube metropolis was the second-largest city in the Reich; the Führer himself described it as a 'pearl' to which he just wanted to give the right setting. Was the post of Gauleiter not in fact a distinction for the Crown Prince, a preparation for higher tasks? Whether Schirach was being sidelined or upgraded, it is clear that, at the age of thirty-three, he was already too old for his former job.

At Schirach's suggestion Hitler appointed Artur Axmann *Jugendführer* of the German Reich and of the Nazi Party. However, Schirach remained Reich Chief of Youth Education in the Nazi Party, which meant he was senior to Axmann. He still wanted a certain involvement with youth.

Vienna was nothing if not a 'difficult' city. The Austrians had certainly greeted the *Anschluss* with jubilation. But the initial euphoria had soon melted away when the 'bloody Krauts'

> When we heard that Schirach was coming to Vienna, we kind of got the idea that it might perhaps mean an easier time for us. Schirach was known for being something of an aesthete, an intellectual, a man of many interests, who appreciated the fine arts; and somehow the Jews at the time thought, it mightn't be so bad.
>
> *Martin Vogel, member of the Zionist youth movement in Vienna*
>
> We were told quite officially that Vienna had to be cleared of Jews. That was the business of Baldur von Schirach.
>
> *Herbert Schrott, Jew from Vienna*

unceremoniously occupied every important official post and immediately brought in their Prussian civil servants from Berlin. The Viennese were accustomed to being regarded as citizens of a metropolis. They did not want to play second fiddle to Berlin and reacted against this demotion with typically snide Viennese humour. 'From a world city to a Prussian province? People of Vienna! Do you accept this humiliation of your city?' was how one leaflet put it. It was a fact that Hitler nursed a deep-seated resentment against the city where he had spent his 'years of suffering', and hated its 'alien mixture of peoples'. Secretly he wanted to promote his home city of Linz, in preference to Vienna. The edgy atmosphere provoked clashes between Reich Germans and Viennese in offices, tramcars, cafés and theatres.

Hitler now gave his paladin orders to raise the level of approval for Führer and Reich and 'to secure once again for Vienna its leading position as a city of culture'. The artistically cultivated Schirach with his aristocratic Austrian title seemed to be the ideal man for the job. But to this was added a further task: in autumn 1940, when the first bombs fell on German cities, Hitler once again placed the wellbeing of children in Schirach's hands. He put him in charge of the *Kinderlandverschickung*, the despatch of city children to the safety of the countryside. By the war's end Schirach's organisation had removed millions of children from areas at risk from air raids to safe country districts. But as so often when the HJ took charge of something, the operation descended into chaos. Organisation had never been Schirach's strong point: children were often sent on their journey alone or ill-equipped, and when they arrived the reception camps were often fully occupied. The fact that not only the HJ but also the Union of Nazi Schoolteachers and the Nazi social welfare organisation concerned themselves with the children meant that there were frequent disputes over areas of authority. As the war dragged on, the difficulties became ever greater and took up a considerable portion of Schirach's working energies.

Straight away, however, Schirach the aesthete fell in love with the city of arts. He had no difficulty in shaking off the role of the brisk youth leader, which basically had always been a pretence for him. Thus, as a former colleague of his writes, 'he changed from restless fighter to sensitive connoisseur, from youth leader to city governor, from man of letters to patron of the arts and from busy executive to guardian of a jewel.'

With his wife Henriette, and the three little children he had by now fathered, Schirach moved into a spacious villa on the Hohe Warte with a view over the Rothschild Park. As his prestigious official premises he chose the palace on Ballhausplatz and set up his office in a large hall where Prince Metternich had convened the Congress of Vienna in 1815. In this vast room, with its imposing gilded décor and six doors, Schirach could reign like a prince. While the bombs rained down on the rest of Europe, Schirach held state receptions and formal banquets, arranged for operas and plays to be staged and summoned renowned artists to Vienna. The Führer was expecting a brilliant performance from his Gauleiter, in order to mollify the Viennese – and the Schirachs took delight in fulfilling this duty. Henriette, in her book tellingly entitled *The Price of Splendour*, dreams nostalgically after the war of 'sweet Vienna, when the spire of St Stephen's cathedral glints like a bunch of orchids, and the pale yellow hall of the Spanish Riding School with its Lippizaners'. She looks back on state receptions with foreign consuls in the 'great white-and-gold hall in Vienna's Hofburg', lit by candles and accompanied by singing from the Vienna Boys Choir.

And now after seventeen years, when the Public Prosecutor asks me what was in my mind when I married Baldur von Schirach, I have no answer to give him. Had I simply said I loved him and it did not matter to me what his job was – even if it had been the craziest job in the world – the Prosecutor would not have understood me anyway. Prosecutors do not want to hear love-stories, they want 'evidence'.

Henriette von Schirach, The Price of Splendour, *1975*

Schirach who, as city chief of Vienna, also had to deal with matters at a borough level, enjoyed this work: 'I got to know the problems of a big city, from water-supply to pensions for street-sweepers. As a local government boss I wasn't at all bad.'

In the relatively open-minded city on the Danube, far removed from Hitler who, in his 'Wolf's Lair' headquarters in East Prussia, was scarcely reachable by his henchmen, Schirach became increasingly remote from the Führer he once so admired. He almost became a rebel. With an eye on Goebbels who, as Propaganda Minister, had a monopoly of culture in the Reich, Schirach requested Hitler expressly to give him a free hand in cultural matters. Hitler agreed willingly. The little Doctor followed Schirach's work with the closest attention, and to begin with was very impressed. Under Schirach's aegis, despite the war, Vienna radiated a new brilliance: with week-long drama festivals, opera productions, and the awarding of newly created prizes, the city regained its old prestige.

However, Schirach's unorthodox cultural policy gave rise to open criticism. Once he opened an exhibition in which paintings were to be seen that came into the category of so-called 'decadent art', including pictures of 'green dogs'. Hitler was furious and ordered the immediate closure of the exhibition. Goebbels wrote carpingly: 'Schirach lacks sound artistic judgement.' New stage productions and films were, in the eyes of the Reich Propaganda Minister, often on the 'borders of illegality'. Schirach invited the playwright Gerhart Hauptmann, who was *persona non grata* with Goebbels on account of the social criticism in his dramas, to Vienna to celebrate his eightieth birthday and held a 'Gerhart Hauptmann Festival Week'. Schirach also celebrated the birthday of the composer Richard Strauss with glittering performances of his music. Strauss had fallen out with the Nazis, but Schirach even dared to kiss the hand of the great man's Jewish daughter-in-law. Goebbels complained bitterly that in the middle of a war against the USSR Schirach played 'that Russian, Tchaikovsky' and even included as much Chekhov as Shakespeare in his programme.

> One gets the impression that Schirach, through sheer lack of experience, is not up to the demands that Viennese cultural policy places on him. He seems bent on repeating all over again the mistakes we have made since 1933 and which we have already grown out of. Sadly, I lack the necessary time at the moment to occupy myself fully with this problem; we had better postpone that until after the war.
>
> *Goebbels, diary, 4 February 1942*

Schirach similarly crossed swords with several Party bigwigs when, in 1942, he convened the 'European Congress of Youth' in Vienna. The plan, derisively called 'Baldur's children's party', met with sharp criticism in Berlin. Ribbentrop, who considered that Schirach was meddling in his foreign policy, declared that the participation of foreign diplomats in the congress was undesirable. The Italian foreign minister, Count Galeazzo Ciano, withdrew his previous acceptance. Goebbels saw to it that the press wrote not a word about the event. Nevertheless the congress, at which the 'Association of European Youth' was founded, turned out to be a success for Schirach. Fascist youth organisations from those European nations which lay in the German sphere of influence despatched their delegates. Italians, Spaniards, Flemings and Walloons from Belgium, Danes, Dutchmen, Frenchmen, Norwegians, Finns, Bulgarians, Roumanians, Slovakians and Hungarians all came to Vienna. Schirach, as ever an idealist in youth matters, still dreamed of a 'community of European nations', the uniting of Europe's youth. Hitler's secretary, Martin

Bormann, complained about the festivities taking place in Vienna while German soldiers were bleeding to death in and around Stalingrad. Goebbels hissed angrily: 'The troops are fighting, but the congress dances in Vienna.'

However, in another pressing matter Schirach remained on course: the deportation of Jews from Vienna. Shortly after taking up office in July 1940 he assigned to his deputy Gauleiter, Scharizer, the task of 'immediately resuming a well-planned and comprehensive resettlement of the Jews', in order to bring under control the 'desperate shortage of housing'. On 2 October a meeting took place in the Reich Chancellery in Berlin, between Hitler, Bormann and the *Generalgouverneur* of Poland, Hans Frank, who reported on the Jewish ghettos in Warsaw and proudly announced that Cracow was 'cleansed of Jews'. Hitler's secretary, Bormann, noted: '*Reichsleiter* von Schirach interjected that he still had Jews in Vienna, whom Frank should take off his hands.' But Frank bristled at this, claiming that the *Generalgouvernement* was already full beyond its capacity. At that time there were still 60,000 Jews living in Vienna. In November their resettlement within the city began. Families, single people and children were indiscriminately crammed into rooms without heating or suitable sanitary facilities. A protest by the Israelite Cultural Community went unheeded.

On 3 December Schirach received the official message from Berlin that Hitler had decided that the Viennese Jews 'should be removed at a faster pace, that is to say while the war is still on'. 'That was pretty much Schirach's job', a survivor of Auschwitz tells us. 'Vienna was to be cleansed of Jews. It felt like "Ten Green Bottles". The number kept getting smaller.' In February and March 1941, on Schirach's orders, the first transports left Vienna for Poland with 5,000 Jews. They were told they were being resettled in small towns. On 15 March the deportations were halted because of the war situation. However, Schirach was very anxious to remove the Jews from the city as fast as possible. On 19 March he protested personally to the *Reichsführer* SS, Heinrich Himmler, about the interruption of the transports. Himmler thereupon decided that every train leaving Vienna for the *Generalgouvernement* should have one coach full of Jews attached to it. Schirach had got his way.

In October another 5,000 Jews were taken to Lodz and murdered in gas-trucks shortly afterwards.

For the rest of his life Schirach maintained that it was only through Himmler's speech to Gauleiters in Poznan in October 1943 that he learned about the annihilation of the Jews. He claimed that on his appointment as Gauleiter Hitler had told him: 'The Jews are being deported. They are being taken from Vienna to new settlement areas.' He had also been assured by Hans Frank that Jews were being put to work on road-building and the manufacture of clothing and shoes. Apart from the fact that Schirach had ordered the deportation of Jewish citizens from Vienna without batting an eyelid – is it possible that a man who belonged to the highest rank of party and state officialdom in the Third Reich could know so little?

> It struck me that Baldur had never condemned a man to death and never locked anyone up in a concentration camp.
> *Henriette von Schirach*, The Price of Splendour, *1975*

There must be a strong suspicion that in retrospect Schirach sought to wash his hands of the crime. At all events he presumably 'knew' about the atrocities sooner than he admitted. As early as 12 December 1941 Hitler had called together his Reichsleiters and Gauleiters to let them in on his plan to destroy the Jews of Europe. It is highly probable that, as a Gauleiter, Schirach was present. At least he had no appointments in Vienna on that day. On 12 May 1942 the Gauleiter of Poznan, Arthur Greiser, came to Vienna to speak to the Nazi officials there about 'the tasks in the Warthegau' (the area of western Poland that had been made into a German province in 1939). Schirach claimed that this visit had taken place later, but a note in the record of his activity as Gauleiter confirms the date and the occasion. Schirach was indeed at this meeting and heard Greiser reporting on the murder operations and 'how Jews were crammed into vehicles and killed with exhaust fumes'. There is no doubt that Schirach was appalled. He finally realised 'what lay behind this whole deportation business'. However, his subsequent claims that he immediately got in touch with Colin Ross and considered how Hitler might be declared mentally unfit to govern, and that he immediately issued orders for all deportations from Vienna to be halted, sound very contrived. That May, soon after Greiser's speech, five transports containing several thousand people left Vienna bound for Minsk and Izbica. For many of them the journey ended in the gas-chambers of Auschwitz.

As one of the deportees remembers: 'We were then told that we were to be shipped off. We went to this school in Sperlgasse, with a suitcase and a bedding-roll, and there we were shown into a classroom with ten or twenty others. We spent a night or two there and then we were led into a yard where a truck was parked and they said: "All of you get in". Then they drove us to Aspang station, a small station in Vienna that was only used for special purposes, so that the local population would find out as little as possible. There we boarded wagons heading for Theresienstadt.' From there, the eye-witness tells us, the transports left for Auschwitz, Treblinka and Maidanek.

Yet it never occurred to Schirach to draw the logical conclusions from his knowledge. In June 1942, when Reinhard Heydrich was assassinated in Prague, Schirach, who had noticeably avoided making violently anti-Semitic speeches in public, allowed himself to be carried away in a furious reaction. At a rally of the German Labour Front on 5 June, he announced: 'This very autumn we will be able to celebrate a Vienna that is free of Jews. We will then be able to turn to the problem of the Czechs in Vienna. As Gauleiter of Vienna, following the evacuation of the Jews, I am issuing the order for the deportation of all Czechs from Vienna.' In the same year, before an audience of hundreds at the International Youth Congress, he said: 'If anyone wants to accuse me of having driven tens or hundreds of thousands of Jews into the ghettos of the east, from a city that was once the capital of European Jewry, I have to reply: I see it as an active contribution to European culture.'

Hitler's loyal helper could still be sure of his Führer's praise. On Schirach's thirty-fifth birthday Hitler sent his warmest congratulations to Vienna in a message that henceforth has been interpreted as a 'telegram to the Crown Prince'. In a letter the Führer described him as 'the best horse in my stable'. Even when sitting in the Wolf's Lair, the 'Greatest Military Leader of All Time' spoke enthusiastically about his young disciple, of whom he expected 'something great again'.

Schirach was an opportunist who, by making verbal attacks against the Jews, hoped to ensure the benevolence of his boss. He did not have the strength to rebel against Hitler. At the same time he did occasionally help a Jewish artist out of a tight corner. 'If I had set myself against the government, those people would of course have been deprived of my protection', he said later in his defence. With embarrassment he admitted: 'We allowed justice to prevail for individual Jews, but not for the entire Jewish people.'

How rapidly a critical remark could arouse the wrath of the Führer, the Schirachs were to experience at first hand. While visiting Amsterdam, Henriette had happened to witness from her hotel window the rounding up and deporting of Jewish women. 'I was woken during the night by loud screams and shouts. I rushed to the window and tried to make out what was going on in the darkness. Standing in the street below me were several hundred women with bundles. They had apparently been rounded up in a hurry and were being guarded by men in uniform. I could hear weeping and then heard a voice commanding sharply: "Aryans remain behind!" Then the column slowly began to move forward.' Her horror grew when an SS officer whom she knew offered her a chance to buy gold and jewellery cheaply from a store where looted Jewish valuables were kept. Nonetheless, it is astonishing that this incident involving Dutch Jews should have made such an impression on Frau von Schirach, when in Vienna Jews were being rounded up and deported outside her front door almost every day. Be that as it may, Henny decided to tell Hitler about this incident – 'he cannot mean this to happen'. Back in Vienna she immediately telephoned the Berghof – the Schirachs could always ask whether a visit by them would be convenient – and Hitler said, as always: 'Yes, of course. Come as soon as you like.'

As usual, quite a large party had foregathered at the Berghof, including Martin Bormann, Albert Speer and the doctors Brandt and Morell. Although Schirach advised his wife against it – 'there's nothing you can do to change things' – late in the evening she told Hitler about her experience in Amsterdam.

Hitler jumped angrily to his feet. 'You're being sentimental, Frau von Schirach! What have Jewesses in Holland to do with you!' An icy silence spread through the room. None of the seventeen men sitting around the fire said a word. Hitler went on: 'My duty is only to my people – you must learn to hate.' The situation became even edgier when the conversation turned to Vienna. Hitler gave full rein to his hatred of the city. 'It was a mistake of mine, sending you to Vienna. I made a mistake in even accepting those Viennese into the Greater German Reich', he told Schirach. Once again Goebbels was jubilant: 'The behaviour of Schirach and his wife brings a certain tension to the evening. Frau Schirach in particular acts like a silly little madam and completely ignores the Führer's arguments.' Schirach later related how the situation had become so untenable that he and his wife hastily left the Berghof in the early hours and travelled back to Vienna. It appears to have been their last visit to the Obersalzberg.

All at once Hitler announced that he felt a 'certain mistrust' towards Schirach. With undisguised satisfaction Goebbels wrote in his diary in May 1943: 'The Führer has a poor opinion of Schirach. The man has gone soft in Vienna. He has allowed himself to become too infected by the Viennese atmosphere. He has shown no feel for politics and he's not even a fully-fledged Nazi. He's spending too much time with artists and it's doing him no good. Anyway, the Führer has nothing big in mind for him. Sooner or later he may force Schirach into a diplomatic career, which is certainly more his line.'

Schirach's position became more serious when, in autumn 1943, he received criticism for failing to prepare Vienna for air raids. Like all Gauleiters Schirach also held the post of Reich Defence Commissioner for Vienna and was thus responsible for fortifying the city. The Allies were advancing up through Italy, and Vienna was increasingly at risk from attack by enemy bomber squadrons. Kaltenbrunner, head of the Security Service, came to Vienna on a tour of inspection and described the defence measures as 'wholly inadequate'; Schirach's preparations for protecting the civilian population were found wanting. 'The Führer is totally dissatisfied with Schirach', Goebbels wrote. 'He wants to replace

I was politically outmanoeuvred when I went to Vienna.
Schirach, interview with Jochen von Lang, 1966

From Vienna I get a report from the SD that a kind of animosity towards the Reich is building up, to some extent behind the shield of the responsible Reich authorities. Developments in Vienna under Schirach give cause for great concern. Schirach is simply not up to coping with Viennese wiles. He lets himself be flattered without knowing and recognising what the Viennese are actually trying to achieve by it.
Goebbels, diary, 14 April 1942

him and is firmly convinced that he would be incapable of handling a crisis in Vienna.' Himmler demanded his removal. Hitler ordered that a successor for Schirach be proposed. He refused to put up with Schirach's 'sloppy leadership' any longer. However, a replacement could not be found overnight and Schirach stayed on.

I felt rather like a kind of fire-brigade. Things are getting hot in Vienna, so off I'm sent. Now it's the cities being bombed, and I have to do something. You step in everywhere, you work everywhere, and everywhere you do what you can.
Schirach, interview with Jochen von Lang 1966

Yet even the Gauleiter's adoration of his beloved Führer had clearly waned. He followed military developments with growing concern. The entry of the United States into the war was something he had already regarded as disastrous. With the attack on the Soviet Union in June 1941 he claimed to have recognised 'that all was lost'. In January 1943, addressing regional HJ leaders in Braunschweig, Schirach attacked German occupation in the east: 'I find today, however, that those in authority there are doing everything in their power to destroy indigenous customs and traditions. And this seems to me to show a certain lack of human culture. It is not, in fact, domination by force that we want to gain for ourselves in Europe. Surely, as the leading power for order in these times, we wish to build up a new order in this region. Yet such order can only be lasting if we succeed in bringing about the voluntary co-operation of the nations.'

It gradually dawned on him that Adolf Hitler was a 'madman'. 'Our policies are going wrong', he told Göring, 'and the war is lost if we go on like this. We must do something otherwise we will be blamed later on.' Schirach claimed to have begged the *Reichsmarschall* to take over. But Göring apparently replied resignedly: 'I can't do that, Schirach. I've already been so downgraded that in situation conferences at the Führer's headquarters I can no longer open my mouth.' Schirach did not even get a chance to talk to other party functionaries. Hitler had made very sure that no opposition could build up against him. In 1943 he had made Robert Ley, the labour chief, announce that any meeting of more than three Gauleiters would be treated as a conspiracy.

However, Schirach was not contemplating open opposition. There was no question of making an attempt on Hitler's life, because in his view 'a political murder of a head of state, which leads directly to war, is never justified'; it would have led to a collapse of the Eastern Front, and Schirach certainly did not want that.

On 24 February 1945 he saw his Führer for the last time. As if to a final roll-call the dictator had summoned the Nazi leadership to the Reich Chancellery to celebrate the day on which the party's programme had first been announced, twenty-five years earlier. On his journey to Berlin, Schirach, now a less credulous disciple, looked in horror at the ruined Reich. 'Dresden was now no more than a heap of rubble. Everywhere little lights were burning to show where the streets had been. The houses had all gone. Nothing but mountains and mountains of bricks under which lay the people who had died in the great air raid.' Berlin too lay in rubble and ashes. Strangely, the hall of the Reich Chancellery, in which the Gauleiters awaited their supreme commander, remained unscathed. Schirach's apocalyptic mood was heightened when his former idol appeared: 'Hitler now enters the room, maintaining his composure with difficulty; his right hand trembles continuously and he keeps grasping it with his left. He is a ghost, someone who has completely fallen apart and is trying desperately to hold himself together.' For a final time Hitler adjures them to fight to the last man. 'What's happening in Vienna?' he asks Schirach. 'The population will do their duty', replies his vassal.

The criticism of his soft leadership style had given Schirach food for thought. He made an effort to discourage this impression and now devoted himself with greater vigour to the defence of Vienna. Despite the denunciation by Bormann, Schirach was very well prepared. Goebbels noted that 'Schirach has in fact caught up tremendously with his air-raid protection measures'. He had conspicuously set up a command-post on the Gallizinberg hill outside Vienna. It was a reinforced concrete building with a kind of lecture hall where approaching aircraft could be tracked on large sheets of glass. From an observation-tower he could survey the whole city. As soon as there was a threat of attack, Schirach and his staff raced to the tower and transmitted their observations by telephone to the command-centre. The air-raid shelters were also improved. For Vienna the war from the air began with a raid on 10 September 1944.

The Gauleiter responded harshly to the opposition which was intensifying against him in Vienna. When a conservative Austrian resistance group was exposed and its members arrested, Schirach showed no mercy. One member of the group, a lawyer named Gerhard Kastelic, was condemned to death, and Schirach saw 'no cause' to grant the pardon that his family petitioned for. Kastelic was executed in April 1944. 'I am glad to see that Schirach is now at last adopting a clear-cut and radical attitude to the war', wrote Goebbels.

By now the war was involving the Hitler Youth to an ever greater extent. For the year 1943 the official slogan was 'German youth goes to war'. In addition to their military training these children were now being detailed for 'war duty'. In the postal service, on the railways and in air-raid defence they filled the gaps created by the war. They collected waste paper, scrap metal and woollen blankets for the soldiers at the front, supervised evacuation from battle-zones and helped in other areas, especially with the harvest. When bombs began to fall on German cities, they were increasingly called on to serve as air-raid wardens, firemen and stretcher-bearers. Yet the war duty of the HJ was not restricted to the Home Front. In November 1943 the order was given for the establishment of the 12 'Hitlerjugend' SS Panzer Division. The boys went into action in June 1944, after the Allied landings in Normandy. In the first four weeks one-fifth of the Hitler Youth soldiers in the SS lost their lives. In the next action only 600 boys survived.

Schirach had been against setting up this SS division but no longer had any influence on developments. However, his claim that he did all he could to keep the Hitler Youth out of the last-ditch fighting around Vienna is self-serving. He deliberately arranged for a battalion of *Hitlerjungen* to be trained in military preparation camps by Wehrmacht officers with combat experience. It seems doubtful that he would later have made efforts to ensure that they were not required to take part in any fighting. What is important is the spirit which Schirach implanted in the young and which drove them to patriotic 'deeds of heroism'. In Vienna *Hitlerjungen* darted through the streets on bicycles with a hand-grenade on each handlebar. It is said that they knocked out some two dozen Soviet T-34 tanks. The HJ chief, Lauterbacher, ordered Viennese girls to crew 88mm anti-aircraft guns. In September 1944, in response to an order from the Führer, Schirach had personally called up the *Volkssturm*, Hitler's last-ditch army of children and old men. Even in the final days when the war had long since been lost, young people were cynically sacrificed. 'It's wonderful', Hitler exulted in his bunker under the Reich Chancellery, 'to see the fanaticism with which the youngest intake is going into combat.'

No government should throw young people, who have not yet had a life, into conflict, into battle. No-one can put a good slant on that. When fifteen- and sixteen-year-olds die, it is an appalling loss.

Schirach, interview with Jochen von Lang, 1966

The youth leader later regretted that so many *Hitlerjungen* died in the last days of fighting. The fact that 'in their zeal and keenness for action the young themselves want to fight' Schirach considered quite normal. 'But deliberately to send them into battle is a biological crime.' He shifted the blame for this on to others. Right up to his death Baldur von Schirach refused to accept that in the fighting in Vienna, Bratislava, Breslau or on the Pichelsdorf Bridge in Berlin, 'the death which the young died in reality was that which he had celebrated in verse'.

The Red Army was now advancing steadily westward. In the middle of February 1945 they launched a massive offensive on the Ukrainian and Byelorussian fronts. Budapest fell into Soviet hands. The Russians were just 150 miles from Vienna.

Right to the end I myself believed the war would have a good outcome. That was idiotic, of course. But that's the way we were trained. We believed we could *not* lose the war, we *had* to win.

To us, death was something sublime, not terrible. We only experienced the terrible side later, when we ourselves were at the front.

Klaus Mauelshagen, former member of the Hitler Youth

On 30 March 1945 Schirach declared a state of emergency in Vienna. The *Volkssturm* had to report for duty. The schools were closed. Meanwhile SS *Obergruppenführer* Sepp Dietrich had arrived in Vienna from Hungary with his retreating 6 Panzer Army. From now on he was to take over the defence of Vienna. But Dietrich could see he was in no position to halt the Russian advance: 'We're called the 6 Panzer Army because we only have six Panzers [tanks] left', he said ironically. Gauleiter Schirach had posters put up everywhere which read: 'Vienna has been declared an area to be defended. Women and children are advised to leave the city.' Leading citizens who tried to declare Vienna a free city met with no success. Schirach dared not act against Hitler's instructions in such an obvious way. This was where Schirach's powers ended. Though still the political governor of Vienna, he had no military authority. He limited himself to slogans of encouragement to hold out, as an officer of the *Grossdeutschland* Division recalled: '"We are now defending German soil", Schirach said. "Think of your forebears. They too defended German soil with the sword. Think of the knights who conquered the east. Think of your mothers, think of your wives. Think of what will happen if the Russians overrun you." Schirach knew that Vienna was about to be captured.'

He simply didn't tell the truth. He deceived us from start to finish.

Karl-Heinz Müller, former member of the Hitler Youth

Meanwhile, in order to escape from the bombs and shells that were raining down, he had a cellar under Vienna's Hofburg palace fitted out as a command-post. On 6 April 1945 the absurd *Götterdämmerung*-like scenes being acted out there were witnessed by the daredevil Austrian SS officer, Otto Skorzeny: 'Magnificent carpets lay on the floor, and the walls were hung with paintings of eighteenth-century battle-scenes and portraits of generals. In the ante-room there was a lot of eating, drinking and noise going on. I was obliged to inform the Gauleiter that I had been unable to find a single German soldier in the city and that the barricades were unmanned. I invited him to join me on a reconnaissance expedition. However, he declined the invitation and, bending over his map, explained to me how Vienna would be saved. Any further discussion was pointless. I took my leave. Schirach looked at me and said: "Skorzeny, my duty can be expressed in three words: win or die!"'

A few hours later the Gauleiter, Reich City Governor and Defence Commissioner of Vienna left the city. It may have been that Hitler himself gave him the order to get away from Vienna along with the fighting forces, or that 'in his helpless state he put himself under the protection of the troops', as Goebbels remarked. Whatever the truth, Schirach fled. The Viennese interpreted his behaviour as cowardice, and on 13 April the fate of the city was sealed.

However, Schirach did not get far. He was in a VW boneshaker heading for Innsbruck on some inscrutable mission with his adjutant Fritz Wieshofer, when the vehicle ground to a halt with gearbox trouble. It was some days later, in the Austrian village of Schwaz, that a wood-turner named Huber heard a knock on his door. As his son remembers, two gentlemen stood outside and asked politely for lodgings. One of them was Schirach. Half his face was covered by dark, horn-rimmed spectacles; in his checked shirt and knee-breeches he looked more like a rambler or a huntsman than one of the most wanted Nazi leaders of the Third Reich. Schirach said his name was Richard Falk, and that he was an author working on a crime novel. Its title was *The Secret of Myrna Loy.* The other man announced himself as a manservant.

Schirach and Wieshofer now settled themselves comfortably in the wood-turner's house. Wieshofer had managed to obtain identity papers for both of them and they believed their aliases were secure. Schirach borrowed a typewriter from his host's wife and tapped away happily, to add credence to his claimed profession. When the Americans drove into Schwaz a few days later, Schirach was unperturbed. He gallantly came to the aid of his landlady when soldiers tried to requisition the house, and explained to them in fluent English with a slight southern states accent that the house was overfull and unsuitable for their purposes. In the evenings the Reich Youth Leader (Retd) sat in the garden with youngsters from the neighbourhood and played the guitar.

The manner in which Schirach then came to be a prisoner of the Americans is cloaked in myth. Schirach himself claims that on 4 June he heard an announcement on the radio: 'All HJ leaders from the rank of *Bannführer* upwards are being placed under "automatic arrest".' Artur Axmann was reported missing, and Schirach was thought to be lying dead under the ruins of Vienna. For this reason, Schirach said later, he decided to assume responsibility and place himself at the head of German youth. Together with Wieshofer, he marched into the office of the US

There are many cases in which the measure of our guilt cannot be encompassed by the law. In a moral sense each of us, even those in less responsible positions than myself, was jointly to blame for millions of atrocities, which lay beyond all imagining.

Schirach in his autobiography, I Believed in Hitler, *1967*

Everyone has their own destiny. I have mine. It is one which in the eyes of my fellow-citizens is perhaps heavier than that of others, but I would not wish it to have been different.

Schirach, interview with Jochen von Lang, 1966

area commandant and handed him a written statement: 'Of my own free will I am placing myself in American custody in order to have the opportunity to answer for myself before an international tribunal. Baldur von Schirach.'

This very noble-sounding version is contradicted by Fritz Molden, the son of a Viennese intellectual and serving as an

Schirach was the one I talked to mostly. He was the second-youngest of the prisoners but in some ways he was a pretty odd character. He solved crossword puzzles every day and he read as well of course, but unlike the others, especially Hess and Speer, he appeared to have no inner strength. He just seemed to want to talk the whole time – with anyone at all, about nothing.

Jan Boon, Dutch warder in Spandau

Just as unreal as the letters were our visits to the prison. In Nuremberg we managed to smuggle Richard [Schirach's son] into the cell, hidden under the greatcoat of a prison chaplain. It was many years before he saw his father again.

Henriette von Schirach, The Price of Splendour, *1975*

American liaison officer at that time. His story is that he was tipped off one day that several top Nazis were hiding out in a mountain pasture near Schwaz. There he found Schirach and Wieshofer who both allowed themselves to be captured without a struggle. Molden says he interrogated his prisoners all night and the next day handed them over to the US authorities. Does this put an end to the heroic myth which the hero himself wove?

Schirach was taken to a prison-camp called Rum, near Innsbruck. The same year he was tried by the War Crimes Tribunal in Nuremberg. He was found guilty of 'crimes against humanity' for the deportations of Jews from Vienna and on 1 October 1946 was condemned to 20 years imprisonment, which he served to the very last day in the gaol for war criminals at Spandau. The indictments relating to his period as youth leader had been dropped. In 1966, at the age of fifty-nine, he emerged blinking in the light of freedom once more, and died eight years later, a broken man, in the village of Kröv on the Moselle. On his gravestone are written the words 'I was one of you'. He was never that.

> I wouldn't want to be the Schirach who once existed. I am happy to be the Schirach I am today.
>
> *Schirach, interview with Jochen von Lang, 1966*

CHAPTER THREE

THE SHADOW

MARTIN BORMANN

The Slavs will have to work for us. The ones we don't need can die.

I'll deal with the Church. They won't know what's hit them.

Let's face it, in the real world it's not honesty that defeats dishonesty. In the hard struggle for existence it is the tough, brazen ability to get one's way that wins out every time.

Theology is not so much a liberal study as applied research on confessional lines.

It can be no good for Party and State to have strong central church authorities established alongside them, which go their own way in leading and ministering to the people.

The Christian religion is a poison that is very hard to get free of and which contaminates the young.

Martin Bormann

I know Bormann is a rough diamond. But everything he does makes sense, and I can rely absolutely and unquestionably on him to carry out my orders immediately and in the face of all obstacles . . . Bormann's proposals are so precisely worked out that I only need say yes or no. With him I can get through a pile of papers in ten minutes that would take me hours with a certain other gentleman.

Adolf Hitler

Bormann's greatest achievement during the war was, as far as possible, to keep the twelve querulous courtiers, and quite a few Gauleiters, away from AH [Hitler]. In doing so Bormann certainly used his elbows without ceremony to make some space around the Führer, so as to prevent the man's nerves from being put under even greater stress.

Hans Severus Ziehler, Bormann's mentor at the start of his career as a Weimar civil servant

Bormann, stocky and boorish, was the embodiment of brutality and treachery.

Albrecht von Kessel, formerly in the German embassy in the Vatican

A clever exploiter of Hitler's every mood, Bormann knew how to trim his little ship of power to Hitler's wind, without steering a course of his own.

Hans Frank, former Governor-General of occupied Poland

Bormann knows all about the Führer's most personal affairs.

Hermann Göring

More and more lawyers were brought into the staff of Bormann's office and a separate legal department was created. With the other Reich departments of the Party it took a little longer for Bormann's competing operations to get under way, but almost all of them ended up with no work to do.

Hans Frank, former Governor-General of occupied Poland

Bormann was always obedient, conscientious and knowledgeable. He didn't waste his time on politics.

Ernst Hanfstaengl, former overseas spokesman for the Nazi Party

His power lay principally in the fact that the only route to Hitler was through him.

Wilhelm Höttl, former SS-Sturmbannführer

No sooner had Hitler expressed an idea than Bormann formulated it as an instruction.

Werner Koeppen, formerly on the staff of Rosenberg, minister for the eastern territories

There is an odd relationship between Bormann and me. I have the feeling he is jealous of me, because I make speeches all the time and he sits at headquarters, writing.

Robert Ley, head of the German Labour Front

He's an ox of a man, but everyone should know this: those who gripe about him are criticising me. And I will see to it that anyone who defies this man is shot.

Adolf Hitler

If cartoonists had drawn him – the figure, the fleshiness, the short legs, the face – then they would have always turned him into a pig.

Baldur von Schirach

The maggot in the apple of the Reich.

Speer

*

It was the night of 1 May 1945: that evening the confidence that he would survive his escape had sunk lower with each minute that brought the break-out from the Chancellery nearer. With the Führer no longer alive the courage of his closest accomplice seemed also to have evaporated. Adolf Hitler had shot himself the day before, Russian tanks had pushed forward to within a stone's throw of the ruined Reich Chancellery in Berlin. While all around *Hitlerjungen* and men of the *Volkssturm* were still fighting for them, Hitler's last remaining henchmen in the Führer-bunker had their minds on escape or suicide. As darkness fell a stocky man in the uniform of an SS *Obergruppenführer* attached himself to one of the small groups that was getting ready for the break-out. Over his black tunic he wore a leather greatcoat, and concealed in his pockets were Adolf Hitler's last will and testament as well as his own private diary. The last entry reads: '1.5, Attempting a break-out.' The choice of words betrays his doubt as to its success. At about 11 p.m. he climbed out of one of the basement windows of the Reich Chancellery and ran off. The man was Martin Bormann, the Führer's 'secretary'.

What happened next, at about midnight, was described by Erich Kempka, Hitler's chauffeur, when he was questioned by the International Military Tribunal in Nuremberg: Martin Bormann tried to creep through the Russian lines encircling the bunker. A German shell hit one of the tanks and blew it up. Shortly before, Bormann had taken cover behind it. Now the jet of flame from the explosion enveloped him, and a powerful pressure wave dragged him away.

At this point there begins a puzzle about the mysterious disappearance of the Führer's aide which lasted for decades. Hitler's chauffeur thought Bormann had been killed. But he did not see the body. This gave rise to the wildest speculations. Could Martin Bormann have got away? Could he even be living abroad under another identity? It is a fact that Hitler's secretary survived the explosion unharmed. It is possible that he might even have managed to escape – as some others did. But Martin Bormann gave up. At about 3 o'clock in the morning of 2 May a momentous discovery was made near the Lehrter railway station by Hitler's national youth leader, Artur Axmann: in the pale pre-dawn light he saw a man lying on the tracks crossing the Weidendamm Bridge. Bending over the body, Axmann recognised it as that of Martin Bormann. There was no question that he could have been mistaken, Axmann said. Bormann no longer wore any insignia of rank on his officer's tunic. He had torn them off and thus removed all indications of his identity. The dead man did not appear to have any injuries. At first Axmann took him to be unconscious. But Bormann, lying motionless on the ground, was no longer breathing. Axmann could not stop to take his pulse.

Someone who is being shelled by Soviet artillery is not interested in establishing the truth for posterity. Axmann knew that the leading figures in the bunker carried ampoules of poison with them. He assumed that Bormann had crushed the cyanide capsule between his teeth. When the former head of the Hitler Youth was interrogated in the late autumn of 1945, no-one wanted to listen to the story he had to tell.

It is hard to believe that a man who had fought his way to the top in the internal feuding of the Party cliques with such cunning, such ruthlessness and such determination, would not have managed to disappear underground when everything collapsed. But the 'secretary' had lost his nerve. Up until the death of Hitler he had known neither doubt nor uncertainty. The 'most loyal party colleague', as Hitler called him at the end, needed his Führer as a larger-than-life source of authority and orders. Without that his need to subordinate himself had lost its objective. 'He towers above us like Mount Everest', Bormann had once pronounced, gazing admiringly at Hitler, then added devoutly: 'Where would we be without him?' Now, faced with the collapse of the Nazi order, the bureaucrat missed that strong and commanding personality, missed the routine of his job and the protection of the bunker – all the things that he could lean on. Now he was leaderless, directionless. Hitler's henchman had lost everything.

It is astonishing how stubbornly the myth of Martin Bormann's survival persisted. Bormann *had* to be still alive. He was sought as a defendant in the Nuremberg war crimes trial and the world's press needed him as a source of money-spinning stories year after year. In the decades following Hitler's dictatorship innocent men all over the world were 'unmasked' from time to time as Bormann, on the basis of ever more fantastic tales. But each time they proved to be like the Loch Ness monster. Closer investigation revealed the sensation as either an error or a fraud. At one time Bormann was said to be living in Egypt, advising the Arabs in the conflict with Israel. Then again he was resident in South America where he owned a large estate. Another version even had him re-employed as a top Soviet spy. Such 'revelations' attracted worldwide attention, particularly in the 1960s and '70s. But the many sensational stories were no more than canards.

Again and again Bormann stories were enriched with those implausible details which lie at the very heart of the myth: the German U-boat which brings Nazi loot ashore in Argentina; the accomplices among South American industrialists or secret meetings in Italian monasteries with Evita Perón, the wife of the Argentinian dictator, who offers Bormann asylum in that country provided he is prepared to cede three-quarters of his treasure to Perón. No-one has yet succeeded in beating a viable path through the jungle of countless suppositions. No more could any of the many master sleuths solve the central problem faced by anyone who wanted to believe in Bormann's continued existence: how was Hitler's confidant able, on the night of 1 May 1945, to elude the Soviet conquerors of Berlin?

The search for the missing man had made his name more famous than it had been during his lifetime. After the war only a few people were in a position to remember having seen him before 1945. To a certain degree the German population could see a reflection of Hitler's violent regime in the two dozen men standing accused before the court in Nuremberg. But who was this Martin Bormann?

He was the man who operated in the background; a man who positively sought the dark. In the shadow of his Führer he had concealed himself from the wider world. The only people who really knew him were those in Hitler's immediate circle. As to the early life of the accused, the indictment contained only a few bare facts, such as might be found in any reasonably good newspaper archive. To summarise: born into a lower middle-class family, this perfectly ordinary member of the Nazi Party rose during the period of Nazi rule to be secretary to the Führer. On the other hand, there was no shortage of accusations against him: Martin Bormann had furthered the power of the Nazi conspirators, taken part in preparations for war and committed crimes against humanity. 'As chief of the Party Office directly under Hitler, Bormann was an exceptionally important factor in the power nexus', in the judgement of the US colonel, Robert G. Storey, a member of the prosecuting authority at Nuremberg. In the context of the trial Bormann was called 'Hitler's evil spirit'. That leads us to suppose that Bormann was the first to draw Hitler into the spell of evil. Yet this misses the point; the Führer's secretary was at most a Beelzebub to Hitler's Satan.

A few days before the start of proceedings at Nuremberg the prosecution had to report complete failure in the search for Bormann. Nevertheless, his indictment stated that he was possibly still alive; and therefore the case against him had to be heard. The court announced that 'a defence counsel will be appointed for the defendant Bormann'. The choice fell on a young criminal defence lawyer named Friedrich Bergold, who was anything but happy about it. He would have much preferred to hand the assignment over to one of his colleagues. To appear in a trial that is being followed with the closest attention throughout the world is of course the dream of every defence lawyer. However, it was clear that this particular case would scarcely make his name. Who was to help the lawyer to refute the charges, if not the defendant himself? Who would be able to nominate the witnesses for the defence? Bergold questioned many witnesses and made every effort to find mitigating evidence. But Hitler's henchmen in the dock were filled with a huge resentment against Bormann. What could be more obvious than to incriminate the missing man in order to exonerate themselves? Now, between the end of the war and the pronouncing of the verdict, they only *appeared* to be sharing a common fate; among themselves they were still opponents and rivals – as they had been in Hitler's day. But no-one was more hated than the Führer's secretary. The mutual mistrust in the top echelons of the Nazi regime was not to be compared with the measure of hatred which was directed against the 'brown eminence' by his innumerable adversaries. Even his personal staff and female secretaries, who surely in any other case would have found at least a few favourable words to say about their superior, refused to make any statement in his defence at Nuremberg. In his days in power Bormann had made himself unpopular. 'A few critical words from Hitler and all his enemies would have gone for his jugular', opined Albert Speer; yet to the end Hitler never uttered a single word of criticism against Bormann – even though every other member of the Hitler entourage had at least occasionally come under critical fire from the Führer.

When the verdicts were announced in Nuremberg on 1 October 1946 the court passed the death sentence on twelve of the accused.

Yet in the early hours of 15 October 1946, when the sentences were carried out, only ten of the twelve war criminals could be led to the scaffold. One, Hermann Göring, had taken poison the night before. The other had never been found. He had always operated in the background and it was there that he vanished.

What of Bormann's career? How did he become, for a few years, one of the most powerful men in Europe? Why was he known to only a few people, and why was he hated by nearly all of them? They were appalled by his 'unpleasant qualities', his 'servility', his 'sexual excesses', his 'malice'. But a man who was equipped with an armoury of power like no other member of the brownshirts, who rose from an 'unknown SA man' to be the right hand of the Führer, must at least have possessed some minor qualities. Certainly he was calculating, sober and conscientious, but that alone is not enough. What was the secret of Martin Bormann?

To look at, the man of the shadows was unimpressive in every respect. Short and squat – only 5 feet 7 inches tall – his figure had grown portly at the banqueting tables of the Third Reich. He stood listening, appraising, often with a sly expression on his coarse features, in the wings of the German and later the world stage. Such people are easily overlooked. But it seems that his unobtrusive presence was one of the means by which he was able to get his hands on the levers of power unnoticed. He embodied the image of anonymous hunger for power at Hitler's court. For despite his ordinariness he possessed the one quality which assured him not only Hitler's unlimited trust, but also superiority over all his rivals: Bormann made himself indispensable.

To his subordinates he was the most unpredictable of bosses. One moment he would treat them in the friendliest and most courteous manner, and minutes later he could absolutely degrade them in a thoroughly sadistic way. He often stormed about to such an extent that you instinctively got the feeling you were dealing with a madman.

Erich Kempka, Hitler's chauffeur

'My father must have been a fantastic man', Hitler's secretary wrote to his wife Gerda from the Führer's Wolf's Lair headquarters, in 1944. The cause of this spontaneous and unconcealed admiration was a photo of his father that had been sent to him by an old friend of the family. The picture showed Theodor Bormann in the uniform of the Halberstadt Cuirassiers. His son Martin liked to boast of his descent from a Prussian military family – not least because his wife Gerda, as the daughter of a former major in the imperial army, might have been disappointed with a less impressive family background than her own. Martin Bormann was therefore careful to conceal his lowly origins. His father was a post office employee and had only briefly served as a bugler in one of the Kaiser's regiments of cuirassiers.

The family circumstances in which Bormann grew up were not uncomplicated. Left a widower at a young age Bormann *père*, with two young children and a house burdened with debt, was compelled to look around for a second wife. As luck would have it, a colleague of his wanted to marry off his daughter Antonie, already thirty-five and no great beauty – but she was lively and full of energy, and not entirely without family means. Their first son was born on 17 June 1900. His parents christened him Martin, after the great Protestant reformer, Martin Luther. A little later, a second son, Albert, arrived. By this time Theodor Bormann, a senior post office clerk, was in poor health. Martin Bormann was three years old when his father died. The son thus lost the model whom he had only just learned to admire. Two decades would pass before Bormann found a new object for his unfulfilled desire to be allowed to venerate a heroic figure. He had no personal memories of his dead father. He learned what he wanted to know from his mother and his stepbrother and stepsister from the previous marriage. In this way he created an idealised image of his father which had little in common with reality.

His mother found it hard to get over the death of her husband. Times began to get hard, particularly on the financial side. The Bormanns were in debt and her widow's pension was scarcely enough to feed the four children. Yet Antonie Bormann found a way out: six months later she married her brother-in-law. His wife, Antonie's sister, had died leaving her husband with five children to look after. The newly established family, now with nine children from three fathers and three mothers, never really grew together. For the rest of his life Martin Bormann wanted as little as possible to do with this family. He rejected his stepfather, a local bank manager named Albert Vollborn, although he had no reason to reproach him. There was no stinting on education; the children were able to go to high schools. However, Martin was a poor pupil. It was not that he lacked application. He was just incapable of following abstract thought processes – then and later. Baldur von Schirach who, like Bormann, was brought up in Weimar, was hardly complimentary about him: 'As far as his education goes, one can really say he was a washout. In literature, the arts, music – virtually zero.'

Part of the intellectual atmosphere in which the high-school boy Bormann grew up and sought his ideals, was an exaggerated glorification of one's own nation: Germany. In the Vollborn household *Deutschland* was definitely put *über alles*. As the saying went: *am deutschen Wesen muss die Welt genesen* (the German character must help the world to recover). How else would it do so? The family were dedicated German nationalists and proud of having worked their way up from poverty to modest prosperity.

Shortly after Martin's fourteenth birthday a war began, but no-one imagined how murderous this war would become. In Berlin, Vienna, Paris and elsewhere the masses greeted the prospect of a world conflagration with cheering. War was to bring salvation: a release from the confines of an age which had been seen as paralysingly tedious. In Weimar, too, a crowd in euphoric mood marched through the streets singing patriotic songs. Among them was the young Martin Bormann.

Later he boasted of his martial courage, which unfortunately was never really put to the test. In the early years of the war he repeatedly volunteered for armed service, but was never accepted. In fact, when aged just eighteen, in the last year of the war, he was conscripted. True, Bormann did not get very far in the Kaiser's army – he remained an officer's boot-boy.

After the war he finally turned his back on his stepfather's family. This new period of his life began on a large country estate, where he worked as an agricultural labourer. Admittedly the 'townie' knew next to nothing about life on a farm. But for someone escaping from his family it was more important that he had some kind of home and three meals a day. All his life he dreamed of one day settling down quietly on an estate in Mecklenburg. His hope was that Hitler would reward him for his services – with a grand country house. For this reason alone, he was delighted as a Party official to be able to administer the Obersalzberg estate, being both industrious and enthusiastic in the role. There, unhindered and unsupervised, he played the gentleman-farmer. Although the farm did not pay its way, Hitler left him to it. 'Excellent!' the Führer beamed with feigned satisfaction. 'It isn't nearly as expensive as I thought. A litre of milk is costing me no more than five marks at the most.' Bormann's management of the Berghof farm was more a matter of prestige than economy. But in any case money was now of no importance.

Two decades earlier the nineteen-year-old Bormann was thrilled to be given employment in the management of a Mecklenburg estate. The landowner, Hermann von Treuenfels, was pleased with his new young recruit, who soon showed his true talents as a rigorously strict foreman. In this early post he already revealed qualities which would make him an exemplary secretary: eager obedience to carry out the will of his superior, an energetic toughness towards his subordinates, but also a gift for administration. The brusque and domineering Martin Bormann was hated by the farm-workers in Herzberg. It was obvious that what mattered most to him was increasing the profit. Politically, too, Bormann was on the same wavelength as his aristocratic lord of the manor, who damned the rulers in Berlin as 'red traitors' and the new state as a 'Jews' republic'. Herr von Treuenfels considered republicans to be nothing but craven cowards, incapable of keeping order in Germany. His sympathy lay with the right-wing *Freikorps* militias. Like other big landowners, Treuenfels took in *Freikorps* veterans and gave them food and work. From his estate manager's desk Martin Bormann acted as a kind of paymaster to these homeless irregulars. Their rallying-point was soon to be the NSDAP, the Nazi Party.

The young, authority-minded manager was attracted by his master's belief that a strong hand was all that was needed to restore the world they had been robbed of. Friedrich Ebert, president of the new German republic, was said to have previously owned a bar; the prime minister, Philipp Scheidemann, was just another 'red weakling'. These were not figures whom Bormann could be impressed by. He had grown up in the muscle-flexing empire of the Kaiser, whereas this new government stumbled from one crisis to the next. Like others who came from a lower-middle-class background, Bormann lived to see his modest wealth disappear. His family was also afflicted; his stepfather had since died and such financial assets as he left behind melted away in the hyper-inflation of the early 1920s. His mother's pension was so tiny that she could scarcely maintain her home any longer.

Disorientated by the loss of the certainties in life in a time of collapsing social order, Martin Bormann turned to crime. He took part in a murder. An elementary school teacher named Walter Kadow was suspected by the *Freikorps* unit on the estate of being a 'Bolshevist informer' – reason enough for him to be killed in a brutal fashion. They smashed his skull with full force and put two revolver-bullets through his brain. It was said that the gun had been provided by Bormann, though his involvement in the murder could not be proved at the time, because a *Freikorps* man covered up for him. He got off lightly with one year's imprisonment.

That was the first time he played the role of a man pulling the strings behind the scenes, a man who left it to others to carry out the deed while he himself remained under cover. But he instigated the plot and made sure it went off smoothly, by supplying the technical means for its execution. One of the accomplices in the murder, who afterwards remained under an obligation to Bormann for the rest of his life, later became commandant of the Auschwitz-Birkenau extermination camp: his name was Rudolf Höss.

Bormann was just what he looked like: an unpleasant, bull-necked character, whom nobody actually liked, not even his closest supporters

Wilhelm Höttl, former SS Sturmbannführer

On his return from custody Bormann allowed himself to be fêted as a patriot who had made a sacrifice in a worthy cause. The landowner slapped him appreciatively on the shoulder. In the Luisenhof inn, where Bormann was said to have slipped the murder weapon to the *Freikorps* men, beer and schnapps flowed freely. Everyone was convinced that they would soon be on their way! The march on Berlin and the end of the republic seemed within their grasp. It was in Munich that the smell of battle was most strongly in the air; it was said that Bavaria's provincial government would join forces with the rebels if there was a *putsch* against Berlin. But Hitler's coup, the march on the Feldherrnhalle, failed. Bormann followed the reports of Hitler's subsequent trial with interest, though not yet with any personal commitment. In his opinion the National Socialists in the south of Germany had been competing with his own party, the 'German Nationalist Freedom Party' in the north. Now that the National Socialists (NSDAP) had been banned and Hitler was in prison, the 'Nationalists' wanted to seize the opportunity to take over.

After his own release from prison Bormann once again tried to establish himself at the Herzberg estate, but he was now no longer welcome there, and was forced to make a cloak-and-dagger escape from the property. Rumour has it that the landowner chased him out because the 25-year-old estate manager was having a secret affair with his wife, Ehrengard von Treuenfels, ten years his senior. There is no proof of this, but we can certainly presume it was the case. Bormann was a Don Juan. What was he to do now? He lacked the money to buy himself a small farm, and his mother certainly could not help him. Bormann was once more without orientation. He idled away his time or else went around with the *Frontbann*, an extreme right-wing group of propagandists and bully-boys. In 1926 he joined the National Socialist Party which, in the right-wing free-for-all following Hitler's release from prison, had retained a narrow lead.

At the weekly newspaper, *Der Nationalsozialist*, until then a one-man business, he was able to earn a few marks helping to keep the paper alive. As book-keeper and van-driver he looked after the circulation side. He also tried his luck as a public speaker. In principle the Nazi Party was grateful for any speakers. But

Bormann lacked Hitler's talent for mobilising the masses. He was a failure as a speaker. Even a small gathering of people was enough to put him off his stride. He became unsure of himself, began to stammer and in the end was unable to string a straight sentence together. When heckled by an audience, eye-witnesses report, Bormann went scarlet with rage and lost control of the situation. When it reached the point where his listeners burst out laughing as soon as he stepped on to the platform, the party finally banned him from speaking in public. In all the years that followed, despite his dogged efforts, Bormann never succeeded in speaking before an audience. In the archives there is no sound-recording to be found of Bormann as an orator.

After these unhappy early experiences he realised that he would have to win people over with other qualities: diligence, will-power, quickness on the uptake, unscrupulousness and, most of all, adaptability. In addition he was a skilful tactician – and he was cunning. These were qualities with which he soon proved himself to be an executive who could be entrusted with more important tasks.

It was at the party congress in Weimar on 26 July 1926 that Martin Bormann met the man whom he was to idolise until the day he died. There is a photograph of Hitler inspecting a parade – standing up in his supercharged Mercedes. Right beside the Führer we can see Martin Bormann in SA uniform. Two years later he received a summons to party headquarters in Munich. As manager of an aid fund, it was his job to support SA members who were unable to pay for the treatment of injuries they had received in brawls on the street and in meeting-halls. He rapidly rose to become an expert in financial provision for the ruffians of the SA. Soon Bormann was talked of as the financial wizard of the Party – an organisation whose leader had no interest in money as long as there was plenty of it available. As an 'artist', Hitler pretended a contempt for money. However, it always had to be there so that he and his entourage could enjoy the bohemian lifestyle of Schwabing, Munich's 'Latin Quarter'. Had this jealous clique recognised Bormann's utter lack of scruple, they might have foreseen that Hitler would further the career of this party zealot. But in the words of Alfred Rosenberg, the Reich minister for the eastern territories: 'The road Martin Bormann took could not have been predicted by even the boldest imagination.' This typifies the astonishment of early colleagues of Hitler at a career which forced its way, not through street riots and meeting-hall brawls, but through office corridors. The arrogant 'old campaigners' made fun of the growing bureaucratic machinery of the aid fund. When, by the end of 1932, Bormann was head of a large department and in charge of a small army of 100 staff, his critics failed to realise that this was just what the Führer found so uncommonly impressive. At that time there was nothing to indicate that the conscientious young manager, so brutal to his underlings and so devoted to his superior, intended to play a political role.

His nature was always the unbalanced product of personal ambition, practical expertise in matters of organisation and administration, including financial affairs, and a strong inferiority complex. As a cold-blooded gambler for his own ends he followed the Stalin model, that is to say he recognised the value of a rigid party dictatorship and systematically built up the Party on that principle.

Richard Walter Darré, Nazi agriculture chief

With a blend of idealism and self-interest Bormann placed himself entirely at the service of the Party. He took an interest in political events only as an observer, not as an active participant. True, he assured everyone that he would much prefer to be wearing a brown shirt and fighting on the front line, perhaps as an SA leader or an agitator; but in reality he clung to his steadily growing bureaucracy which controlled ever larger sums of money. In 1932 the fund was said to exceed 3 million marks. 'I always thought him obedient, conscientious and knowledgeable', was how the foreign press spokesman, Ernst Hanfstaengl, described Bormann's activities in the fighting days of the Nazi Party. 'He didn't waste his time on politics. When he sorted out the aid fund, I was glad that someone was at last looking after that money. Previously, certain people had been filling their pockets from it. Göring and Goebbels definitely had.'

Bormann and Hess fought tirelessly against corruption in the Party.

Ernst Hanfstaengl, former foreign press spokesman of the NSDAP

There was another reason why the zealous administrator earned Hitler's good will. He married Gerda Buch, the daughter of a party colleague from the early days of the NSDAP, whom Hitler had subsequently appointed to be the senior party arbitrator. It was at a party rally in the Circus Krone that the nineteen-year-old Gerda first set eyes on the rather stocky but handsome Party member in his brown uniform; from then on Martin Bormann would shape her life. The couple were complete opposites; the slim, narrow-hipped Gerda was 5 feet 11 inches tall, but it apparently did not worry her that her beau was four inches shorter than she was. She worked in a kindergarten – and the sensitive girl felt most at ease in the midst of a horde of children. But she made the running: after the evening at the Circus Krone, she managed to persuade her father to invite the young man to their house. At first, however, Bormann had no thought of settling so soon into bourgeois conformity. He did not even notice the affection which this well-brought-up girl was showing him. It was well known among the Party leadership that when it came to women he liked to operate as a hunter-gatherer. But that did not fit at all well with the strict Protestant principles of the Buch family. Nevertheless, the Party's chief arbitrator acceded to his daughter's wish. Buch hoped that her feelings would cool off without prompting once she had got to know the awkward young man and his tendency to fits of moodiness. Gerda was not only the opposite of Martin to look at; the shy girl also had quite different interests to those of her intended. She played the guitar, sang folk-songs and liked to bury herself behind mountains of books.

At first it seemed that her father's plan would succeed. But in the spring of 1929, after a trip into the countryside, Bormann surprised everyone by asking for Gerda's hand in marriage. Frau Buch enthusiastically took her future son-in-law under her wing: 'Soon we too will have a Martin in our family', was her delighted comment on the impending wedding. Next to Adolf Hitler, the great churchman Martin Luther was her ideal. Yet it was this same son-in-law who would later emerge as a fanatical opponent of the Church.

The wedding ceremony, at which Hitler and Rudolf Hess acted as witnesses, was greeted with malice by the 'old campaigners'. The upstart from Weimar, they said, had only seduced the trusting young woman in order to become 'acceptable at court' by his marriage. It was a fact that this connection with the Buch family opened many doors in the Nazi Party to the ambitious Bormann. Even before the 1923 *putsch* Hitler had been a frequent visitor to the Buch household and it was as a favour to the Party arbitrator that he took part in the wedding. Anyone who belonged to the Buch family had access to the Führer. Nonetheless, the gentle and extremely attractive Gerda was not indifferent to her husband. Those who knew the couple well say that Bormann also had a high regard for his wife and even loved her in his own way. What is more, he could be certain that the dominant role in the marriage, which he so much desired, would never be questioned and that he had acquired for himself the perfect model of a National Socialist wife. By the time they were wed, she was already – as her husband once boasted later – 'a dyed-in-the-wool National Socialist girl', and no amount of rain or sun would make her lose this colour.

Even as a schoolgirl Gerda had overheard Hitler's tirades in her parents' house and in the process had thoroughly absorbed the roles that would be assigned to her as a German lass, as soon as she reached marriageable age: to be a companion for her husband through thick and thin, and as a caring spouse to maintain domestic harmony and bear lots of children. Her husband Martin was the beneficiary. At times he behaved like a pasha at home. A whistle through his fingers was the summons to his wife to 'hurry up' – that meant dropping whatever work she was doing and coming over to him at the double to take his orders. Despite her husband's remarkable rise, the impression Gerda made on the other Nazi henchmen was of 'a modest, somewhat timid housewife', as Albert Speer described her. But Hitler treated Gerda Bormann with particular consideration. Every year on her birthday he sent her an extravagant bouquet of red roses.

Even Bormann's opponents recognised his incomparable appetite for work. Well-versed in bureaucratic method, he adapted himself to his boss in virtually every respect. He knew how to make Hitler's ideas his own and to interpret them in a way that suited himself. Quietly but steadily and with a dogged determination, he overcame each obstacle, one by one. The methods whereby Bormann engineered his rise were once described by Alfred Rosenberg thus: 'When I went to see Hess, Bormann was sometimes with him – later, he was almost always there. If I went to lunch with the Führer in those years, Bormann regularly appeared at the table, along with Goebbels. Hess was clearly getting on the Führer's nerves and it was Bormann who dealt with the necessary questions and instructions. From that point on began Bormann's progress towards "indispensability".'

> He was hewn from coarser timber than Hess. He no longer let the reins of party management trail on the ground.
> *Count Schwerin von Krosigk, former finance minister*

Among the grandees of the Party the only one actively to further Bormann's career was Rudolf Hess, the 'Führer's Deputy'. In the summer of 1933 – a mere five years after arriving in Party head-quarters in Munich – Bormann moved into new premises there. He exchanged the rooms of the aid fund for Rudolf Hess's office, a rapid promotion from a back room to the executive suite. He rose from chief cashier to chief-of-staff. When Bormann took over Hess's office, Hitler had already consolidated his power, and the new men at the top had already carved up their areas of influence. There was nothing left over for Bormann. The grand title awarded to him sounded good, but in fact there was no important post behind it. The staff intended for him had yet to be created. How Bormann and Hess were to share the tasks and decision-making powers of the new department was something that Hitler had deliberately left vague. He liked to see his paladins fighting under him for power and influence. That ensured that no limits would be put on his position as Führer. Neither at this time nor previously had Hess managed to establish a power-sphere of his own in the labyrinth of overlapping authorities deliberately created by the Party's supremo. Although he was one of the 'old campaigners' he had never been more than a compliant dogsbody at his Führer's side. For that reason the actual task which Hitler assigned to Hess and Bormann was an unimportant one: they were to improve the co-operation between the various departments of a party structure that was growing ever larger.

A further task emerged in a scarcely noticeable way – one which would later provide the foundation for Bormann's key position of power, proving far more important than it at first appeared: as the departments of state were reorganised and increasingly staffed by Party members, Hess's office had to ensure that the exchange of information between the new office-holders functioned without a hitch. Hess and Bormann were to use their authority to prevent any foreseeable squabbling over areas of responsibility. This thankless task produced little but irritation, and Hess sometimes complained that he had been reduced to being the 'agony-aunt of the movement'. Anyone operating in this area who wanted to prevent the office from becoming a superior mail-room for the various Party appeal channels, had to be cunning, pragmatic and unscrupulous. The fact that the office ended up as more than a piece of scenery on Hitler's stage was solely due to its chief-of-staff: Martin Bormann was quick to see that it was precisely the ill-defined nature of his powers that enabled him to involve himself in everything. For someone to act as arbitrator, he must be kept informed, even courted, by the disputants; he appraises the moves of the opponents on the chessboard and sees their vulnerable points. The man who controls this particular game can decide whom he will allow through to the next round.

> Bormann never worked through direct confrontation, but with a careful weaving together of minor events, which only had an effect in their totality.
>
> *Albert Speer, 1969*

Under the pretext of ensuring Party unity, Bormann restricted inch by inch the discretionary scope of functionaries who were less than willing to disclose information. It was during this period that the treasurer of the Nazi Party, Franz Xaver Schwarz, rebelling against what he saw as the ruthlessly enforced transfer of power, expressed the judgement that Bormann was 'the worst egoist and enemy of the Party' whom he even believed 'capable of liquidating old comrades'.

Martin Bormann already belonged to that 'second generation' who, after the seizure of power, forced their way to the trough at which the 'old campaigners' had already fed: a power tactician without a visible trace of emotion, a cold calculating-machine with no interest in ideology. 'Bormann is not a man of the people', Goebbels reassured Hitler's old followers. 'He has only ever worked in administration and so he does not bring the right instincts to the real tasks of leadership.' But that was a misjudgement. For Bormann's influence grew steadily. The days of acquiring power were now over, the rise of the Hitler regime was complete. Hitler now needed a man who knew how to 'manage the assets'. A manager is what Bormann was and always remained.

Devoted and obsequious, Bormann placed himself at the service of his master, and was always careful to relieve the dictator of any distasteful task. In the Reich Chancellery in Berlin he was given a small office of his own. He had now reached his goal. He had placed himself in immediate proximity to the Führer. This gave him the chance to make himself indispensable, and he exploited it to the full. Day and night he was at Hitler's beck and call – always ready to tackle the most impossible job with the greatest zeal. Armed with pad and pencil he took notes unceasingly. Every utterance of the Führer, no matter how trivial, seemed to him important enough to be recorded. With time Bormann accumulated mountains of these notepads. In the end he had filled filing-cabinets with Hitler's words. When he was once asked by Baldur von Schirach what he intended to do with them, the conscientious assistant replied that he wanted to capture whatever was in the Führer's mind: 'Then we'll know that on this particular day the Führer said the following, and so we'll be able to follow his lead properly.' Gradually, Bormann's archive of jottings gave him his own steadily growing scope for independent action. Hitler's statements were certainly often contradictory, and Bormann, who had arranged his notes by key-word, could pull out of his card-index the statement by Hitler that suited him best at any given moment. Thus he could set his little intrigues in motion and send things off in the direction he particularly wanted. Criticism from the ranks of the Party faithful simply bounced off him since among his jottings he had a saying of the Führer appropriate for every occasion.

Bormann knew all about the Führer's most personal affairs. At many afternoon teas only he and stenographers were allowed to be present, and it was there that the most important matters were often decided.

Hermann Göring

But even the most casual remarks thrown out by Hitler were important enough to Bormann for him sometimes to go to absurd lengths to obtain the information requested by his boss. In such instances the 'secretary' would if necessary haul his staff from their beds and keep them on the research task until he was satisfied. If need be, he would even cancel train schedules. For Hindenburg's personal doctor, Ferdinand Sauerbruch, he diverted a train on to another track in order to get the doctor to Bayreuth as quickly as possible. The Führer was already there waiting for him, anxious to know when the death of the gravely ill Reich President could finally be predicted with confidence.

In time Bormann took over all Hitler's financial affairs. At the latter's request he even bought his way into the Führer's private life. The house in Braunau where Hitler was born, his parents' house in Leonding and the entire complex of properties on the Obersalzberg were all transferred into Bormann's name.

The man with his hands on the money is in possession of power – so much quickly became clear to the new financial controller of Germany's dictator. When the 'Adolf Hitler Fund of German Business' was created at the suggestion of the industrial tycoon Gustav Krupp von Bohlen und Halbach, Hitler immediately received a sum of 100 million marks to dispose of freely, without having to account for his expenditure. The 'Reich Association of German Industry' wanted, through this generous gift, to show the new Reich Chancellor that the Nazi Party would have to remain well disposed towards business if it wanted to go on being supported with such donations.

> Bormann was like [Molière's] Tartuffe. When I watched him in the early days as chief-of-staff to Hess, he chain-smoked cigarettes and partook of strong, highly alcoholic drinks.
> In my view Bormann was Hitler's 'evil spirit'.
> *Baldur von Schirach*

Hitler had put the administration of these large sums in the hands of his private office, so that his reputation as the 'Chancellor of modest needs' should remain unblemished. Officially, of course, the 'selfless artist' had nothing to do with money. At the same time, between 1933 and 1945, at least 305 million reichsmarks flowed through his bank accounts. After gaining power by the back door, Hitler had become a wealthy man. Rudolf Hess who, as 'deputy' to the supremo, was actually intended to administrate the donation fund, revealed a dreamy unworldliness when faced with such large sums of money. But fortunately he could rely completely on a chief-of-staff who could already demonstrate his experience as a money manager: Martin Bormann. It was exactly the right job for the secretary.

No-one checked up on how the immense sums in the 'Adolf Hitler Fund' were applied. 'If Hitler needed money for anything, Bormann paid, even if it was for a present for Eva Braun', Schirach tells us. The degree of independence with which Bormann ultimately controlled the millions is underlined by an event which took place on 15 September 1938, when the whole world feared for peace. The Chancellor of the 'Greater German Reich' had announced to the world his claim on the Sudetenland and was threatening 'one way or another' to tear it away from Czechoslovakia. The British prime minister, Neville Chamberlain, hastened to the Obersalzberg in the hope of averting the impending war by talking face to face with Hitler. Chamberlain was still in his aircraft on the homeward flight when Hitler and Bormann turned to more amusing matters. That afternoon the two men enjoyed themselves looking at Bormann's belated 30-million-mark birthday present to his Führer: a house hewn out of the solid rock at the summit of the Obersalzberg. A cable-car took Hitler and Bormann up over 400 feet in less than a minute, to the lobby of the so-called tea-house. The German press was not, of course, allowed to report on this far-from-modest gift.

> Bormann was able to take over the management of Hitler's personal finances . . . Even Hitler's mistress was dependent on him, because Hitler had transferred to him the job of meeting her modest needs.
>
> *Albert Speer*

The 'Donation Fund of German Industry' financed the dictator to an even greater extent: in the village of Altaussee lay Hitler's treasure-chamber. By the end of the war art treasures of immeasurable value were housed here in a salt-mine. Magnificent works from all the most famous museums of Europe were hoarded in the abandoned tunnels: Michelangelo's *Madonna*, the world-famous altar-piece from Ghent, works by Titian and van Dyck. Every one of them had been paid for by the Führer's keeper-of-the-purse, Martin Bormann. They were destined for Linz, Hitler's home city on the Danube, which was to rival Vienna as a cultural metropolis. The Führer planned to construct vast museum halls; Linz was to become his own personal treasure-chest.

Though Bormann had been a member of Hitler's personal staff for years, he still remained largely unknown even to senior figures in the regime. In the diary of one of Goebbels' close associates he appears as 'a certain Party-member by the name of Bormann'. Despite his enormous industry and an overweening ambition to increase his standing with Hitler, Bormann would never have been armed with so much power had it not been for an event which unexpectedly catapulted him over the entire ranks of Hitler's entourage.

In spring 1941, when victory appeared to the servants of the Third Reich to be within their grasp, something happened which threw even the most devout National Socialists into extreme shock. On 11 May 1941 at about 10 a.m. the two adjutants of Rudolf Hess burst into the dictator's outer office on the Obersalzberg and urgently requested to be admitted to see Hitler there and then. They had with them a letter for the Führer from their superior containing an incomprehensible message. Albert Speer, who had allowed the two men to go in ahead of him, was standing outside Hitler's study when he heard a hysterical outburst from the other side of the door. Utterly distraught, Hitler shouted for his amanuensis: 'Get Bormann immediately! Where's Bormann?' The cause of this violent scene was the message from Hess saying that a few hours earlier he had, on his own initiative, flown to Britain – with the obscure aim of bringing the war with the British to an end by personal negotiation. Only minutes later Bormann was accusing his superior of treason. He claimed to have always mistrusted Hess and doubted his loyalty to the Führer. Bormann was afraid that, as chief-of-staff in Hess's office, he might be drawn into the scandal. For his 'friends' were soon asking what he, the 'deputy's deputy', knew about the flight to Britain.

Yet Bormann, too, was totally surprised by Hess's flight. His initial fears soon turned into delight and satisfaction. He sensed that this was his big chance. When his own innocence had been proved and Hess was disgraced in Hitler's eyes, Bormann did everything he could to commend himself to his Führer as the successor to Hess. With typical cynicism he changed the names of his children from Rudolf and Ilse, after Hess and his wife, to Herbert and Eike. Two days later the Reichsleiters and Gauleiters, who had been summoned to the Berghof, learned that a new era had begun. They assailed Bormann, who was already expecting them, with questions. But the secretary kept his counsel and with a studiously preoccupied expression indicated that he simply could not spare the time to satisfy their curiosity. Göring, who Bormann could not prevent from barging straight into Hitler's room as soon as he arrived, asked the Führer whom he would nominate as Hess's successor, and warned him urgently against Bormann, a man loathed by almost everyone in the Party. Hitler reassured the 'second in command' of the Third Reich that Bormann would on no account become his deputy in the Party. On the very same day that the German press reported the flight to Britain, the dictator had a brief notice published: 'The former official department of the Deputy to the Führer, will from now on be designated the Party Office. It reports directly to myself. It is headed, as hitherto, by Party-member and Reichsleiter, Martin Bormann. Signed: Adolf Hitler.'

Bormann now had the same powers as Hess had held. The only thing he lacked was the title: 'Deputy to the Führer', minister without portfolio. Yet Bormann cared as little for titles as he did for honours and decorations. He always dismissed the insignia of power as fatuous; to him they were expressions of vanity, ascribing too much importance to appearances. Sober and coldly calculating, to him power itself was all that mattered. And that is why his new post so exactly suited his personality. Bormann was not interested in representational duties – he never wanted more than to run an office.

A short time later those who had taken part in the momentous meeting on the Obersalzberg received a circular letter marked 'Personal' and 'Strictly Confidential'. It was signed by Martin Bormann. It was apparent that the wily tactician was certain of Hitler's support, for in his letter he told the Gauleiters that he, Bormann, was constantly at the Führer's side and that he alone was in a position, at whichever headquarters was in use, to present 'all current matters of importance' to Hitler. The ambitious bureaucrat ended his missive with the assurance that he had 'worked like a horse. In fact harder than a horse, since a horse has Sundays off and his nights' rest. I have frequently had to go without those.'

Only gradually did his opponents and rivals realise that they had obviously underestimated Bormann for far too long, since in the Third Reich the man who wielded power was above all the one who did not flaunt his authority publicly, and among all the close associates of the Führer Martin Bormann alone seemed to understand this unwritten law. Thus among the leading figures of the Nazi Party he became the 'brown eminence'. He manoeuvred without being observed and was scarcely exposed to attack and intrigue from the ranks of Hitler's entourage. The other paladins were declared rivals among themselves and any pact concluded between two or more of them was never more than a temporary alliance. It was usually only a matter of one of them strengthening his position vis-à-vis another, and thus they held each other in check. On the other hand, Bormann's machinations were hindered by no-one, because so far no-one had noticed them. He had been spared and that made him all the more powerful.

He explained his attitude in a letter to his wife, in which he said he had always 'consciously avoided' any kind of public platform of the kind sought by the other top men in the Party; while they always aimed their appeals directly at the public, his advice reached the summit of power. 'I achieve more, considerably more', he wrote proudly. Behind the new name of 'Party Office' there was now operating in the background a functionary who, more obedient and assiduous towards the Führer than his predecessor, was intent on becoming the second most powerful figure in the Reich. He succeeded; just a year after Hess's dramatic flight he was officially appointed 'Secretary to the Führer'.

> I can't imagine how the Führer would manage without you.
> *Gerda Bormann in a letter to her husband*
>
> Martin Bormann is a frightful man. I think he has gone mad because he cannot tolerate the rarefied atmosphere at the heights of power.
> *Walter Buch about his son-in-law*

Bormann had by now recognised that Hitler played off ministries and Party departments against each other in order to prevent any organisation from becoming too powerful. He saw that he could hold his own better in this power-game if he built up in his Party Office a level of Party supervision over every government ministry.

Naturally he kept this intention secret. No-one was to know that within a short time, using tactics of stealth, he would have filled all key posts with men who owed their position entirely to him, rather than to their own performance or personal qualities. As a 'thank-you' they would have to play by his rules.

Apart from the Führer himself neither the Party machine nor even Bormann had the right to act independently. Hitler's instructions alone were the authority. What was critical for the personal power of all the leading figures in Hitler's inner circle was the quality and intensity of the personal relationship which they could build with Hitler. Here Bormann held the trump-card, for his strength lay in his eager obedience – in his ability to interpret Hitler's often imprecise words in the appropriate manner. Soon no more limits were set on his striving for power. Effortlessly he could now challenge Göring and Ribbentrop, even Goebbels and finally Himmler, those paladins who long before him had belonged to the innermost circle of Hitler's henchmen.

Repeatedly Hitler closed his ears to warnings from his immediate entourage. 'I know Bormann's a rough diamond. But everything he does makes sense, and I can rely absolutely and unquestionably on him to carry out my orders immediately and in the face of all obstacles. Bormann's proposals are so precisely worked out that I only need to say yes or no. With him I can get through a pile of papers in ten minutes that would take me hours with a certain other gentleman. If I say to him: remind me in six months time about this or that matter, I can be certain that this really will be done.'

Such intense devotion sapped Bormann's physical strength: 'This endless sitting at a desk gives me appalling backache', he complained in a letter to his wife. 'And after working a sixteen-hour day, I get a continuous ringing in the ears at night.' In those days the word 'stress' was not in common use.

In the first weeks of June 1941 Hitler's attention was fully taken up with plans for the invasion of the Soviet Union. Soon he would be behind the barbed-wire fencing of the Wolf's Lair, his East Prussian headquarters, and inaccessible to virtually all the senior Party members – but not to Martin Bormann. It was only for the daily situation conferences in the morning that the secretary remained outside the door. The generals would not have appreciated Bormann's presence. During these hours the secretary devoted himself to the mountains of paperwork. A little later, at lunch with the Führer, he would be back on the scene, in his customary place diagonally opposite Hitler, next to Field-Marshal Keitel.

The only time that Bormann saw the conquered territory in the east was when Hitler on two occasions briefly transferred his headquarters to the Ukraine. But the endless tracts of forest, the marshes, and the fields of black earth stretching to the horizon remained for him no more than marks on a map. He took no interest in them.

For Bormann the bureaucrat, the world was a series of desks in windowless bunkers of thick concrete, with artificial ventilation. Apart from routine trips to Berlin, Munich and the Obersalzberg, and occasional side-trips on official business, he scarcely ever left these isolated posts. Only when Hitler retreated to the Obersalzberg was it decreed that Bormann had to follow his Führer into the mountains, often for months at a time.

To this day the anger of the inhabitants of the Obersalzberg about Bormann's ruthless building frenzy has still not abated. The secretary was guilty of destroying one of the loveliest stretches of country in Upper Bavaria. Hitler allowed Bormann a completely free hand in the reshaping of his mountain-top idyll. That is why the secretary earned a reputation as the 'Lord God of the Obersalzberg'. When buying up building land Bormann paid good but never over-generous prices. His zeal and business conduct are typified by an incident in July 1938: when surveying the landscape, Hitler expressed indignation that a small farmhouse at the foot of the Obersalzberg spoilt his view. He then drove off to spend the day in Munich. In the meantime Bormann offered the occupants of the property a cheque on condition that they vacate the house immediately. Hitler's will was done. Bormann had brought workmen and bulldozers with him. There was no time to lose, for the very next day Hitler's gaze must be allowed to sweep unhindered across the broad green meadows – exactly as he had wished.

Bormann's toadying to his Führer knew no bounds. Once, on the Obersalzberg, he had read an unspoken wish in Hitler's eyes: in order that the Führer should not be exposed to the harsh

midday sun when standing outside the Berghof to shake hands
with enthusiastic National Socialists, his amanuensis ordered a
fully grown tree to be brought and planted in front of the house,
so that henceforth Hitler could stand in comfortable shade. The
Obersalzberg staff ironically called Bormann 'Napoleon', because
he bore an astonishing resemblance to the main character in a
popular German film entitled *It's All Napoleon's Fault.*

In the end Bormann himself became a resident of the
Obersalzberg – in a spacious house which offered ample
accommodation for his numerous family. It had to be a large
building with plenty of bedrooms, since his swarm of children
was growing all the time. By now he had become a father for the
sixth time. The positively feudal interior décor cost the owner not
a penny. It was a present that he gave to himself, all paid for out
of the 'Donation Fund of German Industry'. From now on the
Bormann family would move periodically from their principal
residence in Pullach, near Munich, to their second home on the
Obersalzberg. In all this Bormann's wife was not consulted. She
had to go along with it, for it was her husband who determined
when was the appropriate moment for a change of domicile.
Once again Bormann adapted himself to the will of the Führer.
When he was staying at the Berghof, it followed that the entire
Bormann family would move to the Obersalzberg.

Bormann showed his true organisational talent by the amount
of work he got through every day on the Obersalzberg. While
Hitler slept late, his secretary dealt with the daily workload,
checked on progress with the building works and managed the
Party Office. Not until around midday, when the Führer was
ready to get out of bed, did his loyal servant have to make his
report. He certainly needed to tempt Hitler into working.
Bormann managed this by a ruse: reports of success on the
Obersalzberg building sites put Hitler in a mellow mood and
created an atmosphere in which the lazy dictator could be
persuaded to study a few documents. Meanwhile the lunch guests
were arriving – adjutants, doctors, female secretaries, one or
other of the Party bosses, and often Albert Speer, who had also
acquired a property on the Obersalzberg where he ran his
architectural practice.

When he sat at Hitler's table, he very soon found out that smokers were not popular and it was frowned on if someone drank. But I heard from Bormann's circle that he would go out from time to time, sit down with a bottle of schnapps in front of him, and have a serious boozing session.

Baldur von Schirach

The party was usually joined by Eva Braun, whose relationship with Martin Bormann was less than warm, although their mutual dislike was never demonstrated openly. Bormann always greeted her with the same obsequious amiability. She was, after all, the Führer's mistress. To begin with Eva Braun treated the 'secretary' with patronising arrogance, but she soon switched to a more amenable tone, when he proved ever more frequently to be free with money. Bormann knew that her taste ran to more sophisticated things than a brooch with a gold swastika from the Munich shop of an old 'Party comrade' – the kind of present which Hitler used to give her. With Bormann, Hitler's cashier, she could go into a goldsmith's now and again and choose something without having to ask the price. Even when she needed cash she found him a reliable lender. Yet Bormann's co-operation was in vain. No sooner was the 'secretary' out of sight and earshot than she poured scorn on his tubby figure, his fervently paraded diligence and his compulsion to flirt with female staff. At lunch the table arrangement ensured that Bormann had to sit between Eva Braun and Hitler. Bormann was one of the regular guests, yet he knew to what he owed his reputation: with a self-important expression he often offered his last-minute apologies, claiming that an appointment prevented his presence at table. However, when there were female guests of a younger vintage, Bormann found he had ample time to join the meal.

None of the guests was obliged to eat what the Führer ordered for himself. Yet the ever devoted Bormann asked to be served the same vegetarian fare as Hitler. Naturally he praised Hitler's taste above all other, and eulogised about the energy-giving effect of the Hitlerian diet. At home Bormann's preferences were quite different. In his kitchen hung coarse and flavoursome *Wursts* and fat hams.

Right to the end Bormann acted the part of the abstemious man, the true reflection of his master.

Baldur von Schirach

On Hitler's customary outings to the tea-house, Bormann followed him like a shadow. At the subsequent afternoon tea he was always on hand and remained silent when the Führer dozed off in his chair. On the other hand, the building-workers on the Obersalzberg were scarcely given any peace by Bormann. In the afternoon he would rush from site to site. The phrase 'can't be done' was not in his vocabulary, he used to boast. Though a merciless slave-driver, he nonetheless showed understanding for the amorous needs of his workers. As Herbert Döhring, the major-domo on the Obersalzberg, recalls: 'There were three huts in a wood, which Bormann had fitted out as a brothel for the Obersalzberg workers. The girls got a regular salary from the Labour Front that existed then, from the department called "Strength through Joy"'.

Bormann made use of the time during military presentations to make phone calls and deal with the tasks Hitler had given him. At around 8 p.m. he sat down again next to Eva Braun for the evening meal – anxious to hear what the Führer wanted him to see to next. Afterwards he would circulate in the drawing-room or watch a movie. By now Bormann was usually tired out. Most nights he only slept for four hours. In the evenings he often sat in a corner and nodded off. True, he had nothing to contribute to the subsequent discussion about the film, but the hours that followed could be a testing time for him. Whether the Führer was delivering one of his monologues, or laughing and slapping his thighs at the gossip about people who were not present – Bormann was once more wide awake and filling his notebook with entries for his card-index of Hitlerisms. It could also happen that in the middle of the night Hitler needed some piece of information, such as the number of books published in the Kaiser's Germany of 1910, and Bormann gathered the desired information by telephone and telex, even during the night hours when it might seem impossible to get hold of anyone. It gave him immense satisfaction when, a short time later, he was able to report the results of his research to the dictator who was now ready for sleep himself.

> He never dared to go on extended service trips or to take any leave. He was constantly worried that his influence might be reduced.
>
> *Albert Speer, 1969*

His obsequiousness extended to the smallest details. Though he was a chain-smoker, he strictly avoided lighting up when Hitler was nearby. He would often retire to the lavatory for a smoke. He liked to drink and had a heavy hand with the schnapps – but when it was likely that he might be summoned to Hitler, he remained sober. For him the need to be Hitler's constantly available henchman was like an addiction. Whoever was in favour with Hitler also had Bormann as a friend. He behaved ingratiatingly, in order that no word of criticism should ever reach the highest quarter. Where he did not need to be careful, he gave free rein to his temper. He would lay waste to expensive furnishings, but if his chief felt like listening to operetta at midnight, he became as gentle as a lamb: he would even put on the records himself.

Those were the strains imposed on someone who completely subordinated his own personality and needs to those of a 'higher power'. But for Bormann this was no burdensome duty. It was his wish to stand in the shadow of a commanding authority. He felt it a distinction to be closer to the Führer than anyone else had succeeded in being. That was his only objective. He allowed a mightier man to have authority over him, he subordinated himself. Bormann had only one, very personal, reason for doing this: he achieved importance by serving an important person. Only one man remained undisturbed by Bormann's hunger for power: Hitler himself. 'When all's said and done, the Führer is still the Führer! Where would we be without him?' These are the words of the paladin who defined himself as 'Hitler's most loyal

Party colleague'. When Bormann's son Martin once asked him what National Socialism was, his father replied: 'National Socialism is the will of the Führer!'

> Bormann erected a real Chinese wall, through which you were only admitted if you showed that your hands were empty and explained to Bormann in detail the purpose of your visit. He thus had absolute control over the workings of the Reich.
>
> *A visitor to Hitler*

Like Cerberus at the gates of Hades, Bormann kept a watch on all who had access to the dictator. With the aid of lists he monitored Hitler's contacts with the outside world. No-one who wanted to see Hitler could get past Bormann. His motto was: 'A minister's uniform is not a passport.' Even high-ranking visitors had to justify to the 'secretary' the reason for their visit. In this way he could keep a watchful eye on the entire workings of the Reich. In a conversation over tea Hitler once confessed: 'I'm glad to have a doorkeeper like that, because Bormann keeps people off my back.' The secretary would have had to be a paragon of selflessness not to exploit this situation to his own advantage: 'Bormann profited cleverly from all Hitler's moods. He knew how to trim his little ship of power to Hitler's wind, without steering a course of his own', remarked Hans Frank, the governor-general of occupied Poland. So it was that a minor functionary rose to be the secret executor of a despot's decisions. It was more than rumour that the secretary often issued instructions in Hitler's name, which were frequently based on no more than a laconic remark by the Führer at table. Bormann was interpreting Hitler's will – or what he believed that will to be. And who was to contradict him? Bormann was Hitler's mouthpiece, with almost unrestricted freedom of action. The important thing to remember was that nothing was to be made known about Hitler that did not serve to reinforce his heroic image. 'People must not know who I am, where I come from and what my family origins are', Hitler had once revealed to Bormann. Only Bormann knew the whole truth. He saw to it that undesirable traces of Hitler's past were erased, that his background, his previous history, his relationships with his family or with women should remain in the dark. 'To say nothing', Bormann once wrote to his wife, 'is normally the most sensible thing. And one should under no circumstances ever tell the truth, except where compelling reasons make it really necessary.'

> He was uncommunicative, did not seek personal contact and devoted his time exclusively to working for Hitler. No sooner had Hitler expressed a thought than Bormann formulated it as an instruction. He knew everything that went on in the Reich Chancellery and manoeuvred between everyone.
> *Werner Koeppen, formerly on the staff of the minister for the east, Alfred Rosenberg*

Another facet of Bormann's character was his all-pervading distrust. To him, sitting ensconced behind his desk, a man to whom bureaucratic order meant everything, who kept in motion a perfectly functioning machine of papers, orders and decrees – to him the only being who could escape his control was a thinking individual. And loss of control meant danger. That is why, for this too, he had to find a mechanism for imposing order. Thus he placed people in one of two categories: those whom he could exploit and subordinate, and those whose hostility he had to fear. Yet he was suspicious towards everyone. He gathered information relentlessly – on the members of his staff, about members of Hitler's close circle. He sniffed around in their private lives and fed his personnel index with dubious details about intimate escapades, about the strengths and weaknesses of his rivals. In his personal dealings with opponents Bormann was cool, calculating; he lurked like a predator until his prey came within range. That gave him the advantage. Heinrich Himmler, *Reichsführer-SS*, was only one of many who was unable to free himself from the crafty bureaucrat's humiliating power-games. Bormann did not go violently on to the attack. But in the long run his carefully placed pinpricks seldom failed to have their effect. He weakened the authority of his opponent and spun a web of dependence. The

Reichsführer-SS and the Führer's secretary appeared to be friends. In fact the outward show of cordiality was based on a 'favour' which might be called blackmail. Bormann bound Himmler to him by lending him money. Himmler was desperately dependent on Bormann's 'charity', because he had a former mistress and an illegitimate child to support. Bormann's silence protected Himmler from a scandal which might well have cost him his career. It was well known that Hitler did not tolerate extra-marital relationships – even where the *Reichsführer-SS* was concerned. So Himmler approached 'dear Martin', the custodian of Hitler's millions, for a loan. The petitioner received 800,000 reichsmarks. Despite his ministerial salary, the debtor, burdened with two families, had difficulty covering the exorbitant interest payments.

> Bormann has corrupted the Führer and corrupted the ideals of National Socialism. He is Hitler's lickspittle and a servile hack.
>
> *Hans Frank, Governor-General of occupied Poland*

Bormann certainly cared nothing for morality. Like Himmler, he had a mistress himself, who was admittedly tolerated by his wife Gerda. Bormann made no secret of his liaison with the actress Manja Behrens. He did not spare his spouse from glowing descriptions of his apparently successful seductive skills. He told her he found Manja very fetching, she had attracted him enormously; he had set her afire with his kisses, and so they had become lovers. 'You know my willpower', he boasted to Gerda. 'In the long run Manja was no match for it. She is mine now, and it is just for that reason that I feel so incredibly happy in our marriage.' Looking back over so many years, Manja Behrens herself sees this liaison through more sober eyes. 'With him and his family I felt a certain protection.' Joseph Goebbels had also courted the extremely attractive actress. 'I told him I'd rather go and work as a cleaner!' Goebbels immediately crossed her name off the casting list for films. Manja Behrens, for whom acting was everything, was in danger of losing her livelihood. Her acquaintance with the mighty Bormann came at a convenient moment. Once she was at his side, all threats were automatically removed. 'Martin was no charmer, he was rather serious, energetic and, of course, a powerful man who could be very entertaining.' In spite of everything, she claims to have kept up a friendly relationship with Bormann's wife, Gerda. Soon the two women were so close that they could compare notes frankly about their man.

> Of course I'm not angry with you both, nor am I jealous. So terribly few worthwhile men are surviving this fateful struggle, so many worthwhile women are condemned to childlessness because the man in their life has not come back from the battlefield. It would be a good thing if, at the end of this war, a law were passed which granted healthy, worthwhile men the right to have two wives. Then you would always have a woman who was serviceable.
>
> *Gerda Bormann in a 1944 letter to her husband*

At the outset, Manja was smitten with a bad conscience. 'But that's nonsense, since it was I after all, who wanted to have her at all costs', wrote Bormann to his wife, and added: 'Oh, my sweet, you cannot imagine how happy I am with the two of you.' Heaven had certainly been kind to him, he mused: a wife and lots of children, and a mistress into the bargain. 'I must be doubly careful, so that I can keep my strength up.' These words were written without a flicker of irony. The anxiety about his health was meant seriously. Bormann certainly expected undivided affection from his conquests: 'My dear child, it's really quite natural for a man to have several women, but a woman can only belong to one man.' This was the doctrine he preached in one of his letters to another mistress, Maria Rubach, who had dared to keep another lover in addition to the 'Secretary'. He, Bormann, would 'deal none too gently' with her if she continued to amuse herself with this man.

To the pragmatic Bormann, Party ideology simply meant whatever suited his private needs at a given moment. Strange as it may seem, each one of his liaisons had this political flavour. As manager of the Party Office Bormann had his hands on the controls of the centre of power; he now laid down generally applicable guidelines in order to give a semblance of honour to his personal situation. The ideology of National Socialism served only one purpose for him: to provide a camouflage for his activities. Behind it he would be able to conceal not only his craving for power, but also his amours. Gerda Bormann proved amenable. She declared her willingness to accept the mistress, Manja Behrens, into the marital household. In the second half of January 1944 she wrote that the *affaire* with Manja and her husband's twofold happiness 'have given me the idea that after the war every decent man should be allowed two wives by law'. Gerda Bormann pursued this idea in letters that followed. The obedient spouse advised her husband: 'You would be in a position to change this. Then you would have to make sure that Manja had a child one year and I had one the next year, so that you would always have one wife who was in running order.'

It was particularly in the late 1930s that Bormann was so busy chasing every halfway available bit of skirt that he abandoned all caution. A former adjutant from Hitler's entourage still recalls today with an amused shudder how, below deck on an excursion steamer, he once caught sight of Bormann – through a half-open cabin door – actively engaged with a prominent lady of the Third Reich. His trousers were round his knees, 'but he still had his boots on', the eye-witness remembers. These days it would be called a 'Don Juan syndrome' and the sufferer would be prescribed aversion therapy à la Michael Douglas. At that time an outlet for such drives could be found with relative ease in the Nazis' approach to life.

Bormann took much less interest in Hitler's political programme. He cared nothing for ideology. To present his own convictions with enthusiasm, let alone with enough intensity to carry others along with him, were tasks for which he was not equipped. Emotionalism or indeed any effusion of feeling was foreign to him; his own unsophisticated nature would not allow him such indulgence. The intenseness of a Himmler was merely alienating to him. His abilities lay in carrying out instructions, not developing ideas. The political reflections which occasionally appeared in his letters to Gerda were of no significance; it seems that she was rather more of a National

Socialist than he was. It is specifically in his notes on the Party's political programme that an impassioned tone is discernible, which was probably due to the influence of his wife. To him 'National Socialism' was more of an abstract concept than a creed. It was the means to an end since it could be exploited to meet his personal needs. Without inhibition Bormann could satisfy his hunger for power and live out his ambitions. His radical manner of dealing with the churches revealed his true face and showed how obsessed with power he really was. Power and still more power – that was the mainspring driving his harassment of practising Christians. As Bormann's son Martin Bormann Jr recalls: 'In my father's mind Christianity was a religion that stultified the masses. To him Hitler was *the* God. He believed National Socialism and Christianity were irreconcilable.' In Bormann's attacks on the churches there was of course a tactical calculation at work. By his commitment he was demonstrating to his opponents that he too was imbued with the slogans of the Party and that he could manoeuvre with assurance on political terrain – for the ideologues of the Nazi Party were still complaining that the upstart Bormann had not contributed a single idea to the National Socialist world-view.

It was clear that the Church, as a refuge for people wanting to avoid total monopolisation by the Nazis, must be restricting the membership of the Party. It was probable, Bormann feared, that 'the Church with all its capacity for psychological pressure will go into battle against the government'. This thought prompted him to issue his decree of 6/7 June 1941 to the Gauleiters. Unused to drafting his own material, his clumsily formulated sentences in fact reveal more clearly the real, self-seeking reasons for his opposition to the churches – and his urge for power: 'When we National Socialists speak of a belief in God, we do not mean by "God", a man-like being who sits around somewhere in the spheres, as the naïve Christians and their ecclesiastical beneficiaries do. The claim that this universal force can be concerned with the destiny of every individual creature, of every tiny microbe on earth, is based either on a generous dose of naïvety or else on blatant misrepresentation. All influences which might detract from or actively harm the national leadership exercised by the Führer must be neutralised.'

Bormann had known for a long time, from his face-to-face

conversations with Hitler, that for him religion had never been more than the means to an end. If the churches had subordinated themselves to his goals, every priest would have been his friend; but because they refused to do so they became his enemies. He would have made allowances for their faith if they had supported his rule. After the war and victory he planned to get rid of them. Führer-decrees to this effect were already sitting in the steel cabinets of the Party Office. Nevertheless, as regards Bormann's anti-Christian campaign, even ministers were convinced that it was all being done behind Hitler's back. Franz von Papen, former vice-chancellor under Hitler and his 'token Catholic', expressed the opinion, when standing as a defendant at the Nuremberg trials, that 'at that time Hitler himself was quite willing to maintain religious peace, but the radical elements in his party' – and he named Bormann and Goebbels – 'continually pushed him into making renewed sallies against the ecclesiastical sector'.

All through those years there was also serious friction with Bormann's Party Office. The concern there was chiefly with the churches, the work of the foreign service etc. As regards the church problem Reichsleiter Bormann adopted a completely uncompromising attitude. This led to extreme tension with the Vatican, and in Protestant countries as well it mobilised all the ecclesiastical forces against us, a very significant and un-favourable development in foreign policy terms, and one which became ever more severe during the course of the war.

Ribbentrop, notes during the Nuremberg Trial

To begin with, Hitler allowed Bormann to get on with his behind-the-scenes activities. But in 1941 Bormann found himself on a collision course with his Führer, who, in view of the wartime tensions, considered the reprisals initiated by Bormann to be unhelpful. However, the 'Secretary' secretly pressed ahead with his plans. For the first time the loyal Bormann went behind Hitler's back. True, it would be the only example of his disobedience. The confusion of war was precisely what he needed for his planned assault on the churches. He was the 'advocate of all tough measures' and as always was determined to go to the limit. Once he had started something, he pursued his plans until his goal was reached. Bormann's department deliberately pursued the objective of cutting the Church off from its sources of finance. During the war it confiscated large quantities of church assets and demanded higher war contributions; the Church was to levy its taxes without any co-operation from state authorities. In this way the legal status of the churches was to be downgraded to that of private associations, and the religious bodies were to be placed under strict state control.

In the last years of the war Bormann's signature is found on an increasing number of resolutions, particularly those relating to racial legislation and to the treatment meted out to the populations in the east. Bormann was convinced of the truth of that hackneyed propaganda formula, 'the Jews are our misfortune'. From 1941 onward, in his function as head of the Party Office, he was a co-signatory of virtually every anti-Semitic law. He was jointly responsible for the introduction of the race laws and the ordinance on the confiscation of the assets of Jewish emigrants, but in this he was notable less for treachery and cunning than for the painstaking bureaucracy with which he exploited every loophole in the law for Hitler's anti-Semitic purposes.

Goebbels, with his fanatical speeches, fuelled the flames of hatred and drove the campaign of terror continually forward. At the controls of the machinery of annihilation sat Himmler, Heydrich and Eichmann. But what role did the Führer's Secretary play in the genocide? What did Bormann know? How did he behave?

One night in May 1942 Walter Meiendresch, a telephonist in the Führer's Wolf's Lair headquarters, listened in on a revealing high-level conversation. On the line was Heinrich Himmler, who wanted to give Bormann some 'gratifying news from Auschwitz' to pass on to the Führer: another 20,000 Jews had been 'liquidated' there. Himmler immediately corrected himself: 'Er, I mean . . . evacuated.' Bormann was furious. Reports of that nature, he informed the *Reichsführer-SS*, were only to be passed on in writing – by SS officers.

That fact that Bormann was always extremely well-informed is proved by an earlier incident in the autumn of 1940. Poland's *Generalgouverneur*, Hans Frank, had been summoned by Hitler to the Reich Chancellery for a discussion about the occupied regions of Poland, which were being used as reception areas for deported Jews. Needless to say, Bormann was present at the meeting. He noted down Hitler's words and heard Frank boast about 'Jew-free areas'. The numbers who could be dumped in the ghettos, Frank said, were growing ever larger. However, he refused most emphatically to accept into Poland Jews from other countries. His argument was that everything must be done to prevent the ghettos from becoming overpopulated. Yet Baldur von Schirach, the Gauleiter of Vienna, was demanding that the 60,000 Jews still left in Vienna should be deported to the *Generalgouvernement*. Being thorough by nature, Bormann never forgot to make sure that, following discussions of this kind, everything that had been minuted was duly put into effect. Again Bormann was the zealous bureaucrat, whose work-load almost always consisted of duly submitting documents to Hitler with notes on outstanding decisions to be made by him. Bormann drove things forward, acted as the transmitter of messages from Hitler and ensured that those responsible did their work thoroughly. Thus he reminded the dictator that he had indeed planned to have 'the 60,000 Jews still resident in the *Reichsgau* of Vienna' speedily removed to the *Generalgouvernement* of Poland – which was then done. In a documentary note dated March 1942 Bormann replied to the question of how the 'the Jewish problem could be solved', with the laconic words: 'Very simply!'

It was in the spring of 1943 that Hitler finally appointed him officially to be what in reality he had already been for a long time: he made him his secretary. The public announcement was couched in brief terms: 'As my personal administrative assistant Reichsleiter M. Bormann is now designated "Secretary to the Führer".' The paper on which the announcement was circulated bore the words '*Der Führer*' printed in gold lettering and was only used on special occasions. Bormann had now achieved everything he had always strived for: on 12 April he was formally given the function of door-keeper which he had fulfilled for years. Bormann himself made sure that the entire Party leadership learned what this meant in specific terms. He made it known in writing that in future Hitler would not entrust him *only* with personal matters, and that he would be permitted to take part in all discussions; furthermore, Hitler had assured him that that all matters put forward for his own attention would first have to be looked at by Bormann. In plain words this meant that only through Bormann would Hitler have contact with the outside world. The princes of the Party were aghast. Was Bormann now to be arbitrator in disputes between them over areas of authority? To many this was an affront. Now, like a spider at the centre of his web, Bormann held all the threads in his hand. He had moved into a special and unassailable position. The 'Secretary' stood at the zenith of his power. At no time was the relationship between Hitler and his aide closer than in those days. The dictator honoured Bormann with the highest praise: 'In order to win the war, I need Bormann. Anyone who is against Bormann is against the state.'

> Usually Hitler just nodded a brief 'Agreed'. That single word was often enough for Bormann to prepare longer instructions.
>
> *Albert Speer*
>
> Hitler always covered Bormann's back.
>
> *Baldur von Schirach*

To the German people at large he was still a nameless and apparently insignificant functionary. Yet in Hitler's Reich the man in the shadows wielded immense, almost unbounded, power. It went without saying that Bormann insisted on the right to be consulted on appointments and promotions in all areas of state. In the conquered eastern territories he immediately achieved what he had always worked for: he could finally be involved in policy making. Shortly before the invasion of the Soviet Union Bormann gave encouragement to a Hitler plagued with doubts, by telling him to answer the call of Providence and launch the campaign. Hitler listened to his loyal aide. In the senior ranks of the SS the rumour soon arose that Bormann had only persuaded Hitler to take this course because he cherished the hope of soon being made ruler of a vast eastern empire. That of course aroused envy and greed among his rivals. Himmler also staked his claim and it led to a duel between the *Reichsführer-SS* and the Secretary to the Führer. In this trial of strength Bormann started from by far the more favourable position. Himmler had never belonged to Hitler's innermost circle. From his own ranks he received the warning that he would have to break the 'Bormann monopoly'. He never succeeded.

In occupied Poland Bormann and his Gauleiters ruled with harsh brutality. The writ of Reich law did not run here. The law of the stronger prevailed. From his card-index he fished out the names of fanatical and unscrupulous Party members with whom to build an administration. In the occupied regions of Poland extreme measures were turning the much-vaunted 'new national order' into reality. Bormann's implacability and moral indifference took the form of a crude and bullying instruction to Alfred Rosenberg, minister for eastern territories, who was to see to it that in the conquered lands 'under no circumstances should towns be renovated or even tidied up'. In a memorandum of 19 August 1942 he wrote: 'The Slavs will have to work for us. The ones we do not need can die. Fertility among the Slavs is undesirable. Let them use contraceptives or have abortions; the more the better. Education is dangerous. We will leave them their religion as a distraction. As far as food is concerned, they will receive the minimum necessary. We are the masters; we come first.'

> When speaking to a leading Party member, one was very careful not say anything negative about Bormann. One could only risk doing so with people who spoke freely and who often criticised him openly to me.
>
> *Baldur von Schirach*

His opponents had finally realised that this man was dangerous. It was advisable for all of them to secure his goodwill, at the very least. Any conspiracy against the 'Secretary' appeared doomed to failure from the start. Goebbels, for example, had tried in vain to topple Bormann. In common with Göring, Speer and Ley he believed that, with the demand for 'total war', he would be able to inspire the entire population to make an ultimate effort and to show that Bormann was chiefly responsible for the fact that this had not happened long ago. For Goebbels's proposal that the war should be waged in a ruthless manner, by summoning up all the nation's strength, had already been sent to the Führer six months previously. Hitler had left it with Bormann, who had consigned it to one of his filing cabinets. However, Hitler now promised Goebbels that he would soon give the starting-order for 'total war'. He gave the order on 27 December 1942 – to Bormann. This was not what the conspirators had intended. Bormann's position was stronger than ever. It was a humiliation. Of all people, it was Goebbels's rival, Bormann, who passed on to him Hitler's order to force the pace of 'total war'. Goebbels obeyed, promising in future only to approach Hitler through Bormann and not to solicit any more decisions from the Führer independently. Never again would Goebbels dare to defy the head of the Party Office.

In November 1943 Goebbels sent Hitler, via Bormann, a four-page memorandum on the political situation. He counselled making peace with Stalin. But again he was left without an answer. When the Minister of Propaganda tentatively enquired about it, Bormann told him to his face that he regretted to say that the memorandum had not been passed on because the proposal did not stand the slightest chance of being accepted by Hitler.

> Just now Bormann is not on his best form either. Particularly in the question of radicalising our war he has not delivered what I had in fact hoped from him.
>
> *Goebbels, diary, 28 March 1945*

Over the years leading figures of the Third Reich had attempted to trip up the careerist Bormann. They had all underestimated him. When Goebbels and Bormann became closer again, in the final days of the Reich, this happened chiefly because the minister was shrewd enough to see that only with Bormann's approval could he gain a place beside Hitler.

By now the Secretary was seated so firmly in the saddle that only a few people were willing to pick a quarrel with him. With increasing aggressiveness he had managed to force every rival out of the centre of power. His final goal was to make the Party Office the highest court of appeal for senior Nazis – as ever, subject to Hitler's authority. But this remained a pipe-dream.

Following the attempt on Hitler's life on 20 July 1944 Bormann organised a witch-hunt among the officer-corps of the Wehrmacht. He had long suspected treachery, he claimed. He was the first to get on to the trail of the conspirators because he had his informers in the telecommunications staff. They provided him with the crucial information. A sergeant described to him what had occurred: shortly before the bomb intended to kill Hitler exploded, *Oberst* Claus Schenk, Count von Stauffenberg, had apparently left the Wolf's Lair HQ in a great hurry. On the afternoon of the same day, when Hitler was showing the Italian dictator, Mussolini, the devastation at the scene of the explosion, the names of the men behind the attempt were known to Bormann. In the end Bormann even hunted down *Generaloberst* Friedrich Fromm. He put Fromm's name at the head of the list of conspirators although the accusations against him scarcely held water. Fromm had been held prisoner in his house by the conspirators, because he had refused to take part in the assassination. Yet shortly before the matter was closed Bormann still managed to engineer a death sentence on the general. Could it be that Bormann hated Fromm because, as an army batman he always had to make sure that this officer's boots were polished to a particularly high shine?

Yet such acts of revenge no longer served any purpose; the fate of Hitler's Reich had long been sealed. If Bormann's hectic activity was still to have any sense, he had to remain a believer in miracles, trusting in the genius of the Führer. Above all, he must protect his Führer from anything that might distract him from his great task, weaken his determination or detract from his belief that Providence was on his side.

At the end of March 1945 Bormann had achieved yet another objective: the senior officers of the Nazi Party were placed exclusively under his orders. Since the army, the Luftwaffe and even the Waffen-SS had failed, only the Party, as Bormann saw it, could now save Germany. Wherever Bormann discovered a crack in the command structure of the Wehrmacht, he surreptitiously filtered the Party in. In a decree Bormann tried once more to rouse his Party colleagues with tired slogans: 'Anyone who abandons his *Gau* under enemy attack is a miserable bastard. Anyone who does not fight to his last breath will be considered a deserter. The only battle-cry worth anything now is: win or die!' But the exhortations of the 'telex general' from the protection of his concrete bunker in Berlin had as little effect as his threats. Words no longer had any value and he had nothing else to offer. Finally, on 9 March 1945 he circulated a letter to all holders of authority with his recipe for 'strengthening the front by rounding up soldiers who have lost contact with their units'. As far as Bormann was concerned, there was no need for men to be in that situation. Those out of touch with their units only had to head towards the noise of fighting and join a unit there. If they failed to do that they were to be shot as deserters under military law.

Ultimately it was the anger of desperation that drove him on. He had to compel the entire nation to fight, using every means available. Bormann succeeded in becoming involved in the plans for the *Volkssturm*, truly the last contingent: 'Today, after certain birth-pangs, the Führer approved the order for the formation of the *Volkssturm*. I feel like a young mother, exhausted but happy', Bormann had written to his wife in September 1944. Only at this late stage did he betray, at least in his letters to her – and then only cautiously – his growing doubts as to whether the fatal blow could still be averted.

> Bormann is my mortal enemy. The man is just waiting for a chance to bring me down.
>
> *Hermann Göring*

In the final months before the collapse Hitler relied on Bormann as on no-one else. In the gloomy world of the bunker beneath the Reich Chancellery the Secretary was closer to his Führer than at any time before. It was the grotesque tragedy of Bormann the bureaucrat that, as his authority expanded, so at the same time the area in which he could exercise it dwindled. It was now that his position was at its most powerful and unchallenged, but the Secretary could not accept that this dream would only last a few days longer. The Third Reich was now not very much more than a square kilometre of Berlin soil. In order to forget, to suppress things, Bormann numbed himself with alcohol. However, in his sober moments he posed as a man fighting on to ultimate victory. 'We must not be downcast', he wrote to his wife. 'Whatever befalls, we are bound to do our duty. And if it is our fate, like ye olde Nibelungs of yore, to meet our end in King Etzel's hall, let us do so proud and unbowed.' In this letter dated 2 April 1945, the last his wife received, he once again accused the man whom for months he had held responsible for the military catastrophe: Hermann Göring. Now a single thought preoccupied him: revenge on the *Reichsmarschall*. The opportunity came on 23 April 1945, shortly after 10 p.m. On that day Göring had sent a fateful radio-telegram to Hitler in his Berlin bunker. Merely reading the first few lines sent Hitler scarlet with rage: '*Mein Führer*', it read, 'are you in agreement that, in accordance with your decree of 29.6.1941, as your deputy I immediately assume overall leadership of the Reich with full freedom of action at home and abroad?' If this question was not enough of an affront to Hitler, the next paragraph put the seal on the final rift between Göring and the Führer. 'If by 22.30 hours no answer is received, I will assume that you have been deprived of your freedom of action. I will then regard the conditions of your decree as fulfilled and will act for the good of the people and the Fatherland.'

Bormann did not need long to consider this. He recognised his chance for a final intrigue against his most personal enemy. 'Göring is committing treason!' he assured Hitler. 'I've known that for a long time', the latter replied, still red in the face. 'I know Göring is lazy. He let the Luftwaffe go to rack and ruin. He was corrupt. It was his example that made corruption possible in our state. And on top of it all he's been addicted to morphine for years. I've known it all along.'

A short time later in Berchtesgaden *SS-Obersturmbannführer* Bernhard Frank held an order in his hand, which Bormann had hastily scribbled: 'Surround Göring house immediately and overcoming any resistance immediately arrest the former *Reichsmarschall* Hermann Göring. Signed, Adolf Hitler.' On 23 April, at about 10 p.m., Frank clicked his heels in Göring's palatial country house on the Obersalzberg and announced to the alleged traitor: '*Herr Reichsmarschall*, you are under arrest.' Six days later, in his 'political testament', Hitler ordained: 'Before my death I expel the former *Reichsmarschall* Hermann Göring from the Party.' His accusation, that Göring had been negotiating with the Allies behind his back, was groundless. But Bormann had achieved his aim.

> You know, I have had my fill of all the ugliness, distortion, slander, repulsive and deceitful flattery, lickspittling, incompetence, madness, idiocy, ambition, vanity, greed etc, in short, all the unpleasant faces of human nature.
>
> *Bormann in one of his last letters to his wife*

On the morning of 25 April several waves of Allied aircraft bombed the Obersalzberg. Bormann's notebook contains three brief entries for that day. The first line triumphantly reports Göring's expulsion from the Party. The second reads: 'First major attack on the Obersalzberg.' Not a word about the fate of his wife and children, or the fact that their home had been destroyed. The third line reads: 'Berlin encircled!' Not even in the remaining entries, right to the end, is there a single mention of his family. In a later interrogation his son Adolf M. Bormann said that, as far as he knew, his father had actually sent a radio message in those last days, ordering his mother to kill herself and her children with poison, as soon as the father of the family declared the fight to be hopeless. However, Bormann's deputy, Helmut von Hummerl, had not passed the message on.

During the night of 1/2 May 1945 Martin Bormann made his attempt to break out of the Führer-bunker. Achim Lehmann, a messenger with Artur Axmann, the Reich Youth Leader, was able to study Bormann at close quarters in those last hours in the bunker. His impression was 'that the man was a coward and wanted to stay alive. Once Hitler was dead, there was only one thought in his mind: "How can I best get out of here?" He drank a great deal, staggered and his eyes were glazed. When we were discussing the plan for the break-out, Artur Axmann said with a shake of the head: "We can't take *him* with us in that condition!"'

After a few cups of coffee Bormann managed to stand more or less upright again. The escape could begin.

But Bormann did not get far. That same night, in the early hours of 2 May, his fate caught up with him. As early as autumn 1943 he had written to his wife: 'If a memorial ceremony should be held after my death, on no account do I want any cheap display of rows of medals and decorations on velvet cushions. Those things give the wrong impression.' He had fulfilled his wish to remain a shadowy figure in the background, right up to his death. He died only hours after the man who had been glad to grant him his obscure existence.

CHAPTER FOUR

THE LACKEY

JOACHIM VON RIBBENTROP

War goes on even in peacetime. No-one who has failed to grasp this can make foreign policy.

There remains only one way out for us now, to make terms with Russia, if we do not want to be completely encircled.

My peace treaty will make all old-style foreign policy superfluous.

I have been appointed permanent secretary, but have asked the Führer to send me to London.

My appointment as Reich Foreign Minister came as a complete surprise to me.

There is no doubt that there was a Jewish problem in Germany before 1933.

Up till 22 April 1945 Hitler did not say a single word about the killing of the Jews.

Hitler was a man of violent temper who could not control himself.

I can assure you, we are all outraged by these persecutions and atrocities! It is simply not typically German! Can you imagine me killing anyone?

I certainly did not engage in conspiracy, but remained professionally dedicated and personally loyal to Adolf Hitler until the end.

Joachim von Ribbentrop

Ribbentrop was in thrall to Hitler.

Hans von Herwarth, formerly on the
German embassy staff in Moscow

There is nothing human about this good-looking Germanic type, other than the baser instincts . . .

Robert Coulondre, former French ambassador to Berlin

I too wanted a strong Germany, but I hoped to achieve this gradually by way of diplomatic solutions, which the growing power of the Reich made possible.

Ribbentrop

The name of party-colleague von Ribbentrop, as Reich Foreign Minister, will be linked for all time with the elevation of the Germans and the German nation.

Hitler

Ribbentrop was the classic diplomat. At the same time he was very much under Hitler's spell.

Romano Mussolini, son of Benito Mussolini

For once, Goebbels and even Bormann agreed, as soon as the conversation turned to Ribbentrop: that he was a conceited, stupid fool who wanted to do everything himself. The minister's much-discussed vanity was made clear to me when, in nearly every reception room in his official residence, the former palace of the Reich President – which in the middle of the war had been expensively converted – I saw photographs of Hitler in large silver frames standing around on chests-of-drawers, desks and sideboards, each with a long, flattering dedication. On closer inspection the riddle was solved:

Ribbentrop had made multiple copies of his only photograph of Hitler.

Albert Speer, diaries, 23 November 1949

Ribbentrop may replace Neurath as Foreign Minister . . . I'm sorry about Neurath. I consider Ribbentrop a dead loss. I say so frankly and openly to the Führer. He listens to it all in silence. He wants to sleep on it and then make his decision tomorrow.

Goebbels, diary, 1 February 1938

For quite some time Adolf Hitler had been influenced by certain circles, including the Party, into believing that the policy of German-Russian friendship could carry with it disadvantages and dangers to Germany.

Ribbentrop

When the Foreign Office said 'no', the security police abroad could do nothing. Every head office department defended its own sphere of authority very toughly and to the letter. Bureaucracy was rampant and regulations were stubbornly adhered to.

Adolf Eichmann

In 1944 Hitler focused in his public statements increasingly on the conflict with Jewry. In the end he veered off into an obdurate fanaticism about it. But up till 22 April 1945, when I saw him in the Reich Chancellery for the last time, never did he say a single word about the killing of Jews. That is why I can still not believe today that the Führer ordered the killings, but I assume that he was presented by Himmler with a *fait accompli*.

Ribbentrop

. . . The Jews had gained a considerable influence in many areas of the nation's public life. In German cultural life, in the press, in films, in the theatre, and most of all, of course, in business and finance, they held leading positions almost everywhere. A well-known Frankfurt Jew, who had been a friend of my family for many years, often spoke to me with great concern about the way things were developing. He himself was of the opinion that the behaviour of certain German and immigrant Jews would sooner or later lead to great conflict.

Ribbentrop

*

The man coming down the staircase looks anything but self-confident. He hides his face behind a shabby attaché-case. He is trying in vain to shield himself from the photographers' flash-bulbs. Now and then a wan light flickers on him. With difficulty he makes his way through to courtroom no. 602 in the Nuremberg Palace of Justice. There, in the International Military Tribunal, the case will be heard against him: Joachim von Ribbentrop, Hitler's Foreign Minister. His seat in the courtroom is in the front row, between Hermann Göring, 'Defendant Number One', and Rudolf Hess, the former deputy to the Führer.

> If the apparent need to establish responsibility can be satisfied by the voluntary acceptance of it by myself and perhaps by other colleagues of the Führer, and if in this way the intended proceedings against Germans can be prevented, I am prepared, as Adolf Hitler's former Foreign Minister, to take such a step and willingly to take the responsibility upon myself, on behalf of all the men and women who are in custody.
>
> *Ribbentrop, in a written submission to the prosecuting authorities before the opening of the Nuremberg trials*

On this first day of the trial, Joachim von Ribbentrop repeatedly runs a nervous hand through his hair. He is anxious to hide his face from the audience in the hall – as though shrinking from their verdict. Yet on that day, as on every other day of the proceedings, he shows no remorse. Ribbentrop does not feel any guilt. Stonily, with no visible movement, he lets the accusations of the state prosecutor flow over him. No description, no document, no film footage appears to arouse in this once powerful man any feelings of guilt or compassion. Guilty – of what? asks Ribbenstrop. Total defeat? It is not a burden on *his* shoulders. Is it his fault if the generals failed? Had he not forged alliances which strengthened the Reich? And what had he, a diplomat, to do with all the crimes with which the court repeatedly confronts Hitler's henchmen? Woe to the vanquished, says Ribbentrop: it is the justice of the victors. Yet to the last moment he remains an ardent supporter of Hitler.

For this he receives his just deserts: on 16 October 1946 at 1.19 a.m. the door to his cell in a Nuremberg high school opens. He is the first to be executed that morning. Flanked by two American GIs he takes his final walk towards the school gymnasium. Awaiting him there is Joseph Malta, the 'Nuremberg Hangman', beside one of the three scaffolds. He leads the condemned man up seven steps to the platform. Then the one-time foreign minister of the Third Reich has to stand on a trap-door and a noose is placed around his neck. But first he wants to address the German people one last time: 'It is my wish that Germany should fulfil her destiny and that an understanding should be reached between East and West. I wish peace for the world.' The trap-door opens. In the minutes that follow, the few witnesses to the execution are exposed to a gruesome spectacle: Ribbentrop does not die immediately. He writhes in his death-throes. He twitches. His head thuds against the wooden wall of the scaffold. The next man to face his death – Field-Marshal Wilhelm Keitel – is already being led in while Ribbentrop is still fighting for his life. It will take ten minutes before Malta receives the order to pull down on the dangling body in order finally to break the victim's neck with his weight. The Nuremberg Hangman recalls in lurid detail: 'Then I pressed with my right hand behind his left ear – it went *ping* and he was dead.'

This macabre performance is repeated nine times. Later the photographs of the executed Nazi leaders brought severe reproaches down on the Nuremberg Hangman. He had, it was claimed, deliberately prolonged the death-agony. Such an abomination was described as unworthy of an international military tribunal of the victorious powers in the Second World

War. The explanation offered was rather a banal one: in the long weeks of the trial the condemned men had lost a great deal of weight; and this fact had been overlooked in calculating the length of the rope.

Ulrich Friedrich Willy Joachim Ribbentrop was born on 30 April 1893 in the Rhineland town of Wesel. His father Richard had served in a Prussian artillery regiment and had reached the rank of *Oberstleutnant* (lieutenant-colonel). Joachim's mother Sophie, *née* Hertwig, was the daughter of a landowner in Saxony. The Ribbentrop family was considered comfortably off, and the even tenor of their life was adapted to wherever the father's artillery unit was stationed. However, Colonel Ribbentrop's military career came to an abrupt end in 1908 due to political differences with his superiors. Joachim developed an intense relationship with his father, and particularly after the death of his mother, Richard Ribbentrop became the central point of reference in young Joachim's life. As was quite common in those days, Joachim Ribbentrop broke off his school education after the seventh year. His school contemporaries later described him as a 'dim-witted' pupil whose only remarkable qualities were his pushiness and unbridled vanity. Both accusations were to follow Joachim Ribbentrop throughout his life. Nonetheless, the young man developed a particular gift for languages. He learned to speak French and English fluently. Both would serve him well in his political career and compensated for his lack of diplomatic training if only because his master, Hitler, spoke neither language and valued the linguistic abilities of his protégé as proof of his worldly sophistication and diplomatic skill.

After years of peripatetic living between Wesel and the Franco-German cities of Metz and Strasbourg, Joachim Ribbentrop and his younger brother Lothar developed a preference for the English-speaking world. They spent two years in Britain, where they came to know and appreciate the life and customs of the island nation, before setting off in 1910 for Canada. Joachim's experiences there made a lasting impression on him and it was in Canada that he made a decision which would ultimately bring him to the dock at Nuremberg: 'Originally I had only gone there on a visit, but I stayed there for four years, until the outbreak of the

First World War. Had I stayed in Canada then, which would have been a possibility due to my unfitness for military service, what course might my life have taken?' That was the question that the condemned man asked himself decades later in his last jottings. None of Hitler's henchmen was born to be a war criminal. Many made themselves such.

The young man felt at ease in the wide open spaces of Canada. In a surprisingly short time he was taken up by high society there. With the help of the Duke of Connaught, who represented the British crown in the dominion, Joachim Ribbentrop was soon adorning the social life of Montreal and Ottawa. There was scarcely a party at Rideau Hall, the magnificent residence of the British Governor-General, to which he was not invited. 'Patricia, the Governor-General's beautiful daughter', whom Ribbentrop still remembered in his death-cell, seemed to have taken a particular shine to the young German. Ribbentrop joined the Rideau Sports Club and became a member of the 'Minto Six', a figure-skating team whose fame spread beyond the borders of Canada. He also proved to be an accomplished tennis player and golfer and, as a charming ballroom dancer and ladies' man, made the heart of many a well-born young lady beat faster.

Nonetheless, the young German emigrant was not only a socialite; he was also a successful businessman. Using some of the money left to him by his mother when she died of tuberculosis, he set himself up in the wine trade, importing and exporting. In 1913, when starting out on a promising career in Canada, he was struck down by a severe kidney infection. He decided to travel to Germany for treatment. From that time on his health was never very robust. He repeatedly chose to hide behind this fact when confronted by difficult political situations. After some weeks in a German sanatorium he returned to Canada where, in August 1914, the outbreak of the First World War took him by surprise. Although Joachim Ribbentrop could have had himself released from military service because of his kidney complaint, he obeyed the call to the flag and hastily left the country whose hospitality he would still, decades later, regret having spurned. On the eve of his departure he invited his now large circle of friends to a dinner party in the festively decorated rooms of the Château Laurier. The next morning he had vanished without trace. His return to Germany by ship was not without adventure. To this day the rumour surrounding his precipitate departure from Canada is that he had been spying for Germany. A woman who knew him at the time, Jodie Hughson, is still convinced of this: 'In those days everyone knew that "good old Ribb" had been a spy and that's why he'd been able to leave the country so fast. The other Germans were interned the very same day.'

It is a fact that even Germans who were ill were arrested, including Joachim's brother Lothar, who died in Canada in 1918 as a consequence of tuberculosis. The Canadian authorities took away the passports of 'enemy aliens', thus ensuring that they could not fight for the other side. The Canadian press also returned repeatedly to the question of whether yesterday's celebrated guest had in truth been a German spy. On 3 October the Canadian journal *Beck's Weekly* ran an article under the headline: 'A little spy story of our own'. It contained a detailed account of how Ribbentrop, the 'successful businessman and virtuoso violinist', had actually been placed under arrest because 'incriminating material about strategic locations' had been found in his luggage.

The charge of espionage cannot be fully proven, but neither can it be completely dismissed. In Ribbentrop's defence it can be argued that in the papers of the German Foreign Office that have been preserved there is no mention of his name in connection with espionage. What on earth would he have been supposed to find out in Canada? Why would the Kaiser's spymasters have recruited a seventeen-year-old, of all people, the moment he arrived there?

On the other hand, why should they not have done so? Was not a linguistically gifted, patriotic young man like Ribbentrop the ideal candidate for the role of unsuspected spy on His Imperial Majesty's service? Was it not remarkable how swiftly and effortlessly the doors of Canadian high society were opened to this completely unknown youth? Was this not the explanation for his smooth departure from the country on 1 August 1914, while other Germans were less fortunate? In history not every material fact is to be found in the documents.

Joachim Ribbentrop went into the field, lived through the first great international conflict of the twentieth century, was awarded the Iron Cross 1st Class and promoted to *Oberleutnant*. After being wounded in April 1918 and spending several weeks in a military hospital, he reported to the Imperial Ministry of War, which despatched him as their authorised representative to the German consulate in Constantinople. Once again we cannot avoid asking, what was he meant to be doing there, and why was he specifically chosen? He had absolutely no diplomatic training, and his military rank was too low for him to have been suitable for 'high-level assignments'. As in Canada there must be a strong supposition that he had been entrusted with subversive activities. Turkey was Germany's ally in the war and had to be maintained as one the Central Powers at all costs. Within its Middle Eastern empire as many as possible of the Arab tribes had to be stirred up against the British. Could Ribbentrop have been a German Lawrence of Arabia?

The Turks already had their hands full trying to suppress the British-supported revolt of the Arabs against their own rule. Yet even dreams can stay alive for decades, for what had been a failure in the First World War Ribbentrop tried to revive in the second – an *intifada* against the British Empire, from the Middle East to India. But that time, too, his efforts were in vain.

It was in Constantinople that Ribbentrop got to know General Hans von Seeckt, and in the treaty negotiations at Versailles in 1919 he was assigned to the general as his adjutant. However, nothing came of his participation in that momentous conference. As Ribbentrop recalled in his Nuremberg cell: 'When we received the text of the Treaty in Berlin, I spent a whole night reading through it, then I threw it away in the firm belief that no German government could possibly sign a thing like that.' Nonetheless, it was duly signed, and that was a sufficiently devastating reason for Ribbentrop to withdraw both from diplomatic and military life – not to mention espionage. This decision is no surprise: an ambitious social climber like Ribbentrop saw the Weimar Republic as no more than the accomplice of the Allied Powers in fulfilling the terms of the Versailles Treaty, to the cost of a once great and proud Germany. He wanted nothing to do with a republic like that.

In the summer of 1919 he met Otto Henkell, the owner of Germany's largest producer of Sekt, the champagne of the Rhine. This acquaintance was to be the turning-point in both his professional and private life. Little more than a year later Joachim Ribbentrop married Henkell's daughter, Annelies. With the wedding began the remarkable social and financial career of a man who had once had visions of making his life in Canada. The brand-new son-in-law took over as the Henkell company's representative in Berlin and made himself into an independent businessman (once again in import-export). From 1925 onward he was the proprietor of the firm of Schönberg & Ribbentrop and in this capacity the distributor of such famous labels as Johnnie Walker and Pommery. In the same year the swiftly growing wealth of the Ribbentrop family was crowned with true nobility. Joachim's aunt Gertrud von Ribbentrop adopted him and now, with the help of the aristocratic prefix 'von', her nephew gained speedy access to the capital's highest social circles. For the rest of his life Ribbentrop had to pay his aunt a small pension for this act of affection. The charge that he did not always meet this obligation led to much bad feeling in the years to come.

The *arriviste* was helped to climb by an old acquaintance, Franz von Papen. The two had first met in Constantinople and had remained in touch ever since. After several unsuccessful attempts Papen succeeded in getting his newly titled protégé accepted as a member of Berlin's exclusive Union Club. Papen and Ribbentrop also shared political views and frequently acted in collaboration until Hitler had been sneaked into power, with Papen's help, on 30 January 1933. For Ribbentrop the only thing that mattered initially was matching his social prestige to his success in business. This the Union Club enabled him to do with dazzling success. The Ribbentrops were frequently invited to the home of the Guttmann family, whose head was chairman of the Dresdner Bank. His daughter, Marion Whitehorn, remembered the newcomer to Berlin society in the mid-1920s: 'He fitted in very well with those around him. He flattered them and made friends with all sorts of people. He wanted to get to know as many people as possible, so as to sell more of his champagne. But I always had the feeling that no-one really liked him. He had a manner which was rather unattractive.'

Nevertheless, as time went by, the name of Ribbentrop began to count for something in the political circles of the German capital. The champagne salesman cultivated the acquaintance of Hjalmar Schacht, chairman of the Bank of Germany, Gustav Stresemann, the Foreign Minister, and other leading figures of the Weimar years. The Ribbentrops relied on their apparently sophisticated and open-minded style. But for the moment neither of them voiced any political opinions.

It was in Ribbentrop's exclusive Berlin club that all those trends of thought came together, which would eventually ring the death-knell of the Weimar Republic. Here the fear of a pro-communist Germany was cultivated and the rejection of the Treaty of Versailles was common currency. Nationalistic and often anti-Semitic attitudes were articulated, as were the wish for the return of Germany's former colonies and the acquisition of new ones. However, the highest priority was the removal of the Weimar Republic.

All this had a profound influence on the businessman, Joachim von Ribbentrop. Yet in those days allegiances, which today seem surprising, were not only possible but normal. Ribbentrop himself felt committed to the German People's Party which in fact was one of the pillars of the Weimar Republic. He was on friendly terms with its founder and chairman, Gustav Stresemann, the standard-bearer of German democracy. This does not fit the historical stereotype – but it is true. In early October 1929 Stresemann died and with him the last hope of nationalist and republican forces finding common ground. The Wall Street Crash on 'Black Friday', a few days later, simultaneously ushered in the global economic crisis. Its gravest consequences were those suffered by Germany.

The Republic stood at the edge of an abyss; in the streets of Berlin a battle raged over the legacy of Germany's first democracy. In the course of the years 1931 and 1932, as Ribbentrop later wrote in his prison-cell, it became 'clear to me that Germany was bound to fall to communism. I was convinced that the only chance of halting communism lay with National Socialism.'

> Even at this first meeting Adolf Hitler made such a strong impression on me that I was convinced that only he and his party could save Germany from communism.
>
> *Ribbentrop, note during the Nuremberg trial*

In August 1932, for the first time, Ribbentrop met Hitler, the man he ardently revered until his suicide in April 1945. The talks between the Nazi leader and Franz von Papen about a possible power-sharing with the National Socialists, collapsed. The landslide victory of the Nazi Party in the general election of July 1932 – with 37 per cent of the popular vote – meant the conservative and German nationalist parties had to accept catastrophic losses. Yet this fact was not given sufficient acknowledgement in the talks with von Papen. Hitler was simultaneously despairing and enraged, because his 'legal bid for power' had failed despite his sensational success at the polls. The Nazi propaganda chief Goebbels confided to his diary that 'the whole Party had already geared itself up for power'. Yet Hitler's claim to the chancellorship remained unfulfilled and the Papen government continued in office. At that moment, a man like Joachim von Ribbentrop, whom Hitler had not previously encountered, came like an answer to his prayer. Here was a man who knew both Franz von Papen and Kurt von Schleicher, the general with ambitions to be Chancellor; he cultivated social contacts with those advising the venerable Reich President, Paul von Hindenburg. For years he had been in close touch with precisely those people who, in a situation like this, could be of inestimable value. Hitler had none of those things. And what was more, in Ribbentrop he was looking at someone who kept up contacts in France and Britain, had mastered several languages and on top of all that was offering his services as a negotiator in this apparent stalemate.

In a conversation lasting several hours Ribbentrop urged the Führer to adopt his strategy, which was dependent on his old friend Franz von Papen, whereas Hitler favoured the idea of continuing to negotiate with Kurt von Schleicher. Events followed thick and fast. In November 1932 new elections were held; the Nazi Party suffered further losses and power seemed to be receding from its grasp. By dint of emergency regulations and decrees, the overtaxed President Hindenburg, with Papen and Schleicher, ruled a country battered by the persistent economic crisis. On the streets the communists and Nazis jointly organised a strike of Berlin's public transport, but apart from that the savage fighting between them heralded the end of German democracy. While more and more industrialists supported Hitler for the chancellorship, the Nazi Party was weakened by internal conflicts. Not a few prophets saw Hitler's star already in decline.

However, behind the scenes Ribbentrop was tirelessly making new connections and getting his contacts to work for him. Ribbentrop's villa in the fashionable Berlin suburb of Dahlem was the scene of the key meetings in those weeks leading up to Adolf Hitler's back-door filching of power. Hardly a day went by without rounds of talks being held with various different participants. Ribbentrop staked everything on one card, became a member of the Nazi Party and introduced Hitler into his own social circle. He exploited old contacts and new for the benefit of the man he described as 'the saviour of Germany'. In the end he was to fall into an almost slavish dependency on the Führer. Ribbentrop was in thrall to Hitler. For his part, his idol valued the social position and wide network of contacts possessed by his new fellow-traveller. Ribbentrop arranged several abortive rounds of negotiations with Papen, whose government resigned after the November elections. The man appointed as the new head of government was General Kurt von Schleicher. Papen was no longer at the centre of power. But it was now that his links with Ribbentrop became really useful for the first time.

Shortly before Christmas 1932 the former head of government addressed the annual dinner of the Union Club in Berlin's Kroll Opera House. In his speech he developed his ideas about the 'new state' and expressed fervent support for Hitler and his involvement in the new government. Among the audience were both Ribbentrop and the Cologne banker, Kurt von Schröder, one of Hitler's backers. In the six weeks that followed, Ribbentrop finally stepped on to the political stage and launched Adolf Hitler's bid for power. Tirelessly he brought together people of contrary opinions, sat disputing parties round the table again and promoted Hitler's chancellorship.

Annelies von Ribbentrop charted her husband's hectic activity:

'Tuesday 10.1.1933: Discussion with Hitler and von Papen. Hitler does not want any co-operation before the elections in Lippe. Sunday 15.1.: Joachim travels to Oeynhausen. Long talk alone with Hitler . . . Arranged further discussion with Hitler either Monday evening with Schultze in Naumburg or Tuesday in Halle. Wednesday 18.1., 12 noon in Dahlem: Hitler, Röhm, Himmler, Papen. Hitler insists on the chancellorship. Papen again says this is impossible – Joachim puts forward the suggestion that Hitler and Hindenburg's son [Oskar] be brought together. Friday 20.1. Long discussion at Papen's house in the evening. Papen tells us that Oskar Hindenburg and Meissner [chief of President Hindenburg's office] will come to Dahlem on Sunday. Sunday 22.1. at 10 p.m.: meeting in Dahlem. Present: Hitler, Frick [later to be Hitler's minister of the interior], Göring, Körner, Meissner, Oskar Hindenburg, Papen and Joachim. Hitler spends two hours talking alone to Oskar Hindenburg. Followed by a Papen-Hitler discussion. Papen now intends to push through Hitler's chancellorship. Tuesday 24.1.: Tea in Dahlem: Frick, Göring, Papen, Joachim. Decision must be reached as quickly as possible on the formation of a national front and then a meeting to be held at 10 p.m. for a final discussion with Papen. Hitler agrees to proceed on this basis. Saturday 28.1.: Papen states that he [Hitler] should be called back immediately as a turning-point had been reached and he considered that the chancellorship was possible for Hitler after a long discussion with [President] Hindenburg.'

Over the last two days Ribbentrop had kept his own account: 'Sunday 29.1. At 11 a.m. a long discussion between Hitler and Papen. Hitler states that in broad terms everything was settled. However, new elections would have to be held and an Enabling Law introduced. The question of the new elections is discussed. Since Hindenburg does not want elections, Hitler asks me to tell Hindenburg that these would be the last elections. In the afternoon Göring and I go to see Papen. Papen declares that all obstacles have been removed and that Hitler is expecting to see Hindenburg at 11 a.m. tomorrow. Monday 30.1. Hitler is appointed chancellor.'

The team worked well together: Ribbentrop and the initially hesitant Papen cleared away the stones on the path to the Reich Chancellery. Without the indefatigable assistance of his henchman Ribbentrop, Hitler would have had much greater difficulty in reaching his goal. The hectic days of January 1933 showed him for the first time how adroit and tactically inventive, but also how persistent his new servant could be in negotiation. Ribbentrop naturally expected his reward for this but for the moment he went away empty-handed. With the formation on 30 January 1933 of the 'national front', which 'on Papen's advice' did not include Ribbentrop, the course was set for the future. From now on Hitler used Ribbentrop as a mouthpiece and recognised in him a genuinely useful aide, because he unquestioningly turned the Führer's will into political action. Just like Hitler, Ribbentrop tended to indulge in long-winded monologues, and although he put forward a variety of views when talking in private, publicly he always adopted Hitler's ideas and even slipped them into his diplomatic notes or agreements. He always subordinated his own politics to Hitler's wishes. Never once did he step out from the Führer's shadow. On one hand this assured him of Hitler's protection against latent criticism of him within the Party, and on the other it guaranteed him a dazzling career which was unparalleled in the Third Reich.

At first, however, Ribbentrop seemed to have lapsed into oblivion. On 30 January 1933 he had nothing to show personally for having played his part as a facilitator. In the evening following the 'Seizure of Power' he dutifully lined up with the others offering Hitler their congratulations in the Kaiserhof hotel. In the Nazis' feverish victory celebrations he appeared to be just one among the many who had eagerly hoisted the Führer into the saddle. Furthermore, President Hindenburg had insisted that the foreign ministry remain in the hands of his old and trusted colleague, Konstantin von Neurath, and decreed that there should be absolutely no reshuffle in the diplomatic corps. Yet Ribbentrop, whose short-term political aim was to be a permanent secretary in the Reich Foreign Ministry, did not give up easily. In the weeks following the formation of the new government, he had quite frequent meetings with Hitler in order to study his ideas on foreign policy. He rapidly made them his own.

> The policy which I pursue . . . is not mine but that of the Führer.
>
> *Ribbentrop, 1939*

Most European governments reacted with scepticism to Hitler's appointment as Chancellor of Germany. Hitler was happy to come back to Ribbentrop whenever he needed to give the new government an acceptable face abroad. Ribbentrop saw that within the Nazi Party there was no-one who had his effortless access to influential circles in other European countries. While he continued to pursue his commercial ambitions and at the same time carried out 'diplomatic missions' for Hitler in London and Paris on the side, his master hoisted him up to the next level in the hierarchy. In 1934 Hitler appointed Ribbentrop 'foreign policy adviser and Reich government envoy in disarmament matters'. By 1937 his office, the 'Ribbentrop department', employed a staff of over 70; this number was later to grow to 300. In June 1935 there followed his appointment as 'Extraordinary and Plenipotentiary Ambassador of the German Reich'. In the party hierarchy Ribbentrop now formally stood on an equal footing with Alfred Rosenberg's 'Foreign Policy Office'. But while Rosenberg, as an 'old campaigner' and ideological pioneer, held a strong position in the Nazi Party and its organisational structure, Ribbentrop soon found himself being derided by Goebbels and Göring as the 'champagne baron' or 'Ribbensnob', and the victim of intrigues within the Party. However, Hitler was a brilliant exploiter of his deliberately adopted principle of 'organised chaos', whereby party departments of equal status competed with each other to such an extent that none of them could pose any real threat to his own authority. Ribbentrop had direct access to Hitler, who in turn made use of his controversial foreign policy-maker, in order to bypass the official diplomacy of the Foreign Office and pursue his own agenda. And because Hitler stood by Ribbentrop, the latter was protected from his rivals in the Party. Even so, the *arriviste* Ribbentrop had to endure violent and often public ridicule: 'He bought his name, married his wealth and swindled his way into office', was a *bon mot* which swiftly circulated among high-ranking Nazis.

He was openly accused of arrogance and opportunism. Professional diplomats saw him as a parvenu and a witless hanger-on of Hitler, who had to be removed from the political stage as rapidly as possible. It was this situation which made Ribbentrop decide to join the SS, thus linking his political destiny with that of

Heinrich Himmler, whose rise could not yet be foreseen at that time. The swiftly succeeding promotions from *Standartenführer* in May 1933 to *Obergruppenführer* on 20 April 1940, attest to the shrewdness of this decision. True, it did not silence the hostile voices, but the battle-lines were drawn: anyone who acted against Ribbentrop found himself dealing with Himmler.

In return for this, when Ribbentrop later became Reich Foreign Minister, he would fill all the key posts in the Foreign Office with SS men, thereby enabling Himmler to have direct access to the foreign policy of the Third Reich. In the following years this strategy secured Ribbentrop's position in government and Party. Every attempt to have him dismissed collided with the protective shield of his involvement with the SS. Furthermore, he still enjoyed the personal protection of Hitler, though this too had its price. The Führer expected his instructions to be carried out to the letter. Ribbentrop's obsequious behaviour, the political anonymity of a lackey, was part of the price he had to pay in this complex web of mood changes and power-politics. Subordination, not to say subservience, were what guaranteed the impregnability of his position. Ribbentrop could now set his sights on the job for which he was certainly not qualified, but which he was determined to have at all costs: that of Germany's minister of foreign affairs.

> Ribbentrop hadn't a clue about the English psyche.
> *Herbert Richter, on Ribbentrop's staff in the German Foreign Office*

First, however, the ambitious liquor-salesman needed to score some diplomatic points abroad. The first opportunity for this occurred when he was sent by Hitler to London to negotiate a naval agreement with the British. Under the terms of the Treaty of Versailles Germany was prevented from maintaining a fleet of any size, and the path to a new agreement was a stony one. Ribbentrop's shuttle-diplomacy between London, Berlin and occasionally Paris, met with severe criticism, since the British government did not know what to make of a German foreign policy which often went in conflicting directions. The Reich

Foreign Ministry, which played no part in the negotiations, reported that official circles in London were shocked and outraged by the 'indiscriminate and uninspired diplomacy of Herr von Ribbentrop'. If it was really necessary to use a special envoy – the distinctly malicious gossip went – then he should be an experienced negotiator and not some 'jumped-up champagne merchant'. The German ambassador in London, Leopold von Hoesch, whose job Ribbentrop was to inherit only a few months later, complained about his 'inept and unintelligent' performance. Hoesch made no secret of the fact that in future the British government would no longer approve such visits since, in discussions with the special envoy, 'not a single concrete problem' had even tentatively been addressed. The German Foreign Minister, Baron von Neurath, for whom the devastating criticism of his increasingly undesirable rival was just what he had been praying for, passed the information on to Hitler. However, the latter not only continued undeterred to support his overpromoted 'England expert', but even appointed him 'Head of the German Naval Delegation'.

> Psychologically, Ribbentrop is not proceeding with much skill. He should be more aggressive towards Germany's enemies. Less talk and more action.
>
> *Goebbels, diary, 13 April 1937*

Using a 'carrot-and-stick' strategy Ribbentrop on one hand offered the lure of German disarmament while on the other making open threats of accelerated rearmament. On 18 June 1935, after tough negotiations, the Anglo-German Naval Agreement was finally signed; it permitted Germany to build up its fleet to one-third the size of Britain's. Ribbentrop's signature on this document was a milestone in his career. From now on he dreamed of a military alliance with Britain against the communist threat from the east.

The anti-Bolshevik element in the foreign policy that Hitler and Ribbentrop had developed, was based on the notion of a close alliance between a Britain dominant on the high seas and a German hegemony on the continent. While Britain was already fulfilling its appointed role, Germany had yet to achieve its proposed status – either by military action or by diplomacy and treaties. As much as Hitler and Ribbentrop were in agreement about opposing Bolshevism, there was still a profound difference between them. Whereas Hitler's 'anti-Bolshevism' was rooted in racist ideology, for Ribbentrop it simply served as a pretext for advancing German nationalist interests. The logical conclusion of Hitler's theories, namely to wage a racially motivated war of annihilation and 'acquire living-space in the east by conquest', was absent from Ribbentrop's thinking. Although even in this respect he followed the Führer unquestioningly, Ribbentrop was not concerned about a 'struggle between the races'. To him, ideologies of whatever provenance were only important if they could be made to fit in with his own allegiances in the quest for power. What is more, unlike Hitler, Ribbentrop lacked that bloodthirsty anti-Semitism for which the Führer was prepared to gamble everything. Ribbentrop certainly invoked the 'international threat of communism' without cease, but the idea of an eastward crusade of the swastika was (for the moment at least) alien to him. Initially what mattered to him was securing Germany's position in the power structure at the heart of Europe.

This difference between himself and Hitler came most clearly to the fore in their policy towards Britain. When it turned out that the British government was in no way willing to sign a military treaty with Germany, Ribbentrop's foreign policy became thoroughly anti-British: if Great Britain would not join an alliance directed against Bolshevism, then a new grouping of allies directed against Britain would have to ensure that Germany's interests in Europe were safeguarded. With the Anti-Comintern Pact, which he had forged with Japan in 1936, later to be joined by Italy, Ribbentrop was formally declaring himself as anti-Bolshevist, while in fact acting against Britain. At the same time he was bringing into play a promising alternative to Hitler's pie-in-the-sky policy towards Britain. Nonetheless, the Führer left him to get on with it.

In all the diplomatic efforts Ribbentrop made in these months he never lost sight of his own personal advancement. Now a father of five children, he had his large house in Berlin converted and extended at public expense. He acquired the Sonnenburg estate in the Oderbruch district of Brandenburg, and nominated it as the family seat of the Ribbentrops. It was fully equipped with a golf-course and tennis-courts and had a direct road to the nearby railway station of Alt-Ranfft. Here in Oderbruch he intended to establish his ennobled clan, given added prestige by his high office and his now lavish fortune. The Ribbentrop name, he hoped, would one day be linked inseparably with Germany's return to the rank of world power.

He frequently entertained foreign statesmen in his private apartments, and his garden parties and grand receptions underlined the virtual impregnability of his exalted position. As a driving force behind all this stood his wife Annelies who, in the opinion of many contemporaries, had a strong influence on her husband. In those days Emma Fuhrmann was employed in farming the Ribbentrop estate: 'Ribbentrop was here at least once a week, a very quiet man. He was a very talented and also a caring person. Frau Ribbentrop wasn't like that. She was the forceful one.' To crown it all, the family-owned firm, Impegroma, which specialised in 'the import and export of leading brands', was doing tremendous business. The generous endowments which Hitler bestowed on all his loyal vassals completed the picture. Joachim von Ribbentrop was a wealthy man, but still a long way from the realisation of his political dreams.

Back in 1936, during his time as German ambassador in London, he was known as 'Ribbensnob'.
Marion Whitehorn, daughter of the then head of the Dresdner Bank, Guttmann

We thought of him as a *little* man.
Sir Frank Roberts, former German expert in the British Foreign Office

In the middle of 1936 two diplomatic posts became vacant following the death of their occupants. Ribbentrop now saw his chance to scramble up the next rung of the ladder. When, on 26 July, Hitler appointed him Germany's ambassador to London, this might have seemed like a disappointment, since a permanent secretaryship at the Foreign Office had also fallen vacant. However, Ribbentrop himself pictured a different scenario. Hitler had, he imagined, originally wanted to him to succeed Bernhard von Bülow as Permanent Secretary. But in his search for someone suitable to replace Leopold von Hoesch in the London embassy, both had come to the conclusion that he – Ribbentrop – was the right man to have in Britain. At all events, Hitler was convinced of the qualities of his protégé, as is shown by a series of challenges which, according to eye-witnesses, he issued to Ribbentrop at his official farewell party: 'Ribbentrop, bring Britain into the Anti-Comintern Pact for me; that would be my greatest wish. I'm sending you there as the best horse in my stable. See what you can do.'

At this point the Führer had not yet abandoned the wishful thinking that he could draw Britain, the 'Aryan brother', on to Germany's side.

> Ribbentrop is having a certain amount of difficulty in London. He lays himself too open to criticism. But not through his actions, only his words. He does not keep his dignity.
>
> *Goebbels, diary, 7 February 1937*

With Hitler's personal orders in his luggage, Ribbentrop travelled with his family to England, where two eventful and ultimately unsuccessful years as the new German ambassador awaited him. It was particularly disappointing for him to find that he was rejected by most British politicians. The friends he made were – as always – to be found in 'better circles'. In the first three months his neglect of diplomatic duties was downright insolent. He made frequent trips to Berlin in order to show his flag in the centre of power, close to Hitler. A satirical weekly dubbed him the 'Wandering Aryan' in an allusion to the legendary Wandering Jew, while leading officials in the British Foreign Office expressed the indignant view that he presumably looked on his London posting as a part-time job. At a reception on the occasion of the coronation of King George VI, Ribbentrop treated the monarch to a Nazi salute, thus providing the perfect example of the clumsy German diplomat. Soon afterwards, Frank Roberts, then an up-

and-coming man in the Foreign Office, with responsibility for Anglo-German policy, found himself dealing with the man who would later become Germany's Foreign Minister: 'Ribbentrop was the mouthpiece for Hitler's idea of dividing the world up between Britain and Germany. Ribbentrop was disappointed by the reaction of the British, because we wouldn't go along with his "big ideas". He kept on going back to Berlin. I think he was afraid that if he wasn't constantly with the Führer, he would lose his influence.'

Ribbentrop was unable to realise his goal of luring Britain into the Anti-Comintern Pact. On the contrary, his behaviour had such a negative effect that British diplomats saw in him the true cause of the rift between Britain and Germany. Neville Henderson, the British ambassador in Berlin, was later to complain bitterly about Ribbentrop: 'I told the Germans at every opportunity that, during his disastrous two years as ambassador, Ribbentrop did more harm to Anglo-German relations than anyone or anything could have done in a whole generation.'

In countless memoranda to Berlin, Ribbentrop complained that Great Britain was not willing to give up its traditional policy of maintaining a 'balance of power' in Europe. Any military action by Germany which upset this balance on the continent would provoke a military reaction by the British. By the end of 1937 Ribbentrop's view had become a political certainty. After pondering on it for months, he finally plucked up the courage to admit that the concept of an Anglo-German alliance, so fervently desired by Hitler, had finally collapsed. Though his actual mission as German ambassador had failed – much to the delight of his numerous political enemies – Ribbentrop himself was still riding high.

Only a few days later, on 2 January 1938, he wrote in a personal note to the Führer that 'alteration of the status quo in the east,' which Germany wanted, could only be carried out by force. France would abide by its treaty obligations and, thanks to the Anglo-French Mutual Assistance Pact, it could count on support from its neighbour across the Channel. However, since the British were not prepared, despite all his efforts, to recognise Germany's interests in the east, Britain must be put in its place through a targeting of its strengths: 'This might come about, for example, if Britain, through inadequate rearmament or as a result of its empire being threatened by a superior power-grouping (e.g. Germany–Italy–Japan), thus found its military forces pinned down in other parts of the world, and thereby unable to provide France with sufficient support in Europe . . . It would be awkward for Britain, if alone and inadequately armed, it found itself facing the aforementioned power-grouping.'

Ribbentrop's strategy with respect to Hitler was plain to see. Hitler's plan to draw Britain in on his side had admittedly failed, but Ribbentrop continued to pursue Hitler's true aim, the 'conquest of living-space in the east'. Ribbentrop's tactics of *Realpolitik* now came to his aid, for the Anti-Comintern policy which had originally – even by him – been directed against Soviet Russia, now finally turned itself into an anti-British pact, just as he had intended. With this strategy Ribbentrop also intended to mollify Hitler's anger at the failure of his policy towards Britain. This retreat from Hitler's original plans and the turning towards the 'Anti-Comintern strategy', which Ribbentrop could himself subscribe to, without doubt made him the most important man in German foreign policy-making. And that was, after all, the goal of all his efforts. There remained just one problem to be solved: the Anti-Comintern Pact had to enshrine the agreements on military intervention, made between the member-states of the pact. For as long as this did not become a reality, Britain was to be allowed to believe that a peaceful understanding with Germany was still a possibility.

Ribbentrop's memorandum is revealing, if we are to make a judgement on his foreign policy, for the policy which he outlined in it is more or less the one he put into effect when he became Foreign Minister. Thoroughly disillusioned about the chances of coming to terms with Britain, his vision for Europe culminated in the German-Russian Non-Aggression Pact, which Ribbentrop and Stalin did in fact sign in Moscow on 23 August 1939. Yet at the beginning of 1938 Hitler was still showing little interest in adopting the foreign policy course advocated by Ribbentrop, whose disappearance into political insignificance now seemed possible. However, unknown to its author, the 'Note to the Führer' played an important part in nearly all political discussions in the spring of 1938. For in German foreign policy the signs were pointing to change.

This policy, now directed towards massive expansion, had one of its early successes on 13 March 1938, with the so-called *Anschluss* (annexation) of Austria. But at the crucial moment Hitler's warlike plans faced him with a problem that he had to solve without delay. In his pursuit of war could he rely on the traditional policy-making elite? Or would he first have to fill all the key positions of power with men whom he knew to be unquestioningly dedicated to him? The uncooperative attitude of the top officials, especially in the Foreign Ministry and the Ministry of War, with regard to his expansionist intentions, made him realise that with people like that in charge he would not be able to conduct his war. What came to his aid was a social scandal that became increasingly public earlier in the same year.

The Reich Minister of War, Werner von Blomberg, was publicly discredited for having married a much younger woman whose dubious reputation was confirmed by pornographic photographs of her, which were being passed from hand to hand. Furthermore, the commander-in-chief of the army, Baron Werner von Fritsch, was accused of having homosexual tendencies. Both developments were all the Nazi regime could have hoped for; on 4 February 1938 Hitler announced a reshuffle, in which he also took the opportunity to get rid of the anti-war Foreign Minister, von Neurath. The man appointed as his successor at the Foreign Ministry was Germany's ambassador in London, Joachim von Ribbentrop. Hitler then appointed himself commander-in-chief of the army.

This meant that a second major international war in Europe, some time in the next twenty-five years, was inevitable and the Hitler–Ribbentrop duo, who would play the decisive part in this, had been formed. Any serious resistance among the old-guard political elite had been sidelined. The post of Foreign Minister was now in the hands of a man who obeyed the Führer without question. Ribbentrop's abilities as a diplomat played a rather secondary role in Hitler's scheming. More important were the contacts which had been so helpful to him in the past and which in the future would also open up alternative channels of foreign policy. There was also the obvious matter of finding a successor to Neurath, and the immutable certainty that Ribbentrop was the model of a devoted follower.

With the new leadership team in place and to the accompaniment of suitable propaganda, Germany annexed its

Alpine neighbour to the south. Ribbentrop played no significant part in this *Anschluss*. He was not even kept informed about events. On Hitler's express instructions he had previously left for England. Officially he was there to take his leave as ambassador; secretly, however, Hitler wanted to have his 'best horse' in London in order to get an early indication of the mood of the British government as soon as he began his march into Austria.

On 8 March Ribbentrop had innocently set off for London, while behind the scenes in Berlin the final preparations were being made for 'the Vienna operation'. Four days later, while breakfasting with the British Prime Minister Neville Chamberlain, Ribbentrop was taken completely by surprise when news arrived that German troops had marched into Austria.

The German Foreign Minister found himself in an embarrassing and exposed position under the stern gaze of the premier: 'Chamberlain asked me if I had any information at all about the events in Austria', Ribbentrop wrote later. 'I was obliged to say I had none, and tried to explain to him that I could unfortunately say nothing until I had contacted my government, which I would do immediately.'

However, for 24 hours Ribbentrop's attempts to get in touch with his Führer were unsuccessful. Hitler had left his Foreign Minister sitting in London – without information and cut off from his nation's policy-making. A day later his humiliation was complete. It was not even Hitler himself, but Göring, who brought him up to date. Göring's foreign policy ambitions were already a thorn in Ribbentrop's flesh; the large and corpulent Field-Marshal (as he now was) often referred to him tauntingly as '*Ribbentröpfchen*' ('Ribben-drip') and the exultant and patronising way he treated the Foreign Minister on the telephone triggered in Ribbentrop a profound attack of depression.

He felt he had been given the brush-off, even duped. For days he could not shake off the idea that not only Göring, but even his former colleague von Papen, now the ambassador to Vienna, had been intriguing behind his back. By this time his relationship with von Papen had long since cooled. After he had finally received permission from Hitler to return to Berlin, he found to his dismay that the incorporation of Austria into the German federation had been completed without him some time ago. The territorial enlargement of Germany, accompanied of course by the improvement of Germany's own economic prospects, had taken place without any diplomatic complications. Britain had accepted the merging of 'two German states', a fact which both Hitler and Ribbentrop interpreted as a sign of weakness. Ribbentrop went on persistently promoting his anti-British policy. To his Führer the alliance with Britain, which he had once striven for, was now looking less attractive. And Ribbentrop's concept of a policy 'without Britain or against her' gradually established itself without any further action by its originator. Even so, the man who liked to think he could pull strings did not find things easy.

Since in the march into Austria he had been allotted the minor role of backstop, at least in the emerging 'Sudeten Crisis' Ribbentrop wanted to play the leading part, for which he felt eminently suited. His permanent secretary, Ernst von Weizsäcker, considered that Ribbentrop 'monopolised the Czech affair for himself'. But Ribbentrop was still fighting on two fronts. On the one hand he had swiftly to establish his reputation as a maker of foreign policy, in order to strengthen his position with Hitler and within the Foreign Ministry. On the other hand – and this was even more important – he had to silence his critics within the Party once and for all.

From now on Ribbentrop was caught on the horns of a dilemma. His isolation within a Party of 'old campaigners' made him totally dependent on the goodwill of Hitler. The need to cut an impressive figure in his eyes led to exaggerated ambition and arrogant behaviour, which only reinforced his isolation.

> Ribbentrop was a conceited little jerk.
>
> *Albert Speer, diary note*

However, the year 1938 finally brought him the reputation he was looking for. In the 'Sudeten Crisis' which had now been going on for months, Ribbentrop scarcely missed a single opportunity to pour oil on the flames. This time he wanted to hand over a country to his Führer – after the *Anschluss* of Austria there was now to be the

'March on Prague'. Unimpressed by diplomatic reactions from abroad Ribbentrop, with Hitler's blessing, steered his foreign policy towards war. At the end of May 1938 Hitler revealed to some of his generals that he was thinking initially of waging a war in the east, and afterwards in the west. Following this 'clearing of the decks' in east and west, a start would be made on the great 'war for living-space' against the Soviet Union. Hitler adopted Ribbentrop's notion of a piecemeal destruction of the enemies surrounding Germany. Unlike Hitler, however, Ribbentrop feared that a war against Czechoslovakia would be enough to provoke a military intervention by Britain. Hitler, meanwhile, was banking on the weakness that he had already identified in the British government, and therefore anticipated no significant resistance from across the Channel.

The crisis in Europe was coming to a head. Hitler's intention of seeing Czechoslovakia disappear from the map triggered hectic diplomatic activity in the capitals of Europe. The visit by Neville Chamberlain to Germany finally paved the way for the Munich Agreement, which gave the nations of Europe a few months' grace before the catastrophe of a war that was being deliberately forced upon them. The Munich Agreement seemed to demonstrate for one last time the ability of the European Powers to unite. Yet Hitler reacted furiously to the Agreement. In his mind a favourable opportunity 'to wage the inevitable war at the right time' had been thrown away – at a moment when he himself was relatively young and the western Allies were not adequately armed. From Hitler's standpoint Chamberlain was not a cowardly 'appeaser' but a skilful diplomat who at Munich had bought time for his country – time in which to catch up with Germany's military superiority.

This time Ribbentrop emerged as the winner of the day. He had always warned that Britain would never abandon her 'balance-of-power' strategy in continental Europe. Since in 1938 Britain's military strength was far inferior to Germany's, he argued, the British government was obliged to employ delaying tactics in order to hinder Germany's expansion plans. And that was precisely what Munich was really about. From a superficial standpoint his 'anti-Britain' policy had admittedly failed, but Hitler's reaction gave him the certainty that that from now on the Führer would align himself with Ribbentrop's anti-British thinking.

Ribbentrop's policy of strength vis-à-vis the British Isles became the guiding principle of future policy. By the end of 1938 the objective of his foreign policy was clear: 'Enlargement of German living-space in Europe and its guarantee for all time; and the creation of a colonial empire appropriate to the size of Greater Germany.'

This meant that conflict with Great Britain was a foregone conclusion. How was 'Greater Germany' to acquire a 'colonial empire' if not at the expense or at least with the agreement of the British Empire? The British government would not countenance such a request – that much was certain – unless Germany were looking for nothing more than the return of its own former colonies. But Ribbentrop was after more: he wanted to push Britain out of the power-politics of continental Europe and bring about a decisive struggle between the old global empire and the new and ambitious power that was Germany. True to his master's teaching, he consciously accepted the risk of the war which this would involve. There were times when his foreign interlocutors gained the impression that he was quite determined to force them into war. In those months the Italian foreign minister, Count Galeazzo Ciano, noted: 'He has got the idea of war, his war, into his head. He does not know or will not say in which precise direction he is heading. He neither identifies the enemies, nor does he determine the objectives. But he wants war in the next three or four years.'

In the early afternoon Hitler withdrew for about an hour to draft his answer to Chamberlain's letter . . . On other occasions this procedure regularly led to fits of melancholia in Ribbentrop, since it showed him what little influence he had on the decisive steps in Hitler's foreign policy.

Albrecht von Kessel, then in the German embassy at the Vatican

Ribbentrop always tried to find out in advance what Hitler wanted.

Hans von Herwath, formerly on the German embassy staff in Moscow

Until German troops invaded the Soviet Union on 22 June 1941 Ribbentrop's alliance policy and Hitler's expansion policy had the common aim of driving the British into a corner. Czechoslovakia was occupied, Lithuania ceded the Memel region to Germany, Spain joined the Anti-Comintern pact and Germany and Italy concluded the 'Pact of Steel'. Poland was subjugated by military force; Holland, Belgium, France, Denmark and Norway were occupied; Japan and Italy formed the Axis with Germany. German troops advanced in North Africa; Greece and Yugoslavia capitulated. True, Great Britain had declared war on Germany but its encirclement by German-occupied territory or allies was almost complete and the British government was isolated in Europe, since President Roosevelt had up to now refused the request for the USA to enter the war. The first German air raids caused devastating damage but failed in their objective of demoralising the British. The recalcitrant islands were Ribbentrop's nemesis.

I am convinced that Hitler would have devoted the rest of his life to the peaceful building of a social state, if we had succeeded then in reaching an Anglo-German understanding.
Ribbentrop, in a note written during the Nuremberg trial

He relied all the more on Italy, where Count Ciano became his most important negotiating partner. Ciano's diaries show how conscious the Italians in particular were that Germany's foreign policy was ultimately directed against the Soviet Union, though for the moment it was ostensibly anti-British. What Ciano overlooked, but Hitler and Ribbentrop exploited, was the knowledge that the surest way to bring Mussolini in on Germany's side was to let him forge ahead along the road of neo-Roman expansionism. Nothing supported this analysis more than the monstrous pomp with which the undersized *Duce* liked to take the stage.

He had gigantic tablets erected which drew a direct line from the Roman Empire of his forefathers to the one which he was building – and on them every conquest was carefully inscribed. Italy was bound to Germany by a treaty and its neighbours were all either occupied or annexed. And yet the anti-British coalition was not perfect.

Until German troops marched into Czechoslovakia on 15 March 1939, the British government abided by the agreement concluded in Munich six months previously. However, the dismemberment of the Czech state was more than a nationalistic 'home to the Reich' exercise: from now on Hitler could no longer claim to be calling 'Germans back to Germany'. This time the German troops were not welcomed as liberators, but hated as occupiers. The Rubicon had been crossed. 'From then on Chamberlain was a changed man', Frank Roberts recalls. 'He knew that it was now essential to stand up to Hitler. The first way to do this was to try to bring Russia into an alliance with Britain and France, in order to support Poland.'

Ribbentrop and Hitler failed to recognise the British premier's change of mood, and six months later the extent of this error would be revealed. Britain's negotiations with Stalin began immediately and within a short time an Anglo–Soviet alliance lay in the realm of possibility, even probability. This did not go unnoticed by the German embassy in Moscow. Frantic telephone calls and diplomatic activity in Berlin were the result. Ribbentrop tried to make a tactical alliance with Stalin palatable to Hitler, in order to banish the visibly growing danger of a war on two fronts. Hitler gave him the green light. And thus Ribbentrop clambered to the summit of his dazzling ascent from champagne salesman to international statesman. For a few hours at least it was the literal truth.

Once again it was unofficial diplomacy that got the ball rolling. On 7 April 1939 Ribbentrop issued an instruction to his 'eastern expert', Peter Kleist, to activate his personal contacts with relatives in the Soviet embassy in Berlin, in order to sound out the possibility of talks about an alliance. Thus began marathon negotiations lasting several months, from which Ribbentrop would emerge as the beaming victor. The treaty, which was finally sealed with his signature in Moscow on 23 August 1939, staked out the interests in eastern Europe of the two opposing ideological powers. Stalin enlarged his domain in the Baltic states and Poland, Germany assured itself the western half of Poland and the certainty of Soviet neutrality in the event of a European war.

Though Ribbentrop had never understood how to negotiate with the British, he achieved success within a few hours with the Soviets – just as in his Berlin villa in January 1933, despite great difficulties and much resistance, he had been able to help his Führer become Chancellor of Germany.

Stalin, his foreign minister Molotov, and Ribbentrop probably had no idea, on that night in Moscow, what a coup they had achieved. While an astonished world was learning of this pact with the Devil from the early communiqués, a sumptuous buffet was waiting in Stalin's study, with Crimean champagne, vodka and cigarettes. All were consumed with gusto. Stalin even insisted on uncorking the bottles with his own hand and then proposed an endless string of toasts to Germany and Hitler. Ribbentrop later reported that Stalin and Molotov had been very nice to him. 'In their midst', he said, 'I felt as though I was among old Party colleagues' – which caused the chief Nazi ideologue, Alfred Rosenberg, to remark indignantly that this was ' just about the most bare-faced insult that can be made to National Socialism'.

His arrival back in Germany was like the entry of a gladiator. In Königsberg the population laid on an enthusiastic reception for him and Ribbentrop accepted the tribute with a beaming smile. The scene was the same at the Reich Chancellery in Berlin, where Hitler greeted him euphorically. Unusually relaxed and in command of the situation, Ribbentrop stood at the centre of attention; at that moment the prestige he had won in the party and the nation can hardly be overestimated. It was the high point of his career. Ribbentrop enjoyed the ovations not only on account of his coup, but also because he believed that with it he had done Hitler a service he would never forget. Perhaps, as he deluded himself, the Non-Aggression Pact with the Soviet Union would deter the west from entering the war in support of Poland. Perhaps this prize would fall into their hands without having to fight a war on two fronts. But seizing the prize was now top of the agenda.

However, the happy henchman's mood of elation did not last long. Britain treated the Hitler–Stalin pact as a cause for immediate ratification of the treaty of assistance with Poland, and thus made it clear that any attack on that country would automatically entail Britain's entry into the war. Weighing still more heavily than this news was a letter from Mussolini, which was brought to the Reich Chancellery by messenger that evening. In it the *Duce* curtly announced that at this particular moment Italy did not wish to take part in a European war. Mussolini and the Grand Fascist Council in Rome were hoping that matters could be resolved by negotiation. The Reich Chancellery echoed to a stream of derogatory remarks about the 'disloyal Axis partner'. Earlier Ribbentrop had led Hitler to believe that Italy would fulfil its obligations under the alliance.

The dictator, who had already issued orders for the invasion of Poland the next morning, now had to cancel all plans for the advance and could scarcely suppress his fury against the Foreign Minister. Ribbentrop's euphoria had evaporated. True, for a few hours he had turned the international political situation on its head and catapulted himself into the limelight, but now he was forced to watch Hitler's gratitude ebb away. What is more, the coup in Moscow had in fact failed to break the solidarity of the western powers with Poland, although the French were clearly finding it harder to sustain than the stoic Britons.

> With the start of the Second World War, Ribbentrop's influence on Hitler's foreign policy came to an end.
> *Herbert Richter, member of Ribbentrop's Foreign Ministry staff*

What Ribbentrop was really striving for in the unreal atmosphere of those last days of peace can be deduced from a number of clues. Of course he wanted a war against Poland – just as his master did. And of course he would have preferred it if Britain and France had stood aside at the last minute. But not even in the wildest Nazi dreams was that a possibility. So he accepted the fact of a war on two fronts since that would be the inevitable outcome. It was all the easier to do this as on the eastern front they only faced a small and weak Poland, not big red Russia.

His rival Göring, on the other hand, shunned a two-front war as the Devil shuns holy water. 'We've got to stop going for broke', he told Hitler, to which the latter replied: 'All my life I've gone for broke.' Göring's hesitant attempts to reach a last-minute compromise with Britain through the good offices of his friend, the Swedish businessman Birger Dahlerus, failed principally because deep down Hitler was simply not interested in negotiating. He wanted his war – and the sooner the better.

Thus came the great scene on the morning of 3 September, which Ribbentrop's chief interpreter, Paul Schmidt, has described so vividly. Following the German onslaught on Poland, Schmidt brought the British ultimatum to Hitler's study in the new Reich Chancellery. He relates how Hitler just sat there, as motionless as stone. After a while he turned to Ribbentrop who was standing stiffly by the window. 'Well, what happens now?' Hitler asked his Foreign Minister with a look of fury in his eyes, as though wanting to express the fact that Ribbentrop had misled him over the reaction of the British. The Foreign Minister replied in a quiet voice: 'I assume that in the next hour the French will hand us an identical ultimatum.' Whereupon his sworn enemy, Göring, remarked laconically: 'If we lose this war, may heaven have mercy on us.'

> Ribbentrop got the war he wanted.
> *Albrecht von Kessel, then in the Germany embassy at the Vatican*

'This war' was what gradually brought Ribbentrop to the painful realisation that now it was the generals who counted with Hitler, not the diplomats. Certainly, he travelled ceaselessly along behind Hitler in a train that had been specially fitted out for him, the 'Westphalia', yet his influence dwindled from month to month. In the period of the Blitzkrieg he was only useful when called upon to secure military conquests by treaty or, with the arrogance of the strong, to mediate in disputes between satellite states. The Foreign Minister became no more than an agent carrying out Hitler's commissions.

Only once more did Ribbentrop attempt to halt the wheel of history. In December 1942 and again in the summer of 1943, the Soviet Union let it be known through their representative in Stockholm that they were prepared to negotiate a separate peace

> Long discussion with Ribbentrop . . . I leave him looking very sorry for himself. A repulsive fellow, who is nobody's friend. Now he's had it with Himmler too, fortunately.
>
> *Goebbels, diary, 6 June 1940*
>
> He [Ribbentrop] simply isn't an old National Socialist and doesn't give the Führer anything like the necessary consideration.
>
> *Goebbels, diary, 19 August 1941*

with Hitler – in the growing fear that the west was secretly banking on an endless war of attrition in the east. At all events Stalin offered to reinstate the German–Russian frontiers of 1941. Regardless of whether Moscow's offer was only a tactical manoeuvre, or a serious attempt to put out feelers, Ribbentrop urged Hitler to take them up on it. He saw this as the last real chance to save Hitler's Reich from the looming disaster. But the Führer refused to budge: 'You see, Ribbentrop, if I make an agreement with Russia today, I'll have another go at them tomorrow – I simply can't do anything else.' As Ribbentrop recognised, all that was left to Hitler was 'victory or doom'. And secretly Hitler had long ago realised that the great victory in the east was no longer achievable. But he did want at least to win his war against the Jews. For that he needed no diplomats, only soldiers and executioners: the former to hold the front line and the latter, under cover of the front, to carry the genocide to its conclusion.

In the spring of 1945 Ribbentrop's intermediary in the Führer's headquarters, ambassador Hewel, begged the Führer to seize the last chance of a political initiative. Hitler's reply was the last word on the matter: 'Politics? I don't bother with that any more. I find the whole thing rather nauseating.'

What kind of war was left for Ribbentrop? Only a turf war. In the Foreign Ministry his staff had a good laugh about the weeks he spent in childish wrangling over areas of authority. One staff member, Hans von Herwarth, well recalls the details: 'For instance, he waged a bitter war against Rosenberg's Ministry for the Occupied Territories. Not because he considered Rosenberg's policy wrong, but because he said: "*I* will decide what happens in the Soviet Union."'

Ribbentrop, we're winning the war by a short head.

Hitler

If, externally, there was really nothing of importance left to do, at least his 'shop' would have to toe the line. Until 1943 all the key posts in the Foreign Ministry were occupied by SS-men. Ribbentrop, by now a general in the SS, showed his gratitude to Himmler for having supported him in all his internal power-struggles. It was, as it were, a useful byproduct that Ribbentrop was able in this way to part company with traditional career diplomats, who had always been highly sceptical of his dilettantism.

One man who applied for a job with the Foreign Ministry in the middle of the war was Walter Schmidt, later to become a diplomat himself. All the candidates were invited to meet Ribbentrop in Berlin, where he subjected them to a veritable inquisition. Afterwards they were treated to Ribbentrop's expatiation on the future of the Foreign Ministry: everything would have to be completely different. He would establish a staff college for the young ministry intake. He had already selected a senior SS officer to be its commandant. He was to train diplomats in a new mould – 'through tests of courage, boxing, riding, fencing and so forth.'

Ribbentrop still owed a personal debt to the *Reichsführer-SS* for his loyalty in the jockeying for Hitler's favour, so that Himmler accepted his invitations to the Foreign Ministry as a matter of course. It went as far as Ribbentrop clearing all his staff appointments with Himmler. Through this personal connection the Foreign Ministry was closely linked with the SS and with its Central Office of Reich Security. In return the *Reichsführer-SS* was able, by influencing foreign policy, to secure 'by diplomatic means' so to speak, his goal of murdering the Jews of Europe. In all this, Himmler's particular interest was aroused by the newly created 'Domestic Affairs Section II'.

In May 1940 Ribbentrop had appointed, as head of this department, a trusted colleague from his former private office who had until then been dealing with internal Party matters. This man, rather inappropriately named Martin Luther, rose in the next three years to become a permanent undersecretary – proof of his special position of trust both with Ribbentrop and Himmler. Luther immediately filled all posts that became vacant in Section II with Party members. Within a short time the section was no longer run by diplomats but by pliable henchmen whose job was dealing with 'Affairs of the *Reichsführer-SS*' and the 'Jewish Question'. In this way, with the knowledge and active encouragement of the Foreign Minister, significant elements of the Foreign Ministry were gradually drawn into the Holocaust. And that was not all: in the ministry's Wilhelmstrasse offices in Berlin independent initiatives were developed for the 'Final Solution of the Jewish Problem'.

On 3 June 1940 the 'Madagascar Plan' was drawn up in the 'Jewish Department'. Under this scheme the so-called 'western Jews' were to be 'removed' from Europe and resettled in Madagascar, while the 'fertile' and 'Talmudically sound' young generation were to held as hostages by the Germans, so that the Jews of America would be 'paralysed' in their fight against Germany. The originator of this treatise, the department head, Franz Rademacher, asserted triumphantly that the Foreign Minister had approved his plan. However, several small matters stood in the way of the 'Madagascar Plan' being put into action: the complete military subjugation of France, the ceding to Germany of the large French island off the east African coast, and the securing of sea-routes, in other words putting the British fleet out of action. Since none of these conditions could be fulfilled, the plan disappeared into a bottom drawer, due to 'military circumstances'.

During the war Ribbentrop based himself almost continuously in Hitler's vicinity. He was seldom in Berlin.
Walter Schmidt, then in the German embassy in Moscow

Following in the wake of the first victories of 'Operation Barbarossa', the invasion of Russia, the Nazi policy of annihilation acquired a new dimension – and once again the Foreign Ministry was involved to a decisive degree. The war against the Soviet Union had 'now provided the opportunity to make other territories available for the final solution of the Jewish problem', department head Rademacher wrote exultantly in a memo to his colleagues on the Africa desk, who were thus also responsible for Madagascar. What he meant were the conquered regions in eastern Europe, which the annihilators had their eye on. Shortly before this document circulated in Ribbentrop's ministry, the head of the Central Office of Reich Security, Reinhard Heydrich, who had been appointed to carry out the murder of the Jews, had issued his invitations to the Wannsee Conference. The list of participants did not include the name of Ribbentrop himself, but of his close associate Martin Luther. In fact, Heydrich ought to have sent the invitation to the permanent secretary, Ernst von Weizsäcker, but the latter's increasing scepticism towards Ribbentrop was well known, and so he was not a candidate.

The unspeakable gathering discussed the annihilation of eleven million Jews in Europe, using camouflage terms like 'evacuation', 'removal' or 'final solution' for the murders. What was agreed in detail was the co-ordination of the 'final solution in the German-occupied regions by the relevant departments of the Foreign Ministry with the responsible experts in the Security Policy of the SD'. Ribbentrop's proxy at this conference, Undersecretary Luther, asked for diplomatic complications in Scandinavia to be minuted and proposed a temporary postponement: 'In view of the small number of Jews in those countries, this deferment will anyway not represent any significant restriction.'

The Foreign Ministry, the minutes continue, 'did not see any great difficulties for south-eastern and western Europe'. How did Ribbentrop react to the outcome that had long been obvious – the murder of the Jews? He was fully in the picture yet refused to recognise the deadly details. Hitler's lackey knew enough to know very well that he did not want to know more – because it was all too horrible. Late in 1941, when the reports from the *Einsatzgruppen* landed on his desk, he refused to read them – they were too appalling for this man, prone as he was to fits of depression. It was Heydrich who, in an official document, forced the pusillanimous party member to take note of the 'activity- and situation-reports of the *Einsatzgruppen* of the Security Police and the SD in the USSR'. The frankness with which the annihilation measures were described must have made it clear to Ribbentrop that this was nothing to do with 'evacuation' but with extermination. In the knowledge of those secret documents the Foreign Minister issued an instruction, on 24 September, that the 'evacuation' of Jews 'from a wide variety of countries must be accelerated, since it is certain that Jews everywhere are bound to agitate against us and will be responsible for acts of terrorism'.

How great a role was really played by the Foreign Ministry in the destruction of millions of Jewish lives in Europe was proved once more in 1960. Following his spectacular abduction from Argentina, Adolf Eichmann stood before a military court in Israel. As Heydrich's manager of death, Eichmann was bound to know, since he had abided meticulously by rules and areas of authority: 'When the Foreign Ministry said "no", the Security Police abroad could do nothing. Every head office department defended its own sphere of authority very toughly and to the letter. Bureaucracy was rampant and regulations were stubbornly adhered to.'

Eichmann's words tell us no more and no less than that without the consent of the Foreign Ministry not a single operation would have taken place 'abroad'. Put another way: a Foreign Minister who had stood up against the physical destruction of defenceless men, women and children, though he would not have prevented all or even very much of it, would probably have been able to prevent some of it. But to take that kind of action, Ribbentrop would have had to have been a very different man.

Martin Luther was certainly Ribbentrop's 'Final Solution man', but he was also a meticulous bureaucrat. In 1943 a dispute which had been smouldering for months between the minister and his protégé flared up. Luther felt he could no longer cover up the huge sums which his boss was withdrawing from a secret Foreign Ministry fund and used this as a pretext for discrediting Ribbentrop. Up to that point he had tried to conceal the minister's extravagant lifestyle, but now his pretensions had reached such a level that Luther had begun to doubt Ribbentrop's sanity. Among other things, the wallpaper in the Ribbentrops' luxurious home had been changed four times – and this was intolerable, particularly in view of the destruction of the German 6th Army at Stalingrad. In a heated conversation with Hitler, Ribbentrop demanded the head of his permanent undersecretary. The squabble finally ended with the despatch of Luther to Sachsenhausen concentration camp as a 'privileged inmate'; and two other 'defeatists' were sent to the Front.

The Luther affair shed a revealing light on the mental state of the Foreign Minister who, in this period, brought to a fine art his ability to close his eyes to reality. In the last months of the Third Reich Ribbentrop was filled with vague hopes of a rift between the Allies and morbid fantasies of Germany marching alongside the Western Powers in order to defeat the common enemy in the east. But by that time nearly all Hitler's henchmen were cherishing such desperate notions.

> In January 1945 I proposed one final initiative. I told the Führer I was prepared to fly to Moscow with my family, in order to convince Stalin of the honesty and seriousness of our intentions and to offer him a kind of pledge, in the shape of myself and my family. Hitler's only reply was: 'Ribbentrop, don't do a Hess on me.'
>
> *Ribbentrop, note written during the Nuremberg trial*

When Grand Admiral Dönitz began, on 1 May 1945, to dismantle the Nazi regime in Germany, the career of Joachim von Ribbentrop was already at an end. One of the first official acts of Hitler's successor was the dismissal of the Foreign Minister. In order to avoid a protracted dispute Dönitz asked him not to call back until he had a proposal for someone suitable to succeed him. An hour later Ribbentrop was on the line again with the astonishing information that after long reflection there was only one candidate he could in all conscience recommend: himself. Dönitz hung up. Ribbentrop went to ground somewhere in the Hamburg area, where he was soon captured. The British soldiers were not certain of the identity of the man who claimed that he only *looked* like Ribbentrop. They set a trap for him and brought his sister in to identify him. Ingeborg Ribbentrop, unaware of why she had been singled out, ran up to her brother, embraced him and said: 'How wonderful to see you again after so long!' Hitler's Foreign Minister was immediately placed under arrest.

> I wanted to help Adolf Hitler create a strong, thriving Germany. But the Führer and his people have failed. Millions have died. The Reich has been destroyed and our people prostrated.
>
> *Ribbentrop, in an extract from a letter to his wife Annelies, October 1946*

The victors' tribunal found Ribbentrop guilty on all four charges: conspiracy, crimes against peace, war crimes and crimes against humanity.

Joachim von Ribbentrop did not accept any of the four indictments. He followed the 218 days of hearings at Nuremberg sitting almost motionless, his face expressing nothing. He was an unconvincing defendant and in an odd way appeared quite uninterested in the proceedings. He could summon up neither curiosity nor compassion; at best perhaps shame that a man like himself could once have held such power. Witnesses who had known him during the war were all astonished at how much this once strutting and pretentious paladin had changed. He was now letting himself go, both physically and emotionally. Deep down, Hitler's henchman knew he would have to die. And ultimately it was a matter of indifference to him. Without his hero, to whom he had been more completely in thrall than had almost any other man, his existence lacked its magical point of reference. Without Hitler, Ribbentrop his henchman was lost.

> I must freely confess that in all the years of working with [Hitler], although I had shared so many experiences with him, I never came any closer to him as a human being than I was on the first day of our acquaintance. There was in his entire nature something indescribably remote.
>
> *Ribbentrop, note written during the Nuremberg trial*

CHAPTER FIVE

THE HANGING JUDGE

ROLAND FREISLER

We are the panzer troops of the judiciary.

We have only one thing in common with Christianity: we demand the whole man!

The criminal law is a reflection of the psychological attitude of the nation.

The new German law is founded on the German view of life, transformed by the National Socialist revolution.

This indictment is the most terrible ever to have been brought in the history of the German people. For you will hear of deeds of such hideous treachery that anything ever committed by anyone in their life before pales in comparison.

We are soldiers of the home front.

The guardian of the law must know the life of his people.

It is the duty of the German nation and of every individual citizen to practise racial hygiene; any infringement of it is tantamount to treason.

Racial degradation of the German people is something which German courts must counteract with severe penalties.

The crime of which all the traitors of 20 July are guilty is: second-guessing the Führer.

The security of the German people demands the heaviest penalties.

Roland Freisler

Freisler is just a windbag; you never see any action.
Goebbels, diary 26 August 1936

Comrade Roland rose swiftly with the Bolsheviks in Russia.
Fellow-prisoner with Freisler in a Soviet prison-camp

Hitler's guillotine.
Helmut Ortner in his book Der Hinrichter *(The Executioner),*
1993

I am thinking here of the protection of the nation itself, its community of blood and of destiny, as it has grown up over thousands of years. The protection of this blood community – of the race – forms no part of the present criminal law. The protection of this community of destiny hallowed by rivers of blood is something unknown to German criminal justice.

The tombs of our national heroes, the deeds of German armies and their leaders, their commemoration and honour, are more or less fair game under today's criminal law. The era we have just passed through did not recognise the people as a whole living being and therefore the people, its race, its history and its heroes do not appear especially worthy of protection.

Freisler

Freisler possessed a polished intellect, though perhaps lacking any real depth of knowledge and experience, yet sure-footed, quick, imaginative, with an effortless command of language, and with an unbridled delight and conceit in oratory and theatrical performance.

Eugen Gerstenmaier, member of the German resistance

Gifted, brilliant and foolish, and all three to the *n*th degree.
Count Helmuth James von Moltke, leader of the anti-Nazi
Kreisau Circle

Freisler – a face moulded by hard work, theatricality and passion.
Eugen Gerstenmaier, member of the German resistance

Freisler is more brilliant, more adaptable and more diabolical than anyone in the long line of revolutionary prosecutors.
Rudolf Diels

Anyone who even now dares to shake the foundations of our national community, anyone who tries to undermine the concentrated vitality of the people with communist hoaxes, is no misguided dupe but a criminal whom we must put out of action. Anyone who disgraces the race of the German people is an enemy whom we must destroy; anyone who subverts the peace and harmony and thus the productivity of German factories, is no aberrant Marxist ideologue, but a criminal whom we must destroy; anyone who tries in times of shortage to get fat on the hunger of the German people, is a traitor to the people and must be destroyed; anyone who, like a hyena on the battlefield, wants to become rich on the German people's struggle to survive, who drives up prices, is a traitor whom we must eradicate! That is where our duty lies as guardians of the law . . .

Today it is truer than ever, that: justice is whatever serves the German people!
Freisler

The facts or results of investigations on which the charge was based were presented by the presiding judge as categorical statements, formulated in an aggressive and provocative manner in the loudest possible voice. None of the accused was given the opportunity to make a coherent statement. Any attempt to do so was immediately overruled by Freisler and often countered with furious insults. At no stage in the proceedings did any real examination take place. The very appearance of the proceedings – held in the Great Hall of the Supreme Court – was that of a show-trial. Most of the hall was taken up with seating for the invited guests, among whom were many military officers, SS and Gestapo people and war-wounded . . .

Gustav Dahrendorf, anti-Nazi imprisoned by Freisler

I got the impression that with Freisler the verdict was usually fixed even before the start of the main trial.

Eugen Gerstenmaier, member of the German resistance

Freisler was one of Hitler's accomplices; he took the path of evil with no regard to how many people lost their lives along the way.

Georg W. Lindemann, son of the resistance fighter, Fritz Lindemann

*

Seldom can anyone have been so symbolically executed at the scene of his misdeeds as Roland Freisler. On 3 February 1945 he was killed by a bomb-fragment while trying to escape from his law court to the safety of an air-raid shelter. The presiding judge bled to death on the pavement outside the People's Court at Bellevuestrasse 15 in Berlin – less than 24 hours after passing his last death sentence and only a few hours before he was to have passed his next.

The last sentences of death that the President of the People's Court, Dr Roland Freisler, passed on 2 February 1945 were on Klaus Bonhoeffer, brother of Pastor Dietrich Bonhoeffer, and on Rüdiger Schleicher, a senior official in the Reich Aviation Ministry – both men were accused of complicity in the attempt to assassinate Hitler on 20 July 1944.

It was still early on the morning of 3 February 1945 when Rüdiger Schleicher's wife Ursula and their daughter set off for the city, in order to discuss the death sentence with Senior Reich Counsel Lautz. At almost the same time Schleicher's doctor brother, Rolf, set out from his home. He was going specially to

Berlin with the intention of forcing his way in to see the Reich Minister of Justice, Dr Thierack, in the hope that he might still be able to avert the execution. When Dr Schleicher and his relatives, who had met by chance on the train, reached the underground station at Potsdamer Platz, no-one was being allowed though the exit. A few minutes earlier there had begun the heaviest air raid that the German capital had experienced in the entire war. For those trapped in the underground station that day, the minutes dragged by with paralysing slowness. As the last explosions echoed away a doctor was called for, and Dr Rolf Schleicher made himself known. He was taken by several men to the front of the People's Court which lay close by. They spoke of a 'highly placed person' having been hit by a piece of shrapnel as he fled across the forecourt. But the doctor could do no more than pronounce the man dead. Schleicher had recognised him: he was Dr Roland Freisler, who the day before had pronounced the death sentence on his brother Rüdiger. A macabre confrontation.

But the sentence had not yet been carried out. Was there still a chance of preventing the execution? Rolf Schleicher refused to issue Freisler's death certificate. He insisted on being taken to see Reich Justice Minister Thierack. Taken completely by surprise, the minister promised to postpone the execution, to submit a plea for clemency and thus gain time for Rüdiger Schleicher's conviction to be re-examined. Hours later Rolf Schleicher was telling his family what had happened: 'The bastard's dead!' But the hope that with Freisler's death his sentences would be quashed was a vain one. The family's efforts to save the life of Rüdiger Schleicher would continue throughout March and into April. On the night of 22 April 1945 sixteen men convicted by the People's Court were shot by an execution squad of the Central Office of Reich Security. One of them was Rüdiger Schleicher.

The sudden death of Roland Freisler scarcely received a mention in the organs of the Nazi regime. An inconspicuous item in the *Völkischer Beobachter* (National Observer) merely stated that the President of the People's Court, Dr Roland Freisler, had been killed during an air raid on Berlin. A press notice from the Reich Ministry of Justice read: 'Newspapers are to refrain from commenting on or making their own additions to the foregoing report.'

Freisler was not a popular man. As the Grand Inquisitor at the throne of Adolf Hitler he was feared and hated. To the dictator he was a servile lackey. Yet it was only by serving the Führer that he could himself achieve the power he wanted. The Nazi regime offered him the opportunity to act the part of lord over life and death. It was a performance which by 1945 was to cost thousands of human lives.

With diabolical skill he dominated the keyboard of injustice, conducting himself like a virtuoso. He adopted the manner of a maestro – a maestro of death. His masterpiece was the humiliation of the accused. In most cases his final chord was a sentence of death. Yet that was not enough for him. He wanted to destroy the dignity of his victim. 'You're nothing but a shabby crook!' he bawled at Count Ulrich von Schwerin, one of the accused of 20 July.

When Freisler was appointed President of the People's Court on 20 August 1942, justice had long since given way to openly arbitrary decisions. Yet this arbitrariness was capable of being carried to even greater extremes. 'The People's Court', as Freisler wrote to Hitler after his appointment, 'will always endeavour to judge a case in the same way as you, *mein Führer*, would judge it yourself.'

In competing for Hitler's favour it was the done thing to excel oneself in eager obedience.

'Not to administer justice but to destroy the opponents of National Socialism' was in the executioner's view the supreme task of the People's Court. Distrusting the traditional channels of justice, Hitler had, on 24 April 1934, created a 'blood court' to combat political opponents. The Führer had been profoundly irritated by the 'failure' of the Reich Court in Leipzig when it passed sentences he considered 'too lenient' in the trial following the Reichstag fire. For this reason he removed from Germany's highest court the right to hear cases of treason and high treason, as well as all political cases. These matters were from now on in the hands of the 'People's Court' in Berlin. The new men in power thus fulfilled a long-cherished dream of a revolutionary tribunal, an instrument of revenge for the brownshirt Jacobins. A full ten years earlier Hitler had prophesied in *Mein Kampf* that 'one day a German national court of law will have to condemn and execute some tens of thousands of the criminal organisers responsible for the Treason of November [1918] and all that goes with it'. What seemed like a pipe-dream in 1924 was now, step by step, becoming reality.

There is a thoroughly cynical sound to the appeal with which Reich Justice Minister Gürtner concluded his speech at the formal opening of the People's Court: 'Exercise your office as independent judges, dedicated only to the law, responsible to God and your conscience.'

The law was Hitler.

How did Roland Freisler rise to become president of the People's Court? Was he a born henchman? Even by seasoned 'old campaigners' Freisler was considered the fanatical type. Others considered him mentally abnormal. He certainly had a destructive kind of inventiveness. As a Nazi judge he not only applied unquestioningly the law that was placed at his disposal, he himself created law in Hitler's name, thus becoming the symbol of a murderous regime and an inhuman form of justice.

> Someone has to be the bloodhound.
>
> *Freisler*
>
> He was absolute evil in a more or less pure form, because he had the power to give full vent to his malice.
>
> *Countess Tisa von der Schulenburg*

Julius Freisler was proud of his first-born son; 30 October 1893 was a joyful day for the family. They had so much wanted a son. Two years later there was another addition to the family, again a boy, Oswald. Roland's father had done well for himself. The young head of the family, a talented engineer, was soon offered a professorship at the Royal College of Building in Aachen. For Julius Freisler this not only meant the status he had longed for, it also guaranteed him and his family an assured income. Both sons were able to attend a good high school. As a pupil Roland was ambitious and keen to learn. He made an impression with his intelligence and quick wit. No-one was surprised when he came top of his class in the final examinations. His best marks were for application and conduct. His appearance, too, was striking: black curly hair, a slim build and a self-confident look in his eye. Years later this look would strike many in the dock as cold and domineering.

Roland Freisler began his law studies at the University of Jena. However, for the moment he had to postpone his ambitious plans. The outbreak of war in 1914 prompted him to enlist as an ensign in the 167th Infantry Regiment in Kassel. Like most of his contemporaries he was fired by the initial euphoria over the world conflagration. For a young man of his generation it was the natural thing to go to war for the nation. He had been led to believe that the greatness of Germany was at stake, the future of the empire and its people. It was not a duty but an honour to die for the Fatherland.

Hundreds of thousands died on the battlefields of Flanders, where Freisler was sent to fight. He was lucky; he was only wounded and was sent back to German to recover in a military hospital. Afterwards he was sent to another war-zone, one where the Germany armies were still advancing. For his bravery on the Russian front the young lieutenant was awarded the Iron Cross. But he ended up as a prisoner-of-war. It was in a camp for officers near Moscow that he learned of the momentous events of October 1917 and later. Revolution in the Russian capital, uprisings back in Germany, the end of the war, defeat.

In the prison-camp Freisler was soon considered more important than his fellow-captives. The Bolsheviks who now held power made use of him, and as a 'Commissar' he had the privileged job of managing the camp's food supplies. Later there would be considerable speculation about what Freisler had been up to during his imprisonment. According to some rumours, he had learnt to speak Russian and absorbed the teachings of Marxism in order to offer his services as a 'Bolshie'. Others accused him of being a typical opportunist who had adapted himself to the situation and howled along with the Red wolves. Freisler himself rejected all accusations that he had even tentatively approached the hated enemy. But he could never fully escape the stigma of being a 'Bolshie'.

Barely two years after the end of the war Freisler returned to his homeland. It was a very different place, and one which he no

1 'Fear spread through Vienna . . .' Eichmann (background, second from right) during the raid on the Israelite Cultural Community, 1938.

2 'A mediocre pupil . . .' Adolf Eichmann in Linz (*c*. 1915).

3 'He was a stranger to morality and conscience . . .' Eichmann as an SS *Sturmbannführer* in 1941. The description is from a personnel report on him.

4 'He knew they were looking for him . . .' Eichmann after his abduction from Argentina, 1961.

5 'Six million dead accuse you . . .' Eichmann as the court's verdict is delivered in Israel, 1962.

6 '. . . basically a misguided idealist.' Schirach giving his first speech on radio, 1933.

7 'As tough as leather . . .' Hitler and Schirach (centre) inspect the Hitler Youth at the Nazi Party rally, 1938.

8 'I am one of you . . .' Schirach with Hitler Youth boys at the Party rally in Nuremberg, 1938.

9 'Sacrificed for nothing . . .' *Hitlerjungen* honour a dead comrade in Munich, 1943.

10 'An ice-cold calculating-machine . . .' Bormann in 1939.

11 'Modest and rather timid . . .'
A portrait of Bormann's wife, Gerda.

12 'A terrific girl . . .' Manja Behrens, Bormann's mistress, in the film *Suzanne Takes a Bath* (1936).

13 'Guessing what's in the Führer's mind . . .' Hitler with Ribbentrop (left) and Bormann, at the 'Wolf's Lair', Hitler's eastern HQ, in 1943.

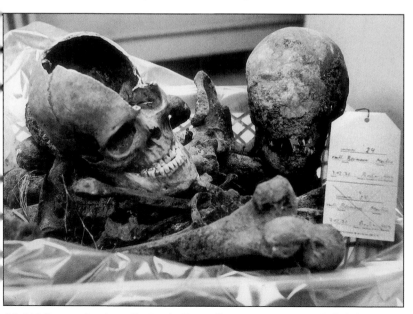

14 'While escaping from the Reich Chancellery . . .' Bormann's skull (left) was discovered in Berlin in 1972.

15 'He hadn't a clue . . .'
Ribbentrop in London, 1936.

16 'The climax of his career . . .' Ribbentrop receives an ecstatic welcome from Hitler after the signing of the Nazi-Soviet Pact, 1939.

17 'He was in thrall to Hitler . . .' Ribbentrop giving a speech in 1939.

18 'Not an individual in his own right . . .' Ribbentrop and Himmler at the Nazi Party rally in 1938.

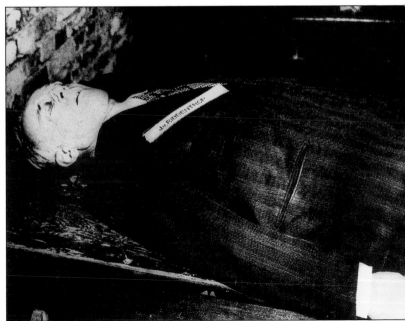

19 '. . . then it went "ping".' Ribbentrop's body after his execution, 1946.

20 'The most bloodthirsty judge of his day . . .' Freisler as President of the People's Court, 1943.

21 'A fanatical Nazi . . .'
Freisler as an attorney with his
client, Gregor Strasser, 1930.

22 '. . . diabolical and adroit.' Freisler at the trial of the 20 July conspirators.

23 'You dirty old man . . .' *Generalfeldmarschall* von Witzleben, on trial before Freisler, 1944.

24 'We're cleverer than you . . .' The White Rose resistance fighters Sophie and Hans Scholl (right) in discussion with a friend, *c.* 1943.

25 'Lord over life and death . . .' Selection on the unloading-ramp at Auschwitz.

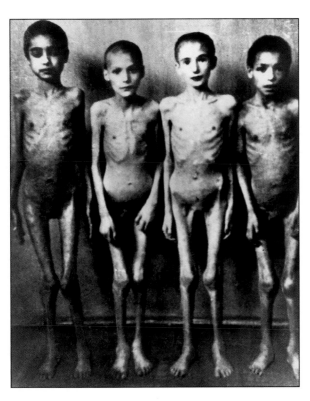

26 'My guinea-pigs . . .' Victims o medical experiments.

27 'We had no childhood . . .' The twins Eva and Miriam Mozes (front row) after being liberated from Auschwitz.

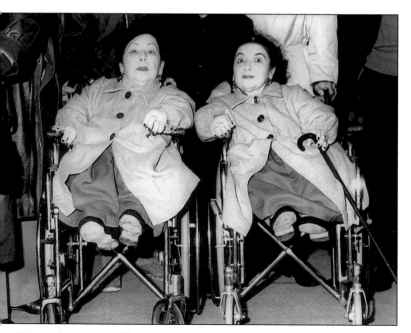

28 'My work on twins will earn me a professorship . . .' Two of Mengele's Auschwitz victims, Elizabeth and Sarah Moscowitch.

29 'So much potential . . .' Mengele's SS identity card photograph, 1938.

30 'It wasn't a good thing to be his son . . .' Mengele with his son Rolf in Brazil 1977.

longer understood. He now devoted himself entirely to his legal studies – with success. At the age of twenty-eight he could not only flaunt his lieutenant's commission but also a doctoral thesis that had been accepted *summa cum laude*.

The young Doctor of Law then completed his period as an assessor in Berlin. In 1924 he returned to Kassel. Together with his brother, who had also decided on a legal career, he built up a flourishing law practice. The two gifted attorneys were never short of clients, since Roland Freisler in particular enjoyed a reputation as a first-class criminal defence counsel. He was a nimble and cunning lawyer with a razor-sharp mind, clarity of expression and rhetorical skill. Yet this defence specialist, much in demand in legal circles, was seen from the very beginning of his career as having a dual personality; whereas in ordinary criminal proceedings he appeared as a sober, correct attorney, dedicated to his cause, in political cases he came across as implacable, intemperate and rabble-rousing, He loved the cut and thrust of courtroom duels; here he had found a platform from which to display his talent as a demagogue. It gave him visible pleasure to pick arguments with the judges.

However, beside jurisprudence Freisler felt another calling. The young lawyer 'wanted to be a politician' – just like that other soldier returning from the war, whom he would come to revere so intensely. In 1924 Freisler entered the state parliament of Kassel as a deputy in the 'National-Social bloc', a right-wing splinter-party. It does not seem to have been particularly hard for him to exchange 'Bolshevist thought processes' for a *völkisch* or extreme nationalist position. The emphases had to be placed a little differently, and a few ideological concepts and slogans swapped around. Apart from that it was just a matter of fighting the democratic 'system' of the Weimar Republic.

As a lawyer Freisler had observed the trial which followed Hitler's failed putsch in 1923 with close attention. The aura of the prisoner in Landsberg Castle had cast its spell over him. Freisler registered with the NSDAP as member number 9679.

The gifts that had proved so effective in the courtroom he now wanted to try out on the political stage. His client was now the Party, the National Socialist movement. And his task was to 'defend' it and advance it with all the tricks and dodges that he had applied so successfully in his legal career. In this he was still driven by personal ambition as well. He saw the Party as a welcome vehicle for his career.

Literally and metaphorically he set himself up as the champion of Party members. In the Weimar years there were clashes a-plenty. Time and again brownshirt hooligans were hauled up before the courts. Freisler made his name as the advocate of a future National Socialist Germany.

Freisler is a slimy charlatan.

Reinhard Heydrich

To my mind Freisler was a one-time communist who was determined to make a name for himself.

Reinhard Spitzy, former Ribbentrop aide

We soon nicknamed him the 'smart-arse' on account of his rhetorical manner.

Willi Belz, former member of the Communist Party in Kassel

With his fanatical behaviour and loud-mouthed over-zealousness he made some friends in the Party, but also enemies. Behind his back the Gauleiter of Hesse-Nassau complained of Freisler's 'temperamental nature, which shows him to be unsuitable for a senior position'. His cosiness and intrigues with deputies, city worthies and businessmen brought him a reputation for mixing private with political interests.

Freisler drowned out all criticism. He fought and shouted his way into the top Nazi echelons in the state of Hesse. As an ambitious advocate he made it plain that the confines of the Kassel city council would soon be too narrow for him. While the 'signs of the new age' were becoming visible in Berlin he did not want to lose contact with the capital. But for the moment, as keenly as he tried, the power-centre of the Party remained closed to him.

With the Nazis' 'seizure of power' all that was to change. When Adolf Hitler became Chancellor, Freisler sensed his chance for the big breakthrough.

Hitler needed henchmen and lackeys in every ministry – reliable Nazi professionals – men like Roland Freisler. Within a week or two, in February 1933, the jurist received the longed-for letter from Berlin: his appointment as a department head in the Prussian state ministry of justice.

He made use of his last days in Kassel to show once more that now a different wind was blowing. In early March he headed a gang of SA men who stormed the City Hall. He wanted to savour the moment of triumph. The very next day he took up position with his men in front of the courthouse and amid ecstatic cheering from the crowd which had rapidly gathered, he hoisted the swastika banner above the building. It was a richly symbolic gesture: the ship of justice was now sailing under a new flag.

The President of the state court of Kassel, Dr Anz, had bravely stood in Freisler's path and prevented the law-courts from being stormed. It was the last time that 'Raving Roland' accepted any resistance to his person. He had been so impressed by Anz's courageous conduct that he wanted to make him president of the German Supreme Court and invited him for coffee at the Prussian justice ministry – at least that was how the newspapers reported it.

Freisler was less accommodating in his treatment of another opponent in Kassel. The Jewish attorney, Dr Max Plaudt, who had been a thorn in his flesh as a rival at the bar, became his first victim. In March 1933, on Freisler's orders, Plaudt was dragged from his house by an SA squad and forced to run the gauntlet through the city streets. He died a week later from the results of the brutal treatment he had received at the hands of the brownshirt thugs.

Two years later Freisler was made an honorary citizen of Kassel.

Aged just forty, with his summons to Berlin, he had taken the first decisive step on his career ladder. The next followed very soon afterwards. Only four months later he was appointed permanent secretary at the Prussian Ministry of the Interior. Here the rapidly rising official gained a reputation, not only as a brilliant jurist but also as an excessively emotional and unpredictable one. At a personal level he could be likeable and charming, but at other times – according to his mood – temperamental, vacillating and cuttingly arrogant. He was a man who could dominate people and terrify them, especially those who opposed his ideas. Freisler's behaviour towards his subordinates left no room for doubt: anyone who shared his National Socialist ideology could count on his goodwill and appreciation, but those who demonstrated non-conformism or opposition to Nazism met with contempt and victimisation.

From the moment Freisler was thrust into the office of permanent secretary he made no bones about his management style. On his first day in the job he challenged the president of the Berlin District Court, Dr Kirschstein. When Freisler interrogated him about his attitude to the principles of National Socialism, the judge faced up to him courageously: 'Throughout my life I have always stood for liberal and democratic principles,' to which Freisler retorted: 'Then I must presume, *Herr Präsident*, that you are not keen on co-operating with us!' Kirschstein answered: 'You're quite right. I have no intention of co-operating in any way with the NS regime.' After this exchange Freisler instructed the District Court president 'to take no further part in official proceedings'. That was the end of Kirschstein's career. He was immediately sent into retirement. As yet, crossing swords with Freisler did not mean putting your life at risk. But anyone who wished to retain the honour of office bowed to the demand for unquestioning loyalty. Most jurists stayed in office, albeit without honour.

The rapid rise of Roland Freisler testified to his zeal, his increasing lust for power and his implacable toughness. Freisler's career was inseparably bound up with the laws of the Nazi regime and the accompanying moral degradation of the German judiciary – a judiciary which acceded, without much scruple, to being stripped of its power. Independent judges turned overnight into compliant enforcers of Nazi violence.

As Hitler's judicial executive, Freisler had no shortage of accomplices. The chairman of the German Association of Judges, Karl Linz, paid tribute to the new direction 'in the name of all German judges': 'We will work together with determination and with all our abilities towards achieving the objectives which the government has set.'

Nazi ideology even penetrated the language of jurisprudence: the words *Volk*, *Rasse*, *Führertum* (nation, race, the concept of

Führer) increasingly displaced the principles of the rule of law. The individual lost his value; all that counted now was the great, collective whole. 'You are nothing, the *Volk* is everything', was the formula to which individual human dignity fell victim. '*Ein Volk, ein Reich, ein Führer*' – the slogan of the regime paved the way for an arbitrary form of justice. Jurisprudence had to be the expression of the Führer's will: one *Volk*, one *Führer*, one justice!

> The separation of powers no longer exists in the NS state. Supreme power rests undivided in the hands of the Führer.
>
> *Freisler, 1933*

From the outset Freisler had not only set himself the goal of interpreting existing legislation in line with Nazi ideology, but he also wanted the 'dawn of the new age' to be reflected in the creation of a new 'system of justice'. In position papers he presented himself as the 'servant of the national community'. Anyone who did not abide by the laws was, he claimed, 'a perpetrator, [and] every perpetrator an enemy of the state' – regardless of whether the act was of a criminal or a political nature. The state was engaged in a war against crime, and criminals were subhuman *Untermenschen* – 'traitors against the state'. In Freisler's eyes treason was the worst of all crimes. Treason was Freisler's trauma from the First World War, the defeat of November 1918. Like so many Germans, he believed the myth of the 'stab in the back'.

Freisler was not interested in a clear and objective judgement of what was 'criminal'. It was not merely a matter of condemning criminals as enemies of the state, said Freisler; they must be eliminated. His paper – 15,000 copies of which were printed and circulated to German lawyers – aimed at a rigorous 'destruction of all forces posing a threat to peace'. What he meant was the peace of the graveyard, a dictator's peace.

Freisler displayed a writing frenzy which further nourished his reputation as 'Raving Roland'. In a flood of documents he created the impression that he just could not wait to subject every area of the law and justice to total dictatorship. As regards the volume of his output, he could scarcely be matched by other leading legal minds of the day. The content, however, was often criticised by his colleagues as superficial and the style as clumsy.

Among many leading Nazis, and by Adolf Hitler himself, Freisler was considered suspect, a presumed 'Bolshie'. This made him strive all the more energetically for recognition, and he tried again and again to prove himself a particularly loyal supporter of the Führer. His methods were boundless devotion and fanatical adulation. Freisler celebrated the shooting of Ernst Röhm in 1934, and the series of killings that followed, as the 'deed of the Führer', and praised the operation as a 'cleansing storm'. Soon he would himself be committing murder by judicial decree.

> The Führer protects the law from the gravest abuse, when in the moment of danger he makes law directly by virtue of his authority as Führer.
>
> *Freisler in a letter after the Röhm affair, 1934*

Among the victims of the bloodletting after the Röhm *putsch* were the former German Chancellor, General Kurt von Schleicher, and his wife. The couple were found shot in their home on 30 June 1934. The Court Assessor Dr Grützner was assigned to investigate the case, but soon afterwards he received instructions to abandon his enquiries and pass the matter over to the secret state police, the Gestapo. Fresh instructions would follow within 48 hours. Grützner did not appear to be the right man to take on this sensitive case. He had been careless enough to say in a telephone call to his office: 'Ex-Chancellor von Schleicher was murdered for political reasons.'

Secretary Freisler intervened officiously. Escorted by three Gestapo men, he went and knocked on Grützner's front door that same night. He instructed him to issue a written report the next morning, and this time it had better be the 'right' one. As Grützner later recalled, there had been no mistaking the nature of Freisler's threats: submit the report or be carted off to a concentration camp. The official announcement, that von

Schleicher had resorted to violence when the police were merely trying to arrest him, was not open to contradiction.

Freisler was a grafter; people acknowledged his competence, his appetite for work. But scarcely anyone in the ministry could abide him, let alone the judiciary and the Party. He was considered shifty. His eyes gave nothing away about what was going on in his mind – until all of a sudden he came out with it. 'Freisler could switch on his fanaticism as other people switch on an electric light', said one lawyer, who knew him well. He himself set little store by the feelings of his colleagues. What mattered to him was the favour of the Führer. He did not mind being the lone fighter – for the great common goal. His view of the world was enough in itself.

He laid personal claim to the Führer-principle in two ways. Firstly he wanted to do the Führer's bidding without question; secondly he behaved like one of the many lesser 'Führers' that Hitler had written about in *Mein Kampf.* Subordinate yourself to the Führer in order to subordinate others to you – that was the general principle of power. Freisler saw himself as the Führer of the courtroom. It was not documents or evidence that were crucial to the verdict, but whatever Freisler defined from his own viewpoint as wrong. It was a complete reversal of all principles of justice.

When Gürtner, the Reich Justice Minister, died in 1941, Freisler was hoping to make the final jump in his career, which would promote him to the first rank of Hitler's entourage. He craved the chance to step into Gürtner's shoes.

Yet this triumph was denied him. It was a setback that Freisler would never get over. Hitler's closest associates detested the over-eager yes-man. The head of the Central Office of Reich Security, Reinhard Heydrich, talked of the 'slimy charlatan' and asked Himmler to turn down his request to join the SS. The head of the Nazi Party office, Martin Bormann, even dubbed him 'the madman'. Only Goebbels was well disposed towards him. Yet when the Minister of Propaganda, who saw in Freisler a soul-mate and ally, proposed him for the post of justice minister at a round-table discussion in the Führer's headquarters, Hitler's dismissive retort was: 'That old Bolshevik? No!'

The stigma from his time as a prisoner-of-war still clung to Freisler. But ultimately what tripped him up was not his

'Bolshevist' past – it was his brother. In the 1930s Oswald Freisler had moved his law practice from Kassel to Berlin. Though a member of the Nazi Party, and much to the annoyance of his brother Roland, he took on the defence of some Catholic lay brothers. ('Their money is as good as anybody's', he said.) When Hitler found out about Oswald Freisler's new clients, he ordered the attorney's immediate expulsion from the Party. Admittedly, the judicial authorities took no action against him until one day he took on the defence of a bank director and – in order to have important incriminating documents destroyed – bribed an employee of the state prosecution service. There was an immediate scandal. When, on 4 March 1939, the police appeared at Oswald Freisler's law office, the official story was that he asked if he could go the lavatory and then threw himself out of the window. But privately a different version began to circulate. He had not voluntarily jumped to his death. The Gestapo had a hand in it. Others said that Oswald Freisler, a diabetic, had taken an overdose of insulin that day. What is certain is that on 4 March 1939 Roland Freisler's brother, aged forty-three, died of unnatural causes.

The mysterious 'incident' contributed to Roland Freisler's failure to achieve the highest office of the Reich judiciary. The Nazis believed in *Sippenhaft*, the punishment of a family for the crime of one member.

The man who did become Minister of Justice was Dr Georg Thierack, previously President of the People's Court, and Himmler's preferred candidate. The passed-over Freisler, who now took over Thierack's former post, tried all the harder to raise his profile: '*Mein Führer*! I beg leave to report to you, *mein Führer*, that I have taken up the office that you have entrusted to me and have now mastered the brief. My thanks for the responsibility you have placed on me; I will be working loyally and with all my strength as a judge, following your example, for the security of the Reich and the internal unity of the German nation.'

The Führer had his reasons for choosing Freisler in particular to be President of the People's Court. His predecessor Thierack had opposed the appointment, but Hitler insisted. He needed a merciless enforcer: 'No, Freisler is going to succeed you,' he told Thierack; he is said to have added: 'It's the last chance I'm giving the old Bolshevik.'

The 'old Bolshevik' was absolutely obsessed with the idea that he had to prove himself. He must remove the distrust of the 'old campaigners' and show he was no less a Nazi than they. In 1942 Freisler took up the post in which, as a lawyer, he could most effectively serve the Nazi mania: he became President of the People's Court.

The People's Court offered the regime persecution and liquidation of any form of opposition; the men in power could rely on that. At its side operated a secret ally, the Gestapo: almost every case of treason that came before the People's Court had been prepared by the secret police. Its influence was so dominant that the People's Court effectively functioned as an extension of the Gestapo. Those arrested often spent many months in custody before trial, during which they were subjected to appalling maltreatment. Torture was common practice – especially in the last years of the war. The judges of the People's Court knew about this. Yet they seldom penalised violent interrogations, even when a defendant retracted his confession in court and claimed it had been extracted by the brutal methods of the Gestapo.

'Someone will have to be the bloodhound', as Freisler quoted Defence Minister Gustav Noske in a letter written shortly before his appointment as President of the People's Court. And Freisler longed to be that bloodhound.

Freisler had never belonged to the intimate circle of senior Party members. Like Speer and Ribbentrop he never succeeded in gaining the respect of the 'old campaigners'. Men like Freisler had no right to express an opinion; they had to listen, obey and carry out their assignments. Among the senior servants of the Third Reich the figure of Freisler was a compliant instrument. Shortly after his appointment the new president requested a meeting with the Führer, in order to report his commencement of duties in person. But the encounter was never to take place. Hitler expressed not the slightest interest in talking to Freisler. The man was to be a judge, enforcer, executioner – nothing else.

On the other hand, Joseph Goebbels stood up for the President of the People's Court: 'It is political expediency, not judicial criteria, that must determine the verdicts of the People's Court in wartime. If it proves politically necessary to remove a defendant, then he has to go, whether or not there is evidence or legal precedent for it.' With these words the propaganda minister addressed the judges of his People's Court, and Freisler was delighted.

In 1935, as permanent secretary in the justice ministry, he had declared to students in the hall of Kiel's Christian Albrecht University: 'Anyone prepared, if only in thought, to betray the Führer, is guilty of high treason; anyone who hesitates, in just a fraction of a thought, to face the Führer's enemies who seek to kill him, is a murderer.' What an attitude! At the time he had been laughed at as 'crazy'. Now the time for retribution had come. Roland Freisler wielded the scythe.

At first no high-profile cases landed on his desk – nothing with which the ambitious judge might have attracted Hitler's attention. For the most part the cases to be dealt with were 'petty' ones: 'defeatists', 'subverters of the armed forces', communists, members of the resistance. He punished them. But he was not satisfied with this routine dispensing of justice. Freisler wanted a grand show-trial. He would not give up until a defendant stood broken and weeping before him. At first his preferred victims were communists. By abusing them he distanced himself from his own past, from the suspicion of being a 'Red' himself.

He once presented himself to the defendant as a shining example of a 'convert', who had found the path to National Socialism – and to the Führer. The accused retorted: 'He's no Führer to me.' Encouraged by the judge's feigned frankness, he went on: 'Can't you see that the clock is at five minutes to twelve?' Freisler then snarled at him: 'We only need three minutes to hang you; so whatever happens you won't live to see twelve o'clock.' Freisler pronounced the death-sentence, stood up and left the court. But his much-loved Führer heard scarcely anything of his activities.

Weeks earlier, on 9 September 1942, Thierack had explained the significance of the People's Court to his successor in writing, with reference to examples: 'In the People's Court, more than in any other, it is apparent that the findings of this highest political court must accord with government thinking. In general the judge in the People's Court must become accustomed to regarding the ideas and intentions of government as primary, and the human destinies which depend on it, as secondary.' Telling that to Freisler was like carrying coals to Newcastle. For a long time he had felt himself in his element. 'Justice is whatever serves the nation.' What mattered was *Führer, Volk und Reich*. Whoever stood in his way would face the implacability of the court. In the struggle towards ultimate victory, even on the home front no verdict was too harsh.

For the erstwhile lieutenant, war was being waged at home as well as abroad. Anyone expressing doubts when faced with the millions of deaths on and behind the fronts, was a traitor to the nation. 'Blackout offences', 'undermining military morale', 'defeatism' – these were the cynical terms which countless thousands fell foul of. Only in a few cases was the death-sentence reduced to one of forced labour. Most of those executed had inadvertently and rashly expressed open criticism: of the Führer, of the armed forces, of the conduct of the war.

So it was that in August 1943 a postal clerk named Georg Jurkowski remarked to a woman: 'All I can say is, the *Duce* is under arrest, and the same thing'll happen to Hitler. By January he'll be dead.' Jurkowski was not, as it happened, opposed to National Socialism. Yet anyone who merely doubted the abilities of the Führer could pay for such opinions with his life. Jurkowski's fate was sealed by Freisler: 'As a subversive propagandist for our enemies, he will be punished by death.' A woman charged with 'undermining military morale', Ehrengard Frank-Schultz, was accused of having the 'audacity' to remark to a Red Cross nurse that a few years under Anglo-American rule would be better than 'the present tyranny'. Freisler's verdict was that her words brought her eternal dishonour and punishment by death.

A ministerial department head named Vollmer drew up a whole catalogue of statements that were 'no longer tolerable and therefore punishable by death'. These included remarks such as 'the war is lost', 'Germany or the Führer has pointlessly or irresponsibly unleashed the war', 'infiltration by Bolshevism would be no bad thing'. Even the perfunctory statement 'the Führer is ill', could be fatal. No, there was no lack of pretexts for the vast number of executions.

Whether the words were uttered in private or in public was irrelevant. The Reich court declared that expressions of opinion in any venue where other guests were present, were to be regarded as public.

In some cases the arbitrary will of the People's Judge went too far even for the Reich Ministry of Justice. A chance remark about the Führer, which a defendant had made to a friend, was declared 'public' by the People's Court, since 'our National Socialist Reich requires every *Volksgenosse* ("national partner") to concern himself with politics and, for that reason, whatever political view is expressed forms part of the nation's fund of political ideas'. The justice minister, Thierack, warned Freisler in a letter of September 1943 that with reasoning like that the 'concept of what is public loses all meaning'. Such timid objections were of little help to the defendant. Freisler had him executed anyway.

The President of the People's Court actually accelerated the pace. The greatest acts of terror were about to begin.

> I am fully aware of the fact that I administer justice in a one-sided way, but I do this for a political purpose. I have to prevent, with all the strength at my disposal, a repetition of the events of 1918.
>
> *Freisler, October 1943*

'Fellow students. It is with horror that our nation looks on the fate of the men of Stalingrad. The brilliant strategy of the world war corporal has senselessly and recklessly driven 330,000 German soldiers to their destruction. Führer, we have you to thank for this. The German people are seething. Are we to go on placing the fate of our German army in the hands of a rank amateur?'

The words of the last leaflet distributed in Munich by a brother and sister, Hans and Sophie Scholl, were, in Freisler's eyes, more than subversion and treason. Seldom had anyone held up such an unflattering mirror to the regime.

The trial of the 'White Rose' group at last gave Freisler his longed-for opportunity to take centre stage in full voice before a national audience. The White Rose, a resistance organisation made up of students, artists, academics and clergy had for a long time been a thorn in the Gestapo's side. On 18 February the janitor at Munich University had observed the Scholls distributing leaflets and had reported them. Following their arrest, other members were taken into custody, among them Christoph Probst, Willi Graf, Alexander Schmorell and Professor Huber.

The trial began in Munich on 22 February 1943. Roland Freisler was in the chair. As usual, the defendants and their counsel were given no time to prepare their case.

In contrast to his normally hysterical behaviour, Freisler kept his temperament largely in check throughout the trial. 'You spun the Gestapo a fine old yarn, and you would have got away with it by a whisker. But', Freisler went on with a triumphant smile at Willi Graf, 'we're just a bit cleverer than you!' Four days later the 'proceedings' had been concluded. Christoph Probst had tried, for the sake of his children, to come out of it alive. Hans Scholl wanted to put in a word for his friend, but he was interrupted by Freisler: 'If you have nothing to say on your own behalf, kindly keep quiet.'

Sophie Scholl withstood the fiendish hostility of the red-robed thug and challenged him with the words: 'You know as well as I do that the war is lost. Why don't you admit it?' However, the fate of the members of the White Rose had long since been sealed. Sophie Scholl was the first to be led to her execution. She went to her death calmly and with dignity, as the hangman himself later admitted. 'Long live freedom!' Hans Scholl shouted before he mounted the scaffold.

If such actions were to be punished other than by death, it would start a chain of events that would end in the same way as in 1918. That is why there was only one just penalty the People's Court could impose to protect the people and the Reich in their struggle – the death-penalty . . . By their treason against our nation the accused have forfeited their civil rights for ever.

Freisler sentencing the White Rose resistance group, 1943

He completely dominated the scene, because in the courtroom he held all the power.

Franz Müller, White Rose resistance fighter

With ruthless harshness the People's Court now passed one death-penalty after another. Freisler himself was lusting for blood. In an 'activity report', which he proudly sent to the Reich Minister of Justice twice a year, he presented the horrific balance-sheet of his 'proceedings': in the first six months of 1943 alone, 804 death-sentences were carried out. This total concealed the true extent of the arbitrariness of the measure taken against the 'instances of subversion among the population', as they were described by the Central Office of Reich Security. In countless cases the accused were denied any legal hearing at all. The 'People's Judge' despatched those under suspicion straight to a concentration camp.

For this procedure the wordsmiths of the Nazi judiciary had a euphemism at the ready: in December 1941 Hitler had issued the so-called 'Night and Fog Decree', which sanctioned the death-penalty for anyone involved in an act of terrorism or sabotage against the regime. The perpetrators were to be picked up under cover of 'night and fog', shipped off and killed – a decree very much to Freisler's taste. In the dispute over the judicial responsibility for these procedures he pointed out officiously that the People's Court was probably the best organ to hear and pass sentence in 'night and fog' cases. And so it got the job.

By the end of 1942 over 1,000 such cases were recorded. Without exception it was now the rule that death sentences were pronounced. No friend or relative was informed, no farewell letter ever reached its addressee. No family found out about what was treated as a 'secret Reich matter'. Everyone dragged off in the 'night and fog' was dead within 24 hours.

Just as the 'Night and Fog Decree' also applied to 'enemies' in the occupied areas of northern and western Europe, so did Freislser now sniff out 'defeatists' throughout the Reich. The proceedings of the court became ever more merciless and ineluctable. Whether a defence counsel would be allowed to plead at all was increasingly left to the judge's discretion. After the end of 1942 those sentenced to death were even denied the comfort of a priest. The defendant was now nothing more than a defenceless cipher.

The disaster into which the German Reich was relentlessly descending appeared to have no impact on Freisler. Like Hitler, he retreated more and more into himself, became more and more self-centred. Even before a trial began at all, he offered the other judges on the bench his view of the case. His fellow-judges were thus reduced to having a walk-on part, denied from the outset any opportunity to object. The way in which the phoney trial then proceeded was largely a question of how the defendant reacted to the charges against him. If he attempted to dispute the evidence, which happened rarely enough, he was subjected to a torrent of abuse, mockery and screaming tirades of hatred. Only a few defendants succeeded, often after long weeks of torture and sleep-deprivation, in facing up to the red-robed demon. One such was the anti-Hitler resister, Count Fritz-Dietlof von der Schulenburg, whom Freisler screamed at as '*Schurke* (villain) *Schulenburg*' throughout his trial for complicity in the 20 July Plot to kill Hitler. When the judge, by a slip of the tongue, addressed him once by his title, *Graf* von der Schulenburg, the defendant ironically corrected him: '*Schurke Schulenburg*, if you don't mind.' Equal courage was shown by the Catholic lawyer, Josef Wirmer. 'If I hang, it is not I who should be afraid, but you!' he retorted to Freisler, who snarled back furiously: 'You will soon be in hell!' To which Wirmer replied: 'I'll be delighted if you soon follow, *Herr Präsident*.'

It is not a matter of dispensing justice but of destroying the opponents of National Socialism.

The task of cleansing is performed with the exactitude of precision machinery.

Freisler

Freisler's penetrating stare left the state prosecution service in no doubt as to the severity of the sentence he demanded. And nearly always the 'representative of the state' met his expectations. It was a barbaric justice meted out in the name of the people.

It was not only a war against the whole world, but every individual death sentence that contributed to a nation's struggle to survive. Woe to him who suicidally questioned that feeling of 'togetherness'. The opponents of the regime were arrested, murdered, or fled into exile – or else awaited their death in a concentration camp. The 'self-purification of the nation' which Freisler so ardently promoted, went on functioning until the bitter end.

The language of the judiciary, which did not permit any true justice but simply gave expression to a purely arbitrary will to destroy, did not find exclusive justification in the demonic nature of the 'hanging judge'. This was not just the blind fury of an individual, it was the language of a tyrannical regime, with Freisler at the summit of its judicial branch.

Roland Freisler was a paragon of industriousness, marital virtue, ostensibly bourgeois propriety and party-political discipline. He even had courage of a kind: he never used any air-raid shelter other than the primitive cellar in Bellevuestrasse, where all the staff of the court took cover when the sirens sounded. Yet he waited for the day when his name would go into the history books. At last his great moment came.

With the attempted coup of 20 July 1944, the military resistance group around Colonel Claus Schenk, Count von Stauffenberg, planned to remove the dictator and thus put an end to the Nazi madness. Yet they failed in their objective. Adolf Hitler survived and the same evening addressed the German people in a radio broadcast: 'A very small clique of ambitious, ruthless and at the same time criminal and stupid officers hatched a plot to remove me and along with me wipe out practically the entire senior staff of the German armed forces.'

These 'officers without honour' were tragic, misjudged heroes without support, who were not borne along by the mood of the people, but only by a sense of duty. They were isolated plotters, who not only wanted to save their own honour, but also the honour of a nation of Nazi fellow-travellers. Most of these patriots wanted a peace that would have left the Reich they held sacred, at least partly intact. But by now that Reich was neither whole nor holy. For even the Wehrmacht was too deeply implicated in the Holocaust, too many murders tainted Germany's name. As Henning von Tresckow, the chief plotter, stated, the only thing that mattered was for the German resistance to risk everything on one throw, in order to face the judgement of history.

The question has often been asked, whether it would actually have served any purpose had the bomb placed under the map-table blown

Hitler to pieces. Germany's unconditional surrender was surely already a foregone conclusion. Just as was the break-up of the Reich into occupation-zones, the brutal amputation of eastern Germany and the expulsion of its people. All this was certain, of course. Nevertheless, the war would have been brought to an end – either by a provisional government led by Goerdeler, or by a military regime. Then millions of soldiers on the European fronts would not have had to die; hundreds of thousands of Jews would not have been sent to the gas chambers; beautiful cities like Würzburg, Dresden, Breslau and Königsberg would not have been destroyed. The successful assassination of Hitler would have made sense.

As it was, the killing went on – and the conspirators were not spared. Hitler wanted to see blood: 'This time I'll deal with them in short order. These criminals are not to go before a court-martial, they'll be tried by the People's Court. They won't be allowed to say much for themselves. And within two hours of the passing of sentence, they must be executed. They must be hanged immediately, without any mercy.'

The criminal evidence against them was clearly to hand. The perpetrators had confessed. Any court-martial would have been able to condemn the principal defendants to death. It would not have required confessions. And since for political reasons Hitler himself had at the outset given the directive that the circle of conspirators should be defined as narrowly as possible, it seemed superfluous to attract a lot of public attention by inventing a far-reaching plot. But that was precisely what Freisler failed to grasp. He simply did not understand what was required: namely to keep the lid firmly on the affair. All he saw was the chance to prove himself. Throughout the whole trial he was mainly thinking of himself.

'These criminals . . . are not to be given the honour of the bullet, they're to be hanged like common traitors!' Hitler ordained. 'A court of honour is to expel them from the Wehrmacht, then they can be put on trial as civilians . . . And the most important thing is that they're not given time to make long speeches. But Freisler will see to that.'

At last Freisler had achieved what he had always dreamed of: he was Hitler's personal enforcer. At last he would no longer be dealing with anonymous 'defeatists'. Before him stood men he could make an example of. Bringing them to trial, forcing them to their knees – this was his moment of triumph. He had some high-powered support: 'The criminal trial which now has to be completed, must be of historical proportions', demanded the propaganda minister, Goebbels.

Freisler will see to it. He's our Vishinsky.

Hitler, 1944

That cheap play-actor can single-handedly turn incompetents into revolutionaries and even make martyrs of failed assassins – just by the absurd way he runs his trials.

Ernst Kaltenbrunner, head of the Central Office of Reich Security

A spectacular show-trial would have been just what 'Raving Roland' liked. And the tribunal was to be preserved for posterity. Freisler did everything necessary to document it.

Hidden cameras, which were concealed behind the swastika banner above the judges' podium, recorded every detail of the macabre drama. Freisler could set them in motion by banging his gavel. As soon as the cameras were running, he subjected the defendants to coarse bellowing in order to capture their total humiliation on film for posterity and especially for his Führer. But what was intended as a carefully staged propaganda spectacle was a failure. Most of the films would later be kept well out of sight. For even a careful selection of footage produced precisely the opposite effect to what was intended. In the face of the judge's frenzied ravings, the upright dignity of his victims was all the more apparent.

We had to tell Freisler that he was shouting too loudly at the defendants, so that the sound-engineer wasn't able to get a good balance between his shrieking and the quiet voice of the defendant.

Erich Stoll, cameraman at the trial of the 20 July plotters

'Two weeks after the event the People's Court is proceeding against eight traitors expelled from the army, who played a leading part in the crime of 20 July!' The newsreel that started with those words was never shown in German cinemas. The Ministry of Propaganda feared a 'disagreeable discussion' about Freisler's conduct of the case. Himmler himself had advised against giving the trial too much publicity. 'You're right, Himmler', Hitler finally agreed. 'If I publicise the trial, I'll also have to let the blighters have their say. Suppose one of them is a good speaker; he might present himself as bringing peace to the German people. That could be dangerous.'

On 7 August 1944, after the first eight accused had been forced to let Freisler's storms of invective sweep over them, an avalanche of further trials rolled into motion. Gestapo and judiciary worked hand in hand and for month after month dragged real and presumed resistance fighters before Freisler's bench. Family members, acquaintances, tenants, no-one who had admitted having had contact with the resisters was safe from persecution.

Henning von Tresckow's children were separated from their mother and taken to a children's home. 'There the name-tapes were cut out of their little shirts,' Tresckow's secretary recalls. A few courageous wives tried to save their husbands' lives. Emmi Bonhoeffer, whose husband Klaus was finally executed on 23 April 1945 after being sentenced by Freisler, later recounted how, shortly after his arrest, she went to see Freisler and told him that her husband's statements were not to be taken seriously, since they had been extracted under torture. Freisler played the innocent: 'What gives you that idea?' – 'I collected his laundry; it was covered in blood!' Whereupon Freisler flipped through his papers and remarked laconically: 'Ah yes, it says here: more intensive interrogation.'

In principle, those conspirators who were in the Wehrmacht should have been tried before a court-martial. However, in the final years of the war, Hitler placed less and less trust in courts-martial, and had the officers arraigned before the People's Court. He summoned a 'court of honour', a shadowy tribunal chaired by his loyal lackey Wilhelm Keitel, Chief-of-Staff of the Wehrmacht. The 'court of honour' expelled the suspects from the Wehrmacht and left them, to the tender mercies of that court in which the Goddess of Justice was indeed completely blind.

Freisler's penetrating voice opened the proceedings: 'This indictment is the most terrible ever to have been brought in the history of the German people. For you will hear of deeds of such heinous treachery that anything ever committed by anyone in their life before pales in comparison. Should it be established that you have committed such deeds, it is unlikely that your life up to that point will be of any interest whatever to us.'

In the very first minutes of the proceedings Freisler took the opportunity to make it clear to the accused that nothing they might say would have the slightest influence on the outcome of the trial. Any attempt to escape their fate was doomed to failure.

After the President had called on the Chief State Prosecutor to read the charges against *Generalfeldmarschall* Erwin von Witzleben, who until 1942 had commanded the German forces in France, Witzleben stepped up before Freisler. In his desperation and fear of death, he raised his right arm in the Nazi 'German salute'.

Freisler reprimanded him: 'You are Erwin von Witzleben. If I were you I would no longer use the German salute. The German salute is used by *Volksgenossen* who are men of honour. In your position I would be ashamed to use the German Salute.'

It gave him obvious pleasure to humiliate the one-time hero of the German Wehrmacht. The *Generalfeldmarschall* was forced to hold up his trousers, since his belt and braces had been taken away from him. Freisler hissed at him: 'You dirty old man. Why do you keep fumbling around in your trousers?'

He addressed General Erich Hoepner with the words: 'In 1938 you were the general commanding the Panzer Corps. What zoological characteristics would you consider appropriate to show the court what you have done? For as regards your intellect you are an ass, and as to your character you are a *Schweinehund*.'

But Freisler's plan did not work out. Ernst Kaltenbrunner, the head of the Central Office of Reich Security, was beside himself with fury at the end of the first day of the hearing and shouted: 'That cheap play-actor can single-handedly turn incompetents into revolutionaries and even make martyrs of failed assassins – just by the absurd way he runs his trials.'

The Nazi leadership had hoped for a settling of scores, which would nonetheless be kept within bounds. But in this they were mistaken. With his hysterical outbursts Freisler merely revealed his inability to match his own ideal of emotionless and soulless killing. What is more, he was going against the directives of Hitler, who had spoken in his address to the nation of a 'small clique'. But by his conduct of the trial he conjured up a much more extensive plot. Thus he unwittingly increased the significance of the anti-Hitler resistance. But he could not see that. He saw only his chance to make a big impact.

> The impression we had of Freisler was of a power-crazed sadist, for it gave him an inordinate feeling of pleasure to see men trembling with fear and to condemn them to death. It is impossible to identify with the motivation of a psychopath like that.
>
> *Otto Gritschneder, attorney*
>
> Freisler's bellowing is not appropriate for propaganda. It would tend to have an offputting effect on the uncommitted.
>
> *Goebbels*

In these trials the upstart gave free rein to his hatred for the old Germany, and for those bearers of illustrious names who now stood powerless before him. Freisler performed for the camera, which was mainly there to record the legal proceedings. All those present except the judge were supposed to be mere props. But they were not that at all. In spite of all the torture and duress, the defendants were not will-less walk-ons, and nor were the selected spectators who followed Freisler's affected posing and sarcastic remarks with impassive and sometimes uncomprehending expressions. But the audience in the courtroom, alas, did not show the appropriate reaction for a propaganda film.

When completed, the film ran to a total of about 150,000 feet. It was cut by the Ministry of Propaganda to 45,000 feet and was only shown to carefully selected Nazi organisations and Gauleiters. Of what use were the harangues of the President, which according to the court record went on four times as long as all the speeches of the accused, the prosecution and the defence put together? The film footage, which was actually meant to show a triumphant Freisler, demonstrated instead the steadfastness of the accused.

Count Peter Yorck von Wartenburg: '*Herr Präsident*, in my interrogation I have already stated that the way in which National Socialist ideology developed . . .'

Freisler interrupts: '. . .was not to your liking! To put it in concrete terms, you told Stauffenberg that in the Jewish question you did not agree with the extermination of the Jews, you did not agree with the National Socialist concept of justice.'

Von Wartenburg: 'The essential thing, which links all these questions, is the state's claim to total authority over the citizen, with no regard to his religious and moral obligations towards God.'

Freisler had been hoping for stammered confessions. But the accused maintained their composure. Scarcely a single defendant broke down under the verbal blows which rained down on them from Freisler.

Count Ulrich Wilhelm Schwerin von Schwanenfeld: 'I have had first-hand experience of the constantly changing attitude towards the Poles.'

Freisler (interrupting): 'And you accused National Socialism of constantly changing its mind.'

Count Schwerin: 'Yes, and of murders. Both at home and abroad . . .'

Freisler: 'Murders? You're a miserable crook. Don't you break down under the weight of your own nastiness? Yes or no? Doesn't it break you down?'

Count Schwerin: '*Herr Präsident*!'

Freisler: 'Yes or no? Just give me a clear answer!'

Count Schwerin: 'No!'

'Do you not see that you are guilty?' Freisler asked Count Helmuth James von Moltke.

You cannot be any more broken-down than you already are, you're just a pathetic little heap that no longer even has any respect for itself.

Freisler to Count Schwerin

'No', he said.

'Why did you oppose the Führer?' Freisler asked the young Hans Bernd von Haeften, a counsellor at the Foreign Ministry.

'Because I see in Hitler the embodiment of everything evil', the defendant replied.

'No, I do not feel that I am guilty', declared *Oberstleutnant* Caesar von Hofacker,' I acted with the same right as that which Hitler claimed on 9 November 1923.'*

'What do you mean: with the same right? That is outrageous. I will not listen to such nonsense!'

As expected, in his closing words the Chief State Prosecutor, Lautz, demanded sentences of death for all the accused. He phrased this without emotion. The remarks of the defence counsel were no more than marginalia. The counsel for *Generalfeldmarschall* von Witzleben, who had been obliged to take on the case, stated in his perfunctory winding-up: 'The act of the defendant stands as fact, and the guilty perpetrator falls with it.' Afterwards, three of the condemned men, Klausing, Bernardi and Stieff, were able to make brief statements. They asked for their sentences to be carried out by shooting. The following day the other members of the inner group of conspirators – with the exception of Yorck von Wartenburg – made the same request. But even before pronouncing sentence Freisler refused them their wish. They were to be hanged.

The sentences were carried out the same day. With their hands tied behind their backs, the men who tried to assassinate Hitler were taken to the execution-room in Berlin's Plötzensee gaol and there, one after the other, they were hanged in the most horrific way with piano-wires from meat-hooks. The executioners were following Hitler's instructions that 'they are to hang like slaughtered animals'.

The death-throes of the condemned men were filmed – at the Führer's personal request. The last agonising moments of the conspirators of 20 July were recorded for a man whose pathological depravity was such that he had the film shown to him several times.

In the reports of the Security Service from all over the Reich Ernst Kaltenbrunner did admittedly state that Freisler's conduct of the trials had impressed large numbers of the population: 'In large

---

* ie the right to overthrow an illegal state.

sections of the working class, the sharp, sometimes ironic and extremely quick-witted style of the president was noted with delight and satisfaction. The criticism which the president heaped on the criminal plans of the accused echoed absolutely the outrage of the population at this base crime.' Yet that was only one side. Kaltenbrunner had to admit that there were also many critical voices. The 'cheap way' in which the president insulted and ridiculed the defendants 'did not fully conform with the dignity of Germany's highest court of law'. He went on: 'In particular, quite a number of opinions were recorded in which there were complaints about the fact that the president allowed himself to get into a debate with the defendant Hoepner as to whether the term "ass" or "*Schweinehund*" was the appropriate description of him.

'Others commented that some of the defendants were personalities who, on account of their great ability in the service of this same National Socialist state, had achieved the highest honours and decorations. It was surely strange that these men, who not long ago had been promoted by the Führer himself and whose actions had been celebrated in the press as deeds of heroism, were now being presented as stupid, demented and indecisive. There must therefore be doubts about the personnel policy at the highest level, since those men had been left for years in important senior positions.'

The fact that Kaltenbrunner's reports were largely cosmetic is no surprise since they went to Martin Bormann and via him to Adolf Hitler. The latter was highly satisfied with the result. Had he not himself insisted that on no account was any mitigation to be granted to the accused? Was it not he who had demanded the severest sentence, the death of the traitors? Freisler had done the job that Hitler had instructed him to do. The hanging judge was the man of the moment.

The trials were not yet at an end. After the rooting out of the military resistance movement, civilians and men in political circles were brought before Freisler's tribunal.

Carl Goerdeler, the former mayor of Leipzig, was forced to wait until 7 September 1944 for his 'trial'. Once Hitler had been removed, the resisters had intended to rely on Goerdeler's talent for organisation. He had already worked out the speeches for radio, with which he would inform the public of the successful coup d'état and the future planned for Germany. With him in the dock were two other active opponents of Nazism, Wilhelm Leuschner, a union leader, and Ulrich von Hassell, the former German ambassador to Rome, who had dreamed in his diary of 'the other Germany'. Now the resisters were to suffer the wrath of the 'present Germany'.

. . . The hearing lasts perhaps one or two hours, it is hard to tell, the time flies by, you feel your heart beating, and ever more clearly the shadow of death descends over Julius Leber.*

Paul Sethe, journalist

You are the Lenin of the German labour movement.

Freisler to Julius Leber

After interminable haranguing, crudeness and insults there followed – it was hardly expected to be otherwise – the death sentence for high treason, defeatism, subversion of the armed forces, and acting to the advantage of the enemy. Freisler's excesses now went too far even for the Reich Minister of Justice, Dr Thierack. True, his concern was not humanitarian, merely for 'the interests of the case'. He complained in a letter to Hitler's secretary, Martin Bormann: 'The conduct of the trial by the president was, in the case of the defendant Goerdeler, unobjectionable and factual. But he would not let Leuschner and von Hassell have their say. He shouted them down repeatedly. This made a thoroughly bad impression, particularly as the president had allowed some 300 persons in to witness the proceedings. Which persons received admission tickets is something still to be checked. That kind of behaviour in such sessions is very questionable. Otherwise, the political conduct of the trial did not give cause for complaint. Unfortunately, however, Freisler addressed Goerdeler like a halfwit and spoke as though he were a complete

---

* Julius Leber (1891–1945) was a Social Democrat member of the Reichstag from 1924 to 1933 and his party's defence spokesman. During the war he joined the anti-Nazi Kreisau Circle. Arrested in 1944, shortly before the 20 July attempt on Hitler's life, he was tried and executed in January 1945. Had Hitler been assassinated, Leber would have been a senior minister, possibly Chancellor, in the proposed new government.

nonentity. The serious nature of this important gathering was gravely damaged by this. Frequent long speeches by the president, whose purpose was purely for propaganda, had a repugnant effect on this audience. Equal damage was done to the seriousness and dignity of the court. The president is completely lacking in cool, restrained detachment.'

Together with other defendants, von Hassell was executed the same day, but Leuschner had to suffer a twenty-day martyrdom in a concentration camp before being murdered. Carl Goerdeler had to bear the heaviest burden. Because it was hoped that he would provide further information about the structure of the resistance groups, his execution was delayed. Not until February 1945, when the Germany for which he had fought had long since been reduced to rubble, was Goerdeler put to death.

While the fronts moved ever closer to Berlin, the murderous machinery of Freisler's People's Court continued to run at high speed. It produced one death sentence after another. Freisler's fanaticism seemed to have lost all sense of proportion. The war which had begun as a Blitzkrieg, with lightning attacks and conquests, then moved to a phase of 'decisive battles', and finally, from 1944 onwards, became a last struggle for survival which was bound to end in Germany's destruction. But the more desperate the situation became, the more hysterically the court demanded the loyalty of the *Volksgenossen*. In all this, Freisler's real enemy was the truth, and in order to suppress it, the 'un-shakeably strong and total belief' in a sense of historic heroism and homeland had to be lauded relentlessly. It seemed as though Freisler were refusing to accept the imminent end, as though it were spurring him on to one more bloody campaign of revenge against all those he believed were responsible for the approaching nemesis.

On the afternoon of 11 September 1944 the first US soldiers were standing on German soil, near Trier. The Führer's decree of 25 September called up the last brigade: the *Volkssturm*. All men aged between sixteen and sixty, who were 'capable of bearing arms', but who had been spared from military service up to now, were drafted. Nothing could have made it clearer to the Allies that the Wehrmacht was shattered beyond recall. Hitler himself scarcely appeared in public any more. From January 1945, the man who called himself 'Wolf' buried himself alone in his bunker underneath the Reich Chancellery in Berlin and, long since marked by illness and dementia, awaited a miraculous change of fortune in the war.

Freisler, however, was still fighting his own battle. Despite the chaotic wartime situation, he retained his manic dedication to work, remained the driving force of a ruthless and unbridled assault on humanity. For him there was no question but that 'holding the internal front' demanded a still more unbending administration of justice. Indeed, hand in hand with the deterioration of the military situation went a relentless ratcheting up of the sentences. Thus it was no longer 'worth the trouble' to investigate cases of 'subversion of the armed forces' at all: the death sentence was imposed indiscriminately. The military situation, Freisler claimed, required trials to be swiftly concluded and the sentences carried out with consistency. Almost daily, blood-red posters throughout the Reich announced death sentences 'in the name of the people'. And even after the death of its victims, the People's Court did not rest. In contrast to previous practice, the bodies of those executed were no longer handed over to the relatives, but were burnt or presented to university medical faculties.

In the last autumn of the war the dream of the 'Thousand Year Reich' began to collapse in rubble and ashes. But Freisler was one of those who still – ignoring any inner doubts – stood uncompromisingly behind Hitler. On 26 October 1944 he wrote: 'In one's innermost self one has to admit that it is no longer impossible that Germany might lose the war. The reprisal weapons [the VI and V2] have not brought the success so passionately hoped for. But we must hold out, at whatever cost; the longer we hold our ground, the sooner this unnatural alliance between the Anglo-Americans and the Soviets will break down. When I look at all that has happened over the last few years, I feel compelled to abandon my belief in a worldwide Jewish conspiracy. That belief is too simple a view. All Germans are now in the same boat; we must all row with the same stroke in order to achieve victory or, if the worst should happen, to guarantee that Germany will rise again in her final, greatest triumph.' Freisler's faith in National Socialism was still unbroken.

The tentacles of Nazi justice continued to reach out for members of the resistance. On 9 January 1945 the trial began of Count Helmuth James von Moltke, Father Alfred Delp and other members of the anti-Nazi 'Kreisau Circle'. It was typified by a scene in the 'proceedings' against Count von Moltke. At one point, when reference to the Criminal Code had to be made, not a single copy of the book could be found in the building.

> Freisler bawled at the court: National Socialism will last for ever, or else it will fall fighting to the last man, the last woman and the last child.
>
> *Eugen Gerstenmaier, member of the anti-Nazi resistance*

'Roland Freisler's defendants are the playthings of his intellect,' a woman who attended the trial of the Kreisau Circle remembers of Freisler's behaviour. 'He juggles with people's lives and provides the unexpected twist, the lighting and colour he needs in order to turn something unimportant into an impressive piece of theatre, to present the tragedy that he has already planned.'

Only rarely, according to his mood and inclination, did he allow his judicial 'clemency' to spare a defendant. 'Seven years, Brigitte my dear!' Countess Freya von Moltke shouted over to Brigitte Gerstenmeier after sentence had been passed on their husbands. In fact, the seven years only applied to Eugen Gerstenmeier. But Freya von Moltke still managed to make her voice sound cheerful. Her own husband had just been condemned to death.

> That pitiful creature Freisler: he could never begin to understand how little he can take away from us!
>
> *Count Helmuth James von Moltke in a letter to his wife*

It was to be less than a month before sentence was handed down in Freisler's own case. On 3 February 1945 he was presiding over the trial of another resister, Fabian von Schlabrendorff, who was to appear as the fifth in a series of 'one-day cases' and receive his sentence. Just before 9 a.m. the air-raid sirens began to wail; everyone in the courtroom made a dash for the shelter. Schlabrendorff was standing near his judge when the latter met his end. Still clutched under

Freisler's arm was a file, the Schlabrendorff file, which would have meant his certain execution. Schlabrendorff survived, but Freisler died, along with 20,000 others, in the midst of one of Berlin's heaviest air raids. Scarcely a single person could be found who really mourned the end of the bloodthirsty judge.

Not even the Minister of Justice turned up for Freisler's funeral. Without a memorial stone of his own, Roland Freisler was hidden in his wife's family tomb. After the war she and her children changed their name and to this day claim to have had nothing to do with him.

Today the name of Roland Freisler stands as a symbol of the crimes which went by the name of justice during the Nazi regime. The verdict of the military court at Nuremberg had called him 'the blackest, most brutal and bloodiest judge in the entire German administration of justice', and listed him along with Heinrich Himmler and Reinhard Heydrich as the men who were among the most 'loathsome' individuals the world has ever seen.

Yet Freisler was a symptom rather than the cause of state-sponsored terror. The regular courts, special courts and courts-martial had also passed death sentences 'in the name of the people'. A people which, by the end of the war, was also being oppressed by the crimes of 'justice'. Of the 258 judges and state prosecutors of the People's Court, 95 were re-employed in the judicial system of the Federal Republic. That is more than one in three.

As late as the 1960s the name of Freisler was still appearing in the press. Marion Russegger, as Freisler's widow now called herself, had initiated proceedings about her pension payments. And she won her case. The Munich social service office granted her a sum of DM400 a month in addition to her pension as a war victim – this was compensation, so the ruling explained. After all, had Freisler not died as the Allied bombs rained down, he could have earned his living in postwar Germany as 'a lawyer or a higher civil servant'.

Under a judicial ruling of the Federal Republic the widows of the men of 20 July received no pension as war victims. Margot Diestel, one of the handful of Freisler's victims who survived, received a one-off payment of just DM920.

CHAPTER SIX

THE DOCTOR OF DEATH

JOSEF MENGELE

On my mother's life, I swear I have never done any harm to anyone.

There are two gifted peoples in the world: the Germans and the Jews. One of these two peoples must dominate the world.

I just had to carry out orders, otherwise they would have shoved me into Auschwitz with the others.

I did not personally kill, injure or physically harm anyone.

The main task of the SS doctor is to filter out those who want to dodge work by choosing to die.

I helped many of the sick in the camp, but nothing is ever reported about the good things I did.

There are no judges, only avengers.

Objectively, none of this affects me much, any more than the rest of the assorted dirt that has been dug up about me over the years.

I've been thinking back over the last three decades: 1939–1949–1959–1969. The comparison is depressing.

Sacred Fatherland, you make things very hard for many of
your sons. But we shall not abandon you; we shall love you
for ever and ever.

Josef Mengele

My father had always been the Josef Mengele who died a
heroic death on the Eastern Front. He was the man of
culture, well-versed in Greek and Latin. But now he was the
Doctor of Auschwitz. That had a very severe effect on me. It
wasn't such a good thing to be the son of Josef Mengele.

Rolf Mengele

How could Mengele, one man on his own, have killed so
many? In reality he saved a number of people's lives in
Auschwitz . . . Mengele did not do the things he is accused
of. He was there to select those who were to live and those
who were to die. Did he not do that in order to save lives?

Ewald Krug, German-Paraguayan Nazi

He had everything going for him. There were so many
opportunities open to him. That's one of things I find so hard,
the fact that he squandered those opportunities. Threw his life
away.

Rolf Mengele

The army doctor at the Front also has to carry out a selection
process, because he decides on the priority of the operations
to be performed and thus on whether a wounded man will
live or die. In Auschwitz selection is done in order to separate
out those capable of work.

Mengele

A highly intelligent and cultivated cynic.
       Ella Lingens, prisoner-doctor in Auschwitz-Birkenau

My first impression of Mengele was of a good-looking, courteous
man who addressed me formally and asked me to take a seat.
       Vera Alexander, prisoner-nurse in Auschwitz

Of all the SS-men I got to know in Auschwitz, he was far and away the most human. None of the others could even be described as responsible individuals. They were nothing more than followers of orders, who salved their consciences with the thought that in Auschwitz they had to do their duty for *Volk* and Fatherland.

Hans Münch, Auschwitz doctor, acquitted in 1947

With Mengele you had the feeling that the National Socialist ideal was extremely important to him. What mattered to him was power and job-performance. Nothing else was of any interest.

Ella Lingens, prisoner-doctor in Auschwitz

Every task he was given he carried out, often under the most difficult conditions, with prudence, stamina and energy to the fullest satisfaction of his superiors, and he showed himself equal to any situation. Furthermore, as an anthropologist he was most keen to make use of such free time as he had left, to improve his knowledge and, using the scientific material available to him by virtue of his position, he made a valuable contribution to anthropological science.

Eduard Wirths, Resident Medical Officer, Auschwitz

It is necessary that in the event of war every country has an institution in which to hold elements representing a danger to the nation: foreigners suspected of being saboteurs, worthless individuals prepared to commit espionage, prostitutes, gypsies and professional criminals.

Mengele

It depresses me to think that a man who believed he was using science for the benefit of mankind, was dedicated to a science which led to the destruction of human beings.

Heinrich von Verschuer, son of the racial geneticist, Otmar von Verschuer

Mengele was extremely ambitious. He was anti-Semitic and did not disguise it.

Hermann Langbein, clerk to the Resident Medical Officer,
Auschwitz

During my period of service I received a number of transfers and commands without ever being asked whether I agreed to them. And when I received my final posting, just as I had finished a spell of duty, I had no idea where I was heading, nor to which new unit . . .

Mengele

*

For one Auschwitz survivor, the search for the Doctor of Auschwitz had become his life's mission. At last Alex Dekel believed he was within reach of his goal. A highly placed Israeli secret service man had promised to tell Dekel everything Mossad knew about the long flight from justice of the concentration camp doctor, Josef Mengele. Auschwitz came back to him again, but, in truth, Auschwitz had always been with him.

'Sometimes I felt that his memories of Auschwitz were more real to him than his actual life was', Dekel's wife Sheila recalls. '"Live in the present", I used to beg him. "Get that tattoo removed from your arm. It makes you perpetually think of the past."'

'I'd rather have my arm cut off', her husband had replied. All his life, Auschwitz would never let Dekel rest. And to him the horror of Auschwitz was personified by the camp doctor, Josef Mengele. Dekel could not and would not accept the fact that the doctor had avoided answering for his crimes by fleeing to South America. As archivist of the Israeli consulate in New York, the concentration camp survivor collected every bit of information about Mengele, no matter how small. Anyone who could provide any clue was welcome in his house. In 1976 he persuaded the editors of *Time* magazine that in the interests of justice Mengele must at all costs be found. The magazine financed him in his research. In Polish archives Dekel uncovered new proof of Mengele's hideous activities in Auschwitz. He himself had experienced and suffered them at first hand. On the unloading ramp at Auschwitz-Birkenau the doctor had sent his mother to the gas chamber. He himself was waved by Mengele into the queue of those who were not to be killed immediately. But the Auschwitz doctor made his childhood a living hell. Alex Dekel was thirteen years old when he was deported to Auschwitz in 1943.

Four decades later, one day in June 1983, he was hoping finally to receive the crucial clue to Mengele's whereabouts. Excitedly Dekel set off for New York's Kennedy airport. It was there that an agent of Mossad, Israel's secret service, wanted to meet him. When he returned home later, he was extremely angry and bewildered. His wife could get nothing out of him about the encounter with the secret agent on which Dekel had built all his hopes. His left arm was giving him pain. His wife urged him to go to hospital. But he refused. 'He always believed he was immune to the ravages of time and fate – after Auschwitz, what could possibly happen to him?' Sheila Dekel remembers. Alex Dekel had suffered a severe stroke. It was followed by a heart-attack. Death came swiftly and abruptly.

Only later did Sheila conclude that the Israeli secret agent must have told her husband what the Israeli government had already known for a long time: that Josef Mengele was dead. 'So in the end I can't help thinking that the hunted caught up with the hunter', she says. 'I'm sure it was knowing this that broke Alex's heart and robbed him of the will to live.'

But Sheila Dekel is wrong. Israel was equally unaware of Mengele's fate. The man from Mossad must have told him something quite different: namely that the Israelis and their legendary intelligence service had lost all track of Mengele. It was probably this news that took away Dekel's last hope and gave him the shock that killed him.

In his long years at large Mengele had become a legend throughout the world. Rumours and stories, sensationalism and speculation proliferated around the terrible concentration camp doctor. At first, though, no-one had paid any attention to him – least of all the criminal prosecution authorities. Then, from the early 1960s, every clue to his whereabouts, no matter how false, was worth a headline. People claimed to have seen him in Bolivia and on the Greek island of Kythnos, even in the United States. On several occasions Mengele was reported dead. But then a newspaper or magazine, or the Nazi-hunter Simon Wiesenthal, thought they had picked up a new trail. Mengele became a phantom, the incarnation of Auschwitz, of the greatest crime of the 20th century. Yet Mengele had not been the only SS doctor in the concentration camp. Many others there betrayed the Hippocratic oath, and daily broke the commandment to preserve life. They were the medical men with the death's-head badge on their caps, who, on the unloading ramp at Auschwitz selected hundreds of thousands for the gas chambers. They 'supervised' the gassings. They tortured inmates with barbaric and pseudo-scientific experiments.

Thus the gynaecologist Karl Klauberg infected the wombs of female inmates with bacteria. His colleague Horst Schumann experimented with a perverted method of sterilisation: by means of a concentrated bombardment with X-rays of men's testicles and women's ovaries, the subjects were deprived of their fertility – all in the name of Nazi racial ideology. The Nazis were 'extremely interested in the development of a cheap and quick method of sterilisation which could be used against enemies of the German Reich, such as Russians, Poles and Jews'. That was a statement by Rudolf Brandt, chief-of-staff of the *Reichsführer-SS*, Heinrich Himmler, at the Nuremberg trial of Nazi doctors in 1947. 'It was hoped in this way not only to defeat but also destroy the enemy. The labour of the persons sterilised could be used by Germany, but at the same time their ability to reproduce would be destroyed.'

Mengele's most dreadful activities in Auschwitz, his human experiments, were thus part of the daily round in the extermination camp; many of his colleagues abused the inmates in agonising experiments. Nevertheless, the case of Dr Josef Mengele is of a different order. There are three reasons for this: the 'subjects' of his experiments, his behaviour in Auschwitz and his mysterious disappearance after the end of the Nazi barbarism.

Josef Mengele generally experimented with twins. Parents are particularly proud of twins. Everyone with normal instincts finds twins lovable, sweet and delightful. Mengele injected their eyes with chemicals, extracted so much blood from them that they died of debility, or killed them with injections of Evipan (hexobarbitone sodium) and phenol. His perverted experiments with little twins have stayed in the minds of Auschwitz survivors as being particularly repulsive.

Yet Mengele concealed his cynical cruelty and inhumanity behind cultivated manners and an elegant exterior. Moshe Offer remembers the day in 1944 when, as a twelve-year-old, he arrived in Auschwitz with his parents and twin brother Tibi. 'Dr Mengele was doing the selecting. He stood there, good-looking and beautifully dressed.' The SS *Hauptsturmführer* with his always perfectly fitting uniform, his high boots polished to a brilliant shine, and his white gloves, he appeared the perfect cultivated gentleman. He looked like 'a host greeting guests as they arrive at his house' according to a witness-statement given to the US Office of the Chief Counsel for War Crimes. 'Elegant and with a slender build', is how the prisoner-doctor Ella Lingens remembers his outward appearance.

Unlike the other SS doctors in Auschwitz, Mengele did not have to drink himself into a state where he could handle the selection process. It was the sound of Brahms and Beethoven that put him in the mood to commit his horrific acts, and in his moments of leisure he liked to listen to Schumann's *Träumerei*. When the terrified deportees arrived in Auschwitz, often after travelling for days without food or water, and stumbled or were dragged from the overcrowded cattle-trucks, Mengele casually directed them with a white-gloved hand to the left or the right. To the right meant life – albeit under the hellish conditions of the concentration camp. To the left lay death in the gas chamber. Often, in the midst of this murderous act, Mengele would absently whistle to himself a waltz or a classical melody. Later, his nickname would be 'the Angel of Death'.

The hunt for the Angel of Death, as spectacular as it was unsuccessful, continued through the 1960s, '70s and '80s and created an aura of horror around him. Alongside the crimes that he had actually committed, even more gruesome deeds were attributed to him – in the understandable desire of the victims at least to put a name to the unspeakable crimes committed against them in Auschwitz. Mengele, the man presumed to be hiding out somewhere in South America, turned into a demonic phantom.

To the end of his life he succeeded in evading prosecution. In this he was aided by governmental indifference and the negligence of the prosecuting authorities. In South American dictatorships he was protected by Germans and local people who shared his unreconstructed convictions, by gullible German emigrants, corrupt officials and again and again by his own family of prosperous Bavarian industrialists.

> He can't possibly have done those things. I'm convinced of it. If he did anything, then it was only because he was acting under orders. I can only think of Mengele as a human being, and as a human being I found him likeable. He was modest and very cultivated.
>
> *Werner Schubius, acquaintance of Mengele in Paraguay*

Josef Mengele was born on 16 March 1911, the eldest of three sons. His father Karl, a qualified engineer, had built up an agricultural machinery factory from a small workshop, in the town of Günzburg on the upper Danube. However, during the First World War he mainly produced military equipment such as pioneer vehicles and ammunition-carts. By the early 1920s Karl Mengele was by far the biggest employer in Günzburg. His eldest son Josef was destined to succeed him as head of the business. But 'Beppo', as his young school-friends called him, already had other ideas. He had no desire to continue his parents' provincial existence. 'He wanted to build his own reputation and not be connected with that already established by his family', says Mengele's classmate Julius Diesbach. 'He didn't just want to be successful, but also to distinguish himself from the crowd. He was passionate about becoming famous. He once told me that one day I'd read his name in the encyclopaedias.'

Mengele's mother Walburga was known for her energy and determination. The workers at the Mengele factory were far more in fear of the appearance at the plant of this robust and matronly woman than they were of their boss. The Mengeles were Catholics and regular churchgoers. The upbringing of their children followed the conservative and Catholic pattern of those days, though it bore little sign of Christian love. An emotional chill pervaded the Mengele household. The parents quarrelled a lot.

An embittered Josef called his father a 'cold person', and his mother 'was not much better where affection was concerned'. Josef developed a cynical contempt towards the Church. Nonetheless, as an SS cadet Mengele was married in a Catholic ceremony and even when he became an officer in the SS he did not leave the Church – chiefly out of consideration for his mother.

Josef was an amenable child, anxious to please. His mother seemed larger than life to him; a corpulent, all-dominating giantess. She was capable of showing maternal instinct but also of fits of fury. She was completely unpredictable. In his autobiographical writings Mengele later recalled how his father came home one day with a big surprise for the family. He had bought a new car. His sons were thrilled and father Mengele wanted to pile the whole family aboard for a test-drive. But Walburga scolded him for daring to spend so much money without first asking her permission. After her husband had tried in vain to mollify her for a while, he exploded and threatened to leave her. Mengele wrote how, rigid with fear, he had listened to his parents quarrelling. When his father left the room, he had run to his mother and promised to stay with her always.

As a child Mengele survived illnesses and accidents by a hair's breadth. At the age of six, while playing, he fell into a deep rainwater barrel and nearly drowned. He also suffered from severe blood-poisoning. When he was fifteen he was struck down with osteomyelitis, an infection of the bone-marrow. At school physics and biology were his favourite subjects. As for anthropology, 'for me that was the most exciting of all', he noted in adulthood.

Overall a rather mediocre pupil, he took his school-leaving examination at Easter 1930. At first he wanted to become a dentist. Mengele was convinced that this would be a lucrative occupation: 'In my home town there wasn't a single dentist.' So a trace of the utilitarian thinking which at Auschwitz he took to perverted extremes was already to be found in the school-leaver. But even stronger was his ambition. Mengele did not want to be a small-town dentist. He wanted to see his name in the encyclopaedias. He decided to study medicine – with an emphasis on anthropology and genetics. His aim was to make a career in research. 'My family will be very impressed when I'm the first Mengele to become a scientist', he boasted to his friend Julius Diesbach.

> Mengele was notably more hard-working and ambitious than other students.
>
> *Kurt Lambertz, Mengele's fellow-student*
>
> He wanted to research what was then the most modern thing: genetic biology, the science of race.
>
> *Hermann Langbein, clerk to the resident medical officer in Auschwitz*

Politically, Josef Mengele followed in the footsteps of his conservative-nationalist father. Karl Mengele was a member of the German National People's Party and of the *Stahlhelm* ('Steel Helmet'), the militant, right-wing ex-servicemen's organisation founded in 1918. In 1927 Josef became a member of the Greater German Youth Federation and in 1931 joined the *Jungstahlhelm*, the youth wing of the *Stahlhelm*. However, the young playboy was less interested in politics than in girls and sporty cars. In November 1932 the nationalist Karl Mengele played host to Adolf Hitler, who was campaigning for the Nazi Party in the general election. Mengele put his factory building at the Führer's disposal for his election address to the people of the Danube town. But only after the Nazi 'seizure of power' the following January did the factory-owner hurriedly join the NSDAP. Then, when the *Sturmabteilung* (SA) absorbed the *Stahlhelm*, Josef Mengele automatically became a member of the SA. However, late in 1934 he left the Nazi bully-boy brigade again, ostensibly because of a kidney complaint. It is more likely, however, that the class-conscious son of an industrialist did not want to be placed on an equal footing with the working- and lower middle-class brawlers of the SA. What is more, their crude anti-Semitic prejudice was alien to his upbringing. Anti-Semitism and racial obsession first impressed him in academic garb; in the lecture-theatres of Munich University. It was there that Mengele embarked on his medical studies. However, he was less occupied with healing the sick than with the cultural origins and development of the human species.

> I think he really believed the slogan 'The Jews are our misfortune', and in the whole National Socialist philosophy.
> *Hans Münch, Auschwitz doctor, acquitted in 1947*

Mengele's first year as a student, 1930, was also the year in which Hitler's deluded ideas had a landslide success at the ballot-box. In the Reichstag elections of September 1930 the Nazi Party increased their number of seats from 12 to 107, making it the second largest party after the Social Democrats. The racial fixation of the Nazis seized on theories of social Darwinism, which claimed that some human beings, for reasons of biological inadequacy, were not worthy of life. The social Darwinists advocated active intervention in the reproductive process. Only the best should remain. People with physiological defects were supposedly unfit to reproduce, indeed unfit to live at all. The exponents of this theory of the 'life unworthy to be lived' were Mengele's university professors.

In 1932 Mengele passed his first medical examination in Bonn, and then continued to study medicine and anthropology in Vienna and Munich. Under the Nazis anthropology became very fashionable. It was to provide scientific proof that all non-Aryan races were inferior – which was the basis of all Nazi ideology. The evil delusion of the 'life unworthy to be lived' acquired the status of 'science'. And Mengele's ambition was nothing less than to be successful in this new 'field of research'.

As a medical student Mengele regularly attended lectures by Professor Ernst Rüdin, who had studied under August Forel, the founder of the theory of 'racial hygiene'. In 1904 Forel wrote: 'When the lowest grade of humanity produces dozens of idiots, criminals, cripples, consumptives and those with various other deformities, we build lunatic asylums, nursing-homes, houses of correction, prisons and institutions for epileptics, the feeble-minded and the aged in order to care for, at our own cost, the worst fruits of their degeneracy. And we fail to realise that this kind of humanitarianism is gradually bringing about the ruin of civilised mankind.' Three decades later Rüdin, Forel's Swiss-born pupil, and one of the authors of 'The Law for Preventing the

Transmission of Hereditary Diseases', was playing a leading part in implementing the theory of 'eradication' of those 'unworthy of life'. The law, which came into force on 1 January 1934, imposed compulsory sterilisation on the mentally ill, epileptics, the blind, deaf and physically disabled, on the 'feeble-minded' and on severe alcoholics. Records kept by the police, social services and hospitals were systematically combed, so that as many as possible of those with 'hereditary illnesses' could be carted off to the operating-theatre – if necessary by brutal police enforcement.

The 'New Age' inspired Mengele's ambitious calculations. He was a keen student, 'notably more hard-working and ambitious than others', as Kurt Lambertz, who studied with him at the time, remembers. In 1935 Mengele graduated in anthropology, the subject so fashionable in Nazi circles. It was the year of the anti-Jewish Nuremberg Laws, in which the Nazi regime embodied a new system of legalised eradication, using pseudo-scientific criteria to determine who was German and who was not. The Jews were no longer counted as Germans. Mengele's dissertation was entitled 'The use of racial morphology in examining the anterior section of the lower jaw in four racial groups'. His aim was to demonstrate differences between 'primitive and progressive' races. Mengele struck the right note: he graduated *summa cum laude.*

After four months as an intern in a Leipzig hospital, the goal he had dreamed of, a career in research, came a good deal nearer. On the recommendation of his supervisor in Munich, Professor Mollison, he was given a post as research assistant in the Reich Institute for Genetic Biology and Racial Hygiene, at the University of Frankfurt-am-Main. The head of the institute was Professor Baron Otmar von Verschuer. He became Mengele's mentor on the road to Auschwitz. Before Verschuer's appointment as director of the institute he had been described as 'non-political' in a reference written by Professor Walter Gross, head of the Nazi Party's Office of Racial Policy. Nonetheless he had a 'completely honourable loyalty' to National Socialism and was making a contribution to the 'consolidation of National Socialist thought'. Gross went on to say: 'I can imagine, furthermore, that it is precisely Verschuer's objectivity and non-political approach to science that will be particularly convincing, so that his appointment could be valuable as propaganda and for enlisting support.' As a Nazi, Gross had been quite correct in his assessment of the eminent geneticist. Verschuer himself advocated 'the pure realm of science', and as a non-political person he meant by this that science should not be tied to any party. But as his own case shows, this could still result in unquestioning submission to the Nazi dictatorship.

Verschuer was delighted by the dubious boom in genetic science. He devoted himself with burning zeal to the Nazis' 'preservation of heredity and race'. As a specialist in the study of twins, as early as 1911 he registered and catalogued all pairs of twins, or the surviving twin, living in the Schwalm region of Upper Hessen. They were classified according to illnesses, afflictions and physical characteristics. These included rheumatism of the joints, heart defects, pneumoconiosis, leukaemia, allergic complaints, diabetes and dwarfism. Twins became the prototypes for Verschuer's narrow and obsessive research. In his mind nearly all chronic diseases were hereditary. The Nazis' totalitarian measures for 'restoring the national body to health' met with his full approval. 'In Germany the findings of research into genetic biology have already been built into the public health care system', Verschuer noted with glee. 'The prevention of hereditary disease through sterilisation, marriage counselling and the ban on certain marriages is prescribed by specific legislation.'

Working with Verschuer, Mengele graduated for a second time – this time in medicine. Under the title 'Research into the cleft of lip, jaw and palate among families' he wrote a thesis on the heredity of the hare lip. When it came to putting the 'specific legislation' into practice, Verschuer and his assistant, Mengele, were at the cutting edge. In court they appeared as expert witnesses in cases of *Rassenschande*, bringing disgrace on the race. Marriage and any sexual intercourse between Aryans and Jews was forbidden. Anyone committing this offence was prosecuted. In cases of doubt, the question of whether someone was a Jew or 'half-Jew' was settled by the evidence of Verschuer and his assistant. So Mengele was engaged in 'selection' long before the first train rumbled into Auschwitz.

The professor and his assistant wrote out their racial certificates with messianic zeal. On one occasion, when a judge failed to take account of Verschuer's expert evidence in reaching his verdict, and acquitted the defendant, the Nazis' official geneticist made a personal complaint to the Reich Minister of Justice, Gürtner.

In 1942 Mengele's supervisor was made director of the Kaiser Wilhelm Institute for Anthropology, Human Genetics and Eugenics, in the Dahlem district of Berlin. It was the institution *par excellence* for Nazi-style genetic biology. The man who founded it in 1927, Eugen Fischer, had taught Verschuer and was co-author of *The Principles of Heredity and Racial Hygiene*. Adolf Hitler read the second edition while in prison in Landsberg. Since 1935 medication had been tested on twins at the Kaiser Wilhelm Institute. Doctors treated them with various chemicals and hormones. Verschuer requested extensive funding for the 'twin research', and this was approved by the German Research Association.

Meanwhile Mengele had exchanged his doctor's white coat for a black SS uniform. This, too, was a deliberate move in his career as an anthropologist and geneticist. The SS was considered the 'guardian' of the nation's 'racial purity'. And on 1 January 1939, before becoming an officer in the Office of Race and Settlement, he married Irene Schoenbein, the tall, blonde daughter of a businessman. While Irene typified the Nazi ideal of Aryan woman-hood, the SS doctor examining Mengele noted his greenish-brown eyes and brown hair. The fanatical Aryan was thus predominantly of 'Dinaric-Ostic' (not pure Aryan) blood.

Yet it was not Mengele's 'un-Aryan' appearance that was a threat to his marital plans; his wife was unable to prove beyond all doubt that there were no Jews among her forebears. The papers relating to her American grandfather, Harry Lyons Dummler, could not be found. It was not until influential witnesses vouched for Irene's 'very Nordic nature', that permission for the marriage could be obtained. But to Mengele's annoyance, there was no question of his being entered in the Nazi *Sippenbuch*, the 'Clan Book' or racial record. This privilege was reserved for those who were able to prove conclusively that their ancestors had been pure Aryan, as least as far back as 1750. The final bureaucratic hurdle was a question on reproduction. 'Is reproduction desirable for the benefit of the *Volk*?' the Office of Race and Settlement wanted to know. The examining SS doctor wrote a clear 'Yes' here and nothing more stood in the way of the wedding.

However, their marital bliss was short-lived. Mengele went off to war as an SS volunteer, eager to do his bit. Initially he was posted to the medical inspectorate of the *Waffen-SS*. He was then sent to a branch of the Race and Settlement Office, in Posen (Poznan), German-occupied Poland, where he wrote reports on the racial suitability of settlers for the newly conquered eastern territories. In January 1942, Mengele was sent to the eastern front with the SS 'Viking' Division. After his spell as an intern in Leipzig, this was only the second time that Mengele worked as a doctor in the true sense of the word. It was also to be the last.

On the eastern front he was operating under the most adverse conditions. The winter was unbearably cold. Thousands were dying every day. There were neither enough bandages and dressings, nor enough medicines, to keep the wounded alive. Pressure of time and shortage of equipment forced him to make 'lightning' choices: to decide who should live and who should not. Determining the fate of German soldiers seemed to Mengele a terrible task, but he performed it to the fullest satisfaction of his superiors. 'Outstanding army doctor' were the words in his recommendation for promotion. Mengele was awarded the Iron Cross First Class, the Eastern Medal 41/42 and the War-Wounded Cross Second Class (with Crossed Swords).

In the summer of 1942 Mengele was wounded, ordered back from the front and posted again to the Office of Race and Settlement. He worked in the office of the Reich Medical Officer to the SS and police. There he learned at first hand that the name 'Auschwitz' meant eradication and extermination: his department supervised medical experiments in the concentration camps.

In Berlin Mengele, now an SS *Hauptsturmführer*, was once again close to Verschuer. And his former mentor reported with great satisfaction to his predecessor at the Kaiser Wilhelm Institute, Professor Fischer: 'My assistant, Mengele, has been posted to a job in Berlin, so he can do some part-time work at the Institute.' The researcher into twins still had 'big things' in mind for Mengele. He needed his favourite assistant to build up a central collection of genetic material for the breeding of 'supermen'. Mengele's son Rolf is convinced today that Verschuer, the Nazis' genetics guru, gave the decisive impetus for his father's posting to Auschwitz. The medical historian, Benno Müller-Hill, who has had an opportunity to examine Verschuer's personal papers, is also in little doubt that Verschuer persuaded Mengele to give his career as a researcher a new and decisive direction: 'He may well have said: "There's a great opportunity there for science. There are many races there, lots of people. Why don't you go? It'll be in the interests of science."'

Verschuer obtained access for Mengele to a 'researcher's paradise', unique in the world. In Auschwitz the SS doctor had unlimited 'human material' at his disposal, tens of thousands of potential guinea-pigs. Concepts like 'worthy of life' and 'the right to live' were unknown in the inhuman world of the Auschwitz camp. It was there that Mengele reported for duty on 30 May 1943 – eager to make his mark, obsessed with his career and unhampered by any moral or ethical scruples. For those no longer applied in the Nazi Reich.

The Auschwitz concentration camp had been built in a remote part of south-west Poland, not far behind the eastern front. In summer the earth was scorched by the sun. The stifling air was thick with the acrid stench of burnt flesh. In winter blizzards swept across from the river Vistula. Wooden barracks and unheated brick halls did not offer the slightest protection against the icy cold. In 1943 and 1944, when the machinery of death was running at maximum speed, there were five gas chambers and five crematoria in operation. In them, more than 9,000 human beings could be gassed and burned every day. On clear days the flames shooting from the chimneys of the crematoria, and the billowing black smoke, could be seen for miles around. The principal purpose of Auschwitz was mass extermination.

Yet the concentration camp also 'supplied' forced labour to thirty-four German companies which ran factories in the area. In the evening, when the prisoners returned from their slave-labour to the camp – often utterly exhausted, maltreated, beaten until they bled – they dragged or carried their companions, who had collapsed half-dead or had succumbed to the terrible hardship. It was a procession of shadows and corpses. But the camp orchestra, made up of other prisoners, played them on their way. The dead were laid out on the parade-ground, since the camp officers took meticulous care to see that the number of prisoners returning to camp matched the figure in their card-index.

Slave-labour, experiments on humans, mass extermination – such was the hideous trade of Auschwitz. When Mengele arrived there, the camp was crammed with 130,000 inmates. The so-called 'Moslems' – people who were no more than skin and bone and so weak they could scarcely stand – were 'outsorted' by SS doctors and sent to the gas chambers. The sick, and even pregnant women, were sent to be gassed. Yet every day trains brought hundreds of new prisoners from all over Europe. Their fate was decided on the unloading ramp. As soon as they stumbled out of the cattle-trucks, SS doctors were there to determine who would, for a while, be allowed to live as slave-labourers, and who were to be gassed immediately.

> On the ramp he didn't say a word, but softly whistled some aria or other and – as if he were conducting an orchestra – moved his hand to the left and right, left and right . . . making his selection.
>
> *Vera Alexander, prisoner-nurse in Auschwitz*

This selection process was Mengele's main job. For tens of thousands of prisoners, arriving after days of travelling in appalling conditions, the dapper SS *Hauptsturmführer* was the first man in uniform they came face to face with in Auschwitz. 'We all had to get out and line up in long rows, the men separate from the women and children', as the twins Yitzhak and Zerah Taub recall. 'There, in front of us, stood that man Mengele, in an erect, Napoleonic pose, sending the stronger ones to one side as labourers. The ones to be killed went to the other side. As children we weren't part of the labour-force; we had stand beside our mother along with the people who were going to die.'

On the unloading bay Mengele kept an eye open for human material, for guinea-pigs. Twins were his favourite subjects for experimentation. As Yitzhak and Zerah Taub tell us, he sometimes fetched them back at the last minute, after other SS men had inadvertently sent them with their mothers into the death-line. In other cases, the mothers guessed that there was no hope of escape for themselves, but that their twins had a chance, since they were something special in the hell that was Auschwitz. 'My twin brother and I were on our way to the gas chambers with our mother, and suddenly she said: "Children, go and see those Germans. Run back to where they're looking for twins!" I assume that her instinct had told her we'd be safer if we were separated from her,' Eva Kupas recalls. 'While our mother and our little brother went on walking towards the crematoria, we ran back to the unloading ramp. There stood Dr Mengele.'

> He was a slim man, always immaculate; he toyed with a riding-crop in his hand and whistled Dvorak's *Humoresque* during the selections.
>
> *Claude Lehmann, prisoner-doctor in Auschwitz*

Other mothers insisted on keeping their twins with them. 'No-one knew if it was a good or a bad thing to be a twin', says Menashe Lorinczi, ten years old when he was deported to Auschwitz in 1944. 'The SS overseers were running around looking for twins, but the families were afraid to give up their children voluntarily. Many twins died because their parents refused to be parted from them. A lot of mothers went straight to be gassed with their twin children.'

> . . . Those Jews in prison clothes shouted 'twins out', and looked for dwarfs and people who were deformed. They came up to us as well. My brother and I aren't twins, but we did look very alike. They dragged us out of the line and said: 'You'll at least stay alive.'
>
> *Auschwitz victim, Ephraim Reichenberg*

Little children resisted and screamed as they were torn away from their parents. Mengele spoke to the mothers with an affable smile, attempting to calm and reassure them. He wanted to make them believe that their children would be in good hands.

Sometimes the mothers were also allowed to go with their twins to the right – and to life. The 'Angel of Death' put on a cherubic demeanour while playing his diabolical game of hypocrisy: 'Madam, you're tired and ill from the long journey; give your little boy to this lady. You can pick him up later from the nursery', he lied to one anxious mother.

> We were people who'd also been given a death-sentence, though it wasn't carried out straight away. Instead of killing us there and then, they made guinea-pigs of us, doing what is done these days in laboratories with cats or rats.
>
> *Auschwitz twin, Menashe Lorinczi*

As a prisoner-doctor, Ella Lingens remembers that in Auschwitz Verschuer's one-time research-assistant was 'a great collector of material', and his favourite 'material' was twins. But he was also looking for triplets, dwarfs, hunchbacks and all those who deviated from the norm. 'Even people like me – Jews who looked like pure-blooded Aryans', as Mengele's pursuer, Alex Dekel, told the American journalist Lucette Matalon Lagnado, shortly before his premature death.

As he made his selection on the unloading ramp, Mengele was sometimes jovial, sometimes taciturn, and would often whistle waltz tunes to himself, or songs from operetta. But he was never coarse. The well-brought-up industrialist's son liked to observe the formalities. Deep down he had probably never been able to shake off the dominating influence of his mother Walburga. When sorting the prisoners, the spruce and immaculate Mengele 'looked a bit of a mother's boy', as Ella Lingens remembers. 'It was as if his mother had said to him: "Mind you don't dirty your best Sunday jacket". And he was following his mother's bidding.'

The woman doctor from Vienna had been sent to Auschwitz as a punishment for 'showing favour to Jews'. Dr Lingens had tried to help Austrian Jews to escape. The status-conscious Mengele, who always took an interest in his imprisoned fellow-doctors, reacted with blank incomprehension: 'How on earth could you imagine you would get away with it?' he asked Ella Lingens, and she replied: 'Well, in some cases I did it by bribing the Gestapo.' Mengele, not in the least perturbed, had a ready explanation: 'Of course we sell Jews. We'd be stupid not to. But why get involved in things like that? What did you gain from it? Now you're in here.'

When Mengele and the SS doctor Fritz Klein made their selection, they did it quite cold-bloodedly. Other camp doctors drank to give themselves courage, or dosed themselves with stimulants. After a selection the SS men involved were rewarded with 'special rations': a large measure of schnapps, five cigarettes, a quarter-pound of wurst and bread. Mengele was the unscrupulous 'collector of material' for his perverse experiments, while Klein, filled with anti-Semitic hatred, wanted to take his revenge on all Jews for a personal slight – in his student days, a Jewish classmate had seduced his fiancée. Yet Mengele, too, thoroughly approved of the annihilation of the Jews. Not that he considered the Jews to be in any way inferior – quite the reverse. In Mengele's view, the greatest threat to the superiority of the German race was posed by the Jews. 'He once told me there are only two gifted nations in the world: the Germans and the Jews. One of these two nations would have to dominate the world,' Ella Lingens tells us. 'Mengele wanted the Germans to be masters of the world, and not the Jews.' That was why the Jews had to be destroyed. Mengele saw them as competition to the German 'master-race'. He was a devout disciple of the propaganda about the 'Final Solution of the Jewish problem' – and became one of those who enforced it.

Mengele considered himself a cut above his fellow medics. Had he not proved himself on the Russian Front? He was very proud of his war decorations and wore them prominently on his uniform, as the SS doctor Hans Münch recalls. Mengele often talked about his combat experience on the eastern Front and cloaked himself in a special aura. His war service stood in obvious contrast to the deskbound careers of the other doctors in the camp. And he made sure everyone was aware of it. Not even the senior camp officers escaped the scathing tongue of this elitist know-all. Münch remembers Mengele describing them as 'ignoramuses', who 'didn't have a clue about anything'.

Apparently Mengele's superiors did not know what he thought of them. At all events, the Resident Medical Officer, Eduard Wirths, praised his subordinate in a performance review: 'Every task he was given he carried out, often under the most difficult conditions, with good judgement, stamina and energy to the fullest satisfaction of his superiors, and he showed himself equal to any situation.' Mengele's human experimentation was described in the appraisal as a spare-time hobby: 'Furthermore, as an anthropologist he was most keen to make use of such free time as he had left, to improve his knowledge and, using the scientific material available to him by virtue of his position, he made a valuable contribution to anthropological science. His achievements must therefore be described as outstanding.' With a military crispness, Wirths ended his evaluation: 'As an SS doctor he is universally popular and respected.'

Having previously fought at the Front, Mengele rated duty very highly. Yet in Auschwitz he more than fulfilled his 'duty'. While other doctors in the concentration camp did only as much as was required of them, Mengele perpetually took on new assignments in the nightmare world of Auschwitz. That is why, even today, a number of survivors believe he was the chief medical officer of the camp. But he was not. Eduard Wirths was. It was he who appointed Mengele senior doctor in the women's camp at Auschwitz-Birkenau.

Even in those surroundings of suppurating misery, dirt and disease, Mengele was always to be seen in his superbly tailored SS uniform, ever the suave ladies' man. In the women's camp he was hated and feared – but also admired. Eva Kor remembers that some of the women even admitted – albeit grudgingly and with shame – that they found him attractive. In their desperation a number of women even tried to use their own sex-appeal as a means of escape. They patched up their ragged prison clothes and forced themselves to smile – simple feminine gestures that, for them, were from another life. At one selection process in Birkenau the women had to undress and walk up and down naked in front of Mengele. From their appearance alone he decided who was healthy enough to be allowed to live a little longer.

While at Auschwitz, Mengele arranged for his wife Irene to visit him twice. They went for walks together in the surroundings of the camp. Irene picked blackberries, which she made into jam.

Mengele saw himself as fulfilling a special mission, that of scientific research.

This was another reason why he ostentatiously kept himself apart from the other camp doctors. Dr Hans Münch was the only one of his medical colleagues with whom he talked regularly. Münch worked in the SS Institute of Hygiene in Rajsko, a satellite-camp of Auschwitz. As Münch recalls, Mengele gave a great deal of thought to his 'duty', which he took to mean the annihilation of the Jews. But beyond this, the murdering doctor had always wondered: 'Are there other aspects which should be taken into account?' Münch tried to follow Mengele's thought-process. One thing is certain: ethical principles, such as the right to life, played no part in Mengele's mental world.

> Dr Mengele came in. He was wearing a white coat but underneath it you could see his SS uniform and boots. He gave me a candy then he gave me an injection, which hurt terribly. 'There's nothing to be afraid of', Mengele said to me.
>
> *Auschwitz twin, Moshe Offer*

Münch tells us that Mengele often tried to amuse twin children, especially girls, by taking them for a spin in his car along the camp roads. A few days later the same children lay on Mengele's dissection-table – murdered in the name of research. Child corpses to be made use of as he pleased. 'That was something we just couldn't understand. But for Mengele it became the most natural thing in the world', says Münch. Quite a number of the children called Mengele 'Uncle'. He gave 'his' twins candies and a big smile. And in the end he had them killed and the bodies cut up.

'My guinea-pigs' is what he sometimes called his twins. His relationship with the children was that of a laboratory assistant to his experimental animal: it is a cute little creature but it has to be killed. However, as long as it remains alive, the doctor has a kind of affinity with it. Indeed the doctor sometimes even strokes it. But ultimately the children were never anything more than subjects of experiments. Mengele had as much sympathy for his twins as a researcher for laboratory rats. The member of the 'master-race' had complete discretion over his human zoo. Those to be imprisoned in it were personally selected by him as they climbed out of the cattle-trucks and on to the ramp.

Dr Münch, with whom he so often conversed, refused to take part in the selections, and Mengele was unable to talk him into it. That is one of the reasons why, at the Auschwitz trial in Cracow, Hans Münch was the only SS doctor to be acquitted. And there was another reason: in the 'Institute of Hygiene' Münch had given a number of prisoners fictitious jobs to do, thus saving them from the gas chamber.

After one selection, Münch's colleague, Dr Hans Delmotte, refused to take part in any more. He had been profoundly shocked by the heart-rending scenes on the unloading ramp of weeping mothers and children screaming with terror, being bludgeoned by SS-men. Delmotte was overcome by fits of weeping. The camp commandant, the resident medical officer and Mengele all gave him a talking-to. Mengele told him that an army doctor at the Front had to make similar selections, since he decided in what order the operations had to be performed, and thus whether the wounded men lived or died. At Auschwitz selections had to be made in order to pick out those capable of work. Münch remembers Mengele's boundless cynicism: the main job of the SS doctors, he lectured them, was to filter out the work-dodgers for whom death was preferable. Delmotte continued to work at the camp.

Münch also avoided the selections, not because of crying fits, but by going by the rule-book. He complained to his boss in Berlin that his assignment at the 'Institute of Hygiene' in the battle against epidemics was simply too important. It left no time for selections. Münch remembers how his chief, who felt that the decision to put his subordinates on to selection duties had been made over his head, grabbed the telephone and berated the 'bureaucratic jackasses' in Auschwitz. With the Nazis, official channels even reached the death-camps. Münch continued to be spared the selection process on the ramp.

The 'Institute of Hygiene' had been set up because typhoid, typhus and dysentery were a threat to SS personnel as well. In the prison-huts there was only one way of 'combating epidemics': the 'destruction of bacteria along with their human carriers', the Jewish doctor, Aron Bejlin, tell us. Münch explains how this was done: 'As soon as we knew there was a new outbreak of typhus or some other epidemic in one of the blocks, all the inmates of the block were gassed. The building would then be disinfected with chlorine or some similarly inadequate agent, and filled with other prisoners. Once, in order to 'stamp out' typhus, Mengele sent an entire block of 600 women to the gas chamber. That way he had an 'empty block', Dr Ella Lingens remembers. 'Then between that block and the next one he placed a bathtub filled with disinfectant. The inmates of the next block had to undress completely, get into the bath naked and then go to the empty block, which had previously been fully disinfected.'

The prisoner-doctor Ella Lingens had to look after as many as 800 sick people unaided. Out of a total of 10,000 sick women in the women's camp, 350 died every day in the winter of 1943–4. 'During the day the dead women were piled up in layers between the block where I worked and another block', Dr Lingens tells us. 'The official supply of medication was virtually zero. Everything else had to be brought in illegally by the female prisoners themselves. These medicines probably came almost exclusively from the death-transports.' It was just one example of the perverse way in which the sick were treated in Auschwitz. Medicines which had been taken from those condemned to death on the unloading ramp, before they were herded straight into gas chambers, secretly reached those also condemned to die in the filthy and louse-ridden huts for the sick – and helped some of those there to survive.

Not only were medicines taken from the prisoners, but everything else they had brought with them: family photographs, watches, jewellery, blankets. They had to hand over their clothes and shoes and were put into prison uniforms and wooden clogs. Their heads were shaven and they had an identity-number tattooed on their arm. Human beings were reduced to numbers, their fate to symbols.

Only Mengele's twins were allowed to keep their clothes, and their hair was not shorn – an outward sign that their fate had not been sealed from the first moment. They had a small chance of survival, because they were twins. They were the 'chosen ones', because they were Mengele's property. Admittedly they too, like all the rest, were sentenced to death from the outset. But the sentence was not carried out immediately. Mengele gave them a period of grace – only to abuse them as 'guinea-pigs'. On days when there were no experiments he took them for walks, gave them toys to play with and generally played the 'kind uncle'.

> When we were strapped down on Mengele's operating-table, we never knew what would be done to us next. We felt a cold hand on our backs, a stethoscope and then an injection that was dreadfully painful. We were utterly terrified.
>
> *Auschwitz twin, Kalman Braun*

He gave the twin boys a child-minder of their own: he was Zvi Spiegel, also a twin, who was twenty-eight years old when he arrived in Auschwitz. He had been an officer in the Czech army and appealed to Mengele, the highly decorated 'soldier from the Front', because of his habit of standing very straight. The children called Spiegel 'Twin-Father'. He recalls how, when twins first arrived in their special barrack-hut, a questionnaire from the Kaiser Wilhelm Institute immediately had to be completed, which included questions about family background. Weight, height, age, hair- and eye-colour, state of health and physical peculiarities all had to be entered on the forms, which were then sent back to Berlin. The institute there first received statistical information about the twins, then blood samples. These were followed a little later by their skeletons and organs, wrapped in parcels on which was written 'Urgent – War Material', for further examination at Verschuer's renowned institute.

The closeness of the co-operation between Mengele in Auschwitz and the Kaiser Wilhelm Institute is shown by a project run by Dr Karin Magnussen, an assistant of Verschuer. She worked in Berlin on research into anomalies of the eye. The items for examination were sent to her by Mengele, direct from Auschwitz: eyes from prisoners killed by injections to the heart. A Hungarian prisoner-doctor named Miklos Nyiszli had to perform autopsies on the bodies. As Nyiszli later noted: 'Organs which might be of interest to the Anthropological Institute in Berlin were placed in jars of alcohol, packed carefully and sent off by post.'

A further instance of this intensive collaboration was the project known as 'Specific protein solids'. This was financed by the German Research Association. On 20 March 1944 Verschuer reported to the association as follows: 'In this branch of research I have the collaboration of my assistant, Dr Med. and Dr Phil. Josef Mengele. He is serving as *Hauptsturmführer* and camp doctor at Auschwitz. With the permission of the *Reischsführer SS*, anthropological experiments are being carried out on the wide variety of racial groups in this concentration camp, and blood-samples are being sent to my laboratory for processing.' Itzak Taub recalls how blood was taken from both arms of twins simultaneously, ' and this went on until they sank to the ground like empty plastic bags'. At Verschuer's institute the blood-samples thus extracted landed on the desk of the biochemist, Dr Günther Hillmann, who carried out further research on them. 'Dr Hillmann is a biochemist specialising in protein research', Verschuer went on to state in his report. In those years Auschwitz was a satellite establishment of Germany's foremost institute for genetic research.

With the financial subsidies from the German Research Association, Mengele had a pathology laboratory built right next to Crematorium II in Auschwitz-Birkenau. The dissection-table was made of polished marble. The fiendish laboratory of the 'Angel of Death' was state-of-the-art. The most modern Swiss precision instruments were available to the Polish anthropologist, Dr Martina Puzyna. For Mengele's 'twin research' she had to take precise measurements of the twins' heads: circumference, distance from nose to ear, distance between the ears; every detail. Dr Puzyna was lying in the prisoners' hospital block, suffering from typhus, when she attracted Mengele's attention. Before the war she had been assistant to the Polish professor of anthropology, Jan Czekanowski, who had developed a system for measuring the external features of different racial groups. Mengele pricked up his ears at this. He asked Dr

Puzyna what she had been doing in the camp up till then. 'Heaving stones about', she replied. Mengele laughed and said: 'Well then, you'd better come and work for me for a while.'

The measurements were only a prelude to the human experiments. In the last arrest warrant against Mengele, issued by the State Prosecutor's Office in Frankfurt-am-Main on 18 January 1981, his crimes were briefly summarised in fourteen pages: a catalogue of death written in matter-of-fact German legal language. These are extracts from the 'evidence of criminal medical experiments': 'In summer 1944, killed twins with injections of chloroform and Evipan'; 'following the natural death of one twin, deliberately killed the second twin for purposes of comparison'; caused the death of Hungarian twins by 'surgical intervention to the head'; 'killed a pair of twins born in the camp, by lethal injections'; 'in late 1944 the witness J. claims he performed experiments on her newborn baby, which left its eyes unrecognisable as such, but were only red lumps'; 'clear suspicion that he experimentally transplanted bone-marrow in live prisoners'.

All I want to know is: what have I got in my body? We were injected with poison. To this day I don't know what it was. As a result of the experiments I'm two-thirds disabled. I have tremors. I get epileptic fits. What kind of a life is that?

Auschwitz twin, Moshe Offer

In our camp there were 100 to 200 pairs of twins, dwarf twins and so on. Mengele was neutral towards us. He didn't cause us physical pain. He examined us. We had to do various movements. The other tests were done by his assistants. Mengele never gave us injections.

An Auschwitz twin

Yet Mengele did not just use surgical instruments to commit murder. According to the arrest warrant, he also shot people with his own hand. For example, he is said to have killed a pair of twins 'by shooting them through the neck from behind'. A sixteen-year-old girl, fearing for her life, escaped from the gas chamber on to a roof, where Mengele allegedly shot her.

From all the eye-witness statements against Mengele we get a completely divided and contradictory picture of the perpetrator. On one hand he was 'the murderer with clean hands', who left his subordinates to carry out the orders to kill. On the other hand we see a cruel and sadistic murderer, who took delight in torturing and killing. A prisoner-doctor, Gisella Perl, tells us how she saw Mengele punch a woman prisoner in the neck and beat her over the head 'until it was a bloody mass. I saw her two lovely, intelligent eyes disappear behind a stream of blood. Her ears had gone; he must have torn them off. And within a few seconds her straight, slender nose was nothing but a flat, crushed and bleeding lump.'

'Is it not conceivable that Mengele combined both aspects in himself, that he simply had a split personality, and that he behaved in completely different ways at different times?' asks historian Zdenek Zofka, who has written a 'typology' of the Nazi criminal. 'Or can the contradictions in the image of the man who is said to have done these things be explained by sometimes mistaken or exaggerated witness statements?'

There are many statements accusing Mengele of sadistic murders such as the shooting of children. In contrast to these we have evidence like that from the medical auxiliary Kazimierz Czelny, who never saw Mengele hit or shoot anyone: 'He never got his hands dirty.' The Polish prisoner-doctor, Tadeusz Sniesko, also testifies: 'I never saw Mengele hit anyone or directly kill anyone.' The historian Ernst Klee, who has documented human experiments and other crimes committed by the Nazi medical profession, points to a problem in many of the reports from Auschwitz: 'The eye-witnesses understandably get confused about dates; they project crimes on to perpetrators, who no doubt were murderers, but who could not have committed that particular crime. With Mengele we get the additional factor that he is one of the prominent Nazi perpetrators who eluded capture after 1945. And so many people try – for psychological reasons that are only too easy to understand – to make their own anonymous and largely ignored fate more interesting, by claiming that they were victims of, or at least witnesses to, horrific acts by the famous Nazi monster.'

He was the nice camp-doctor. At the time I didn't yet know who he really was.

Vera Alexander, prisoner-nurse in Auschwitz

I thought of him then and I think of him today as a cultivated person.

Josef Köhler, senior block inmate at Auschwitz

The thoughtful prisoner-doctor, Ella Lingens, does not see Mengele as a sadist but as coldly cynical: 'It is in the nature of a sadist to take pleasure in his victims' pain. But with Mengele you had the impression that he wasn't even aware of their pain. He just didn't notice it. Because to him the prisoners were guinea-pigs, rats, whose inner life and suffering were of no concern – in other words, his was the completely detached attitude of a professional to his work. That is how I saw Mengele.' Dr Lingens warns against placing him on a pedestal as someone 'super-evil' and thus inaccessible to any kind of analysis. Even in Mengele's case, the truth is that evil was dreadfully banal. Mengele did not go to Auschwitz as a murderer but as a researcher. Yet even medical science subsequently made 'Doctor Auschwitz' into a monster and thus outside the bounds of his chosen profession. At the same time we forget that there were even doctors who were not in the SS, but who nevertheless applied for permission to carry out experiments in Auschwitz – in obedience to the demand by Professor Eugen Fischer, the founding director of the Kaiser Wilhelm Institute: 'No constraints on research'. Fischer was one of those who eagerly adopted Hitler's racial paradigm and paved the way to Auschwitz. It was from there that researchers now received their 'material'. Scientific ethics and morality no longer had a part to play.

However, not only in Germany but in almost every other European country, there was a eugenics movement based on social Darwinism, which promoted prejudice in the guise of scientific fact. Until 1940 this was the case in the USA as well; in 1923 Harry Laughlin, then director of the eugenics department at the Old Spring Harbor Laboratory in New York state, claimed before the US Congress that people from southern and eastern Europe were more prone to criminal behaviour than northern Europeans. And as late as 1938 Laughlin was praising the compulsory sterilisation programme in Nazi Germany as an example to be followed. Even in Roman Catholic Poland the 'care and cultivation of heredity' was officially encouraged. This is what the psychiatrist Wladislaw Luniewski wrote in 1935: 'If economic motives alone were to decide the fate of the mentally ill, then, compared with sterilisation, the poisoning or shooting of all those affected would be a much more effective method.' Just four years after these terrible yet prophetic words were written, mental patients in Poland were being shot by German 'cultivators of heredity' in SS uniforms.

In the 1920s and '30s irresponsible eugenicists in many countries actively promoted an obsession with racial selectivity. But everywhere the law imposed restraints on untrammelled scientific hubris. Everywhere except Germany. There the ugly term 'disposal of lives not worth living' was elevated by the Nazis to the status of official doctrine. Traditional ethical concepts such as an unconditional right to life were perverted; humanity and compassion were despised as 'muddle-headed altruism'. Scientists should be allowed to get on with their research without inhibition or restriction. 'Anything is good if it serves the nation' – the 'master-race'. The slogan 'No constraints on research' became a grim reality. Personal careerism added further impetus. Then doctors began walking over corpses.

Mengele wanted to go down in the history of genetics, with his own 'geminology' or study of twins, and a professorship to go with it. His experiments were not cloaked in secrecy – he circulated his 'research findings' with great pride, for instance at a scientific convention held at the concentration camp on 1 September 1944. In front of his colleagues the Doctor of Death expatiated on 'examples of the anthropological and genetic work done in Auschwitz concentration camp'. Mengele believed he was able to use genetics to create the perfect Aryan specimen. In his human zoo he intended to breed nothing but fair-haired, blue-eyed children. That is why Mengele's experiments were designed to alter the eye- and hair-colour of twins. Continuous analysis of the hair was carried out on each twin and comparisons made with the hair of the other twin. Solutions were injected under the scalp to dye dark hair blond, and dyes were injected into the eyes to turn them from brown to blue.

When the experiments were completed the twins, too, were destined for the gas chambers. In January 1945 the latest death-list had been neatly typed out and stamped. But those named on the list survived, for the Red Army was advancing relentlessly westward. On 17 January, as Stalin's soldiers approached the camp, 67,012 prisoners lined up for their final roll-call. Those of the adults who could still walk were forced to begin a death-march westwards through the icy Polish winter. Those too weak to go were either shot or left to their fate in the eerie silence of the camp.

> When a loved one dies and you go and bury them in a cemetery, you know you can go back and visit the grave. But for Miriam and me – and for all Auschwitz twins – there was no cemetery. There was just the memory of the last time we saw our mother, our father and our sisters.
>
> *Auschwitz twin, Eva Mozes*

The majority of SS men thought only of escape. The 'Angel of Death' was among those who abandoned the scene of their crimes. On the cold winter night of 17 January 1945 he made his getaway, carrying all the notes on his pseudo-research. He also took two crates of papers from the office of Dr Puzyna, where the experimental measuring of twins had begun. His car was already waiting outside. Mengele was now in a great hurry. Some of the documents that he now hastily bundled together he had shown, four months earlier, in September 1944, to his colleague, the prisoner-doctor Ella Lingens. 'I say, doctor, did I ever show you the results of my research work?' Dr Lingens remembers him asking. There were ring-binders full of anthropological measurements and sketches of body-parts. 'Isn't that beautiful?' Mengele said as he showed her each drawing. Finally he mused: 'Isn't it a pity that all this will now fall into the hands of the Bolshevists?'

On 27 January 1945 Soviet troops marched into the camp. It was liberation at last. Of Mengele's 3,000 twins, just 180 had survived. Among them were Eva Kor and her sister Miriam. Their parents, two other sisters and almost all their relations had suffocated in the gas chambers of Auschwitz-Birkenau. It is Eva and Miriam who we see in the first row, on that famous piece of film that shows the twins after their liberation, accompanied by nurses as they walk along the double electric fence around the camp. Russian soldiers had dressed them in striped prison jackets to look more authentic. But the identification-numbers tattooed on the children's arms are genuine enough. The Russian film director had made the twins roll up their sleeves and show the numbers to the camera. We can see in their young faces that they could not comprehend what the doctors of the 'master-race' had done to them.

> When I came out of the camp I no longer wanted to live. I could not bear the thought that my whole family had died.
>
> *Auschwitz twin, Moshe Offer*
>
> From 1945 to 1949 I lay in a hospital bed. They had to teach me to walk again. To this day Auschwitz causes me suffering. I'm an invalid. Prematurely pensioned. Our lives have been ruined.
>
> *An Auschwitz twin*

By the time those pictures were taken in Auschwitz, Mengele had long since arrived at another concentration camp 180 miles to the north-west: Gross-Rosen, in Silesia. There prisoners-of-war from the Red Army had been cruelly subjected to experiments connected with bacteriological warfare. The responsible investigator at the Office of the US Chief Counsel for War Crimes, David Marwell, found out that at Gross-Rosen Mengele once more slipped into the familiar role of camp-doctor. He was now nearly thirty-four – an old hand when it came to medical practice in the death-camps. But Mengele's sojourn at Gross-Rosen was a brief one. A week before the arrival of the Red Army he left the camp and mingled with the battle-weary soldiers of a retreating Wehrmacht unit. He had exchanged his black SS uniform for the field grey of a regular army officer. The man who had once been lord over life and death became a refugee in the chaotic cortège of Hitler's defeated armies.

On 2 May 1945, with the Motorised Field-Hospital No. 2591, he met his one-time colleague from the Reich Institute for Genetics and Racial Hygiene in Frankfurt, Dr Hans Otto Kahler. On seeing Mengele in a Wehrmacht uniform, Kahler did not speak to the former SS officer but instead put in a good word for his former co-worker with the commanding officer. Mengele was allowed to stay with the field-hospital. Every doctor was urgently needed.

In his new unit Mengele got to know a young nurse. A mild flirtation turned into an intimate relationship and Mengele trusted the nurse so completely that he handed over to her his cherished 'research notes' from Auschwitz for safe keeping. Mengele expected to be taken prisoner and the papers would have exposed him as a concentration camp doctor. After the war he recovered them and deposited them at his parents' house in Günzburg.

The medical unit fled ever further westwards ahead of the advancing Russians, and near the town of Weiden in Bavaria Mengele was finally captured as a perfectly 'ordinary' fighting man, and was registered under his correct name. At first, the GIs who held him prisoner did not know they were dealing with a war criminal. They did not even recognise Mengele as a former member of the SS. Ironically, it was his vanity that protected him from being unmasked. SS men bore an unmistakable mark of identity: their blood-group was tattooed under their armpit. But not in Mengele's case. When he joined the SS he had refused to have this done. The tattooing was unnecessary, he argued; since before giving a blood transfusion every doctor would carry out a cross-check and not rely solely on the tattooed blood-group information. But his wife Irene knew the real reason behind his refusal: Mengele had the habit of washing in front of a full-length mirror and admiring his smooth skin. He did not want this skin tinkered with. However, the fact that concentration camp inmates were branded like cattle did not upset him in the least.

By now word of Mengele's evil activities had got around. As early as April 1945 Mengele's name was on the Americans' list of war criminals. He was also listed on the 'Central register of war criminals and people under suspicion as security risks', drawn up by the Allied Supreme Command in Paris for distribution to all prisoner-of-war camps. Yet the absolute chaos of those days in the summer and autumn of 1945, when Germany lay in ruins, often prevented information about war criminals from being passed on quickly. What is more, the internment-camps were filled to overflowing. The Americans wanted to get rid of their prisoners as rapidly as possible. And every able-bodied man was needed to rebuild Germany from the rubble.

In the camp, Mengele approached one of his fellow-prisoners, a military doctor, *Oberst* Fritz Ulmann, and complained to him of a deep depression without concealing the reason behind it: his great fear of being exposed as 'Doctor Auschwitz'. Ulmann was sympathetic and helped Mengele to adopt a new identity. He was in the ideal position to do so. The Americans had appointed Ulmann to represent the prisoners in the central camp administration. It was there that release documents were prepared. Using his own name, Ulmann organised a second set of release papers for Mengele, who rather amateurishly altered the name Ulmann to 'Hollmann'.

So it was that on 30 October 1945, under the name of 'Fritz Hollmann', the ex-prisoner Mengele found a job on the farm of Georg Fischer in Mangolding, a little village near Rosenheim in Upper Bavaria. Farmer Fischer grew wheat and potatoes and kept a dozen dairy cows. In Germany's 'Hour Zero', anyone who was able to work could get bed and board. That was all Josef Mengele needed, and thus the doctor became a farm-hand. The former SS *Hauptsturmführer* whose boots were always polished to a shine, now 'selected' potatoes and mucked out the stables. Once, for the refugee children from Sudetenland living in the neighbourhood, he knocked together a wooden pony-cart and painted it in festive colours. Ever the 'kindly uncle', he would sometimes hum tunes to the kids on a comb and paper. At Christmas he played Santa Claus. Otherwise, in his free time he kept to himself and read a lot. Alois, the farmer's brother, soon noticed that the new farm-hand was 'a cut above' the usual. For Mengele washed his hands frequently and filed his fingernails. But no-one questioned him closely about his past. He said he was a soldier from Görlitz; that was good enough for the Fischers.

Mengele detested the heavy work around the farm. He amused himself with ridiculous brain-teasers, which he revelled in with a scientist's meticulous precision. Thus, as he later wrote about his potato-selecting on the Fischer farm: 'One had to adopt a scientific approach to the sorting of potatoes into those for the table, for fodder and for seed. The frequency of the different sizes follows the Gaussian curve of normal distribution. The medium-sized ones make up the bulk, and the very large or very small ones are far less frequent. But since they wanted more medium-sized potatoes I simply shifted the selection-limit for table potatoes accordingly and that way I got more table potatoes than usual. That's how I kept my mind alert.'

At first Mengele scarcely ever left the farm. But after a while he went away more often. Then he began meeting his wife Irene near Rosenheim. But the estrangement between them grew greater on each occasion. An Auschwitz war criminal disguised as a farm labourer from Mangolding – this was not the man Irene had married before the war. 'I had known Josef Mengele as an utterly honourable, decent, conscientious, very charming, elegant and amusing man, otherwise I wouldn't have married him. I came from a good, well-to-do family and had many opportunities to marry. I believe it was his ambition that ruined him in the end', she wrote in a letter in 1984.

For Irene the marriage became more and more of a burden. She resented having to cover up for her war-criminal husband. He was someone she had scarcely lived with and who had never brought her the longed-for happiness of family life. Yet she remained a part of the conspiratorial group who knew that Mengele was alive and who never breathed a word of this to anyone: it included Mengele's family in Günzburg and his school-friend Hans Sedlmeier, who by now was company secretary of the family farm-machinery firm. In the summer of 1946 Irene received her first visit from the American military police. But she maintained an implacable silence. With her son Rolf on her arm – he had been born in 1944 – Irene told the two soldiers what she had already told everyone else: her husband was missing and probably dead. She even went to church dressed in black and asked the priest to pray for her husband's soul.

Mengele, meanwhile, was following the proceedings and verdicts of the Nuremberg War Crimes Tribunal from a safe distance, by reading reports in the local paper, the Rosenheim *Advertiser*. There he actually saw his own name mentioned by someone who knew all about his war crimes: Rudolf Höss, the commandant of Auschwitz. Höss, as a witness in the defence of Ernst Kaltenbrunner, the head of the Central Office of Reich Security, was replying to the question: how much did he know about medical experiments in the concentration camp: 'In Auschwitz there were, for example, experiments on sterilisation, which were carried out by Professor Klauber and Dr Schumann; there were also experiments on twins by the SS medical officer, Dr Mengele.'

After the sentencing of the principal war criminals, attention turned to the SS thugs in white coats. On 9 December 1946 the trial of doctors began in the US military court in Nuremberg. The defendants were twenty-three members of the medical profession including medical assistants and administrators. On 20 August 1947 the court sentenced seven of the accused to death, five to life imprisonment, and four to prison terms ranging from ten to twenty years. The other seven were acquitted. Mengele was not even tried *in absentia*. And a few months later the chief US prosecutor, General Telford, closed the Mengele file. 'We wish to inform you that, according to documents in our possession, Dr Mengerle (*sic*) has been dead since October 1946', he wrote on 19 January to Dr Gisella Perl, the former Auschwitz prisoner-doctor. She had repeatedly drawn the attention of the American military authorities to Mengele's crimes and urged them to arrest the camp doctor and put him on trial.

Irene's story about her husband being dead had worked. But it was not just the family cover-up that saved Mengele; with the USA's new political concerns about the onset of the Cold War, the butchers of the Hitler period were gradually sinking into oblivion.

Nevertheless, in his disguise as a farm-hand, Mengele was in constant fear of being caught and taken to court. In the autumn of 1948 he asked his family accomplices in Günzburg to organise his escape to South America, and on Maundy Thursday 1949,

Mengele boarded a train for Innsbruck. In his head he carried a detailed escape-plan which had been carefully prepared by a well-paid network of people-smugglers. In Innsbruck the Doctor of Death spent the night in a house near the station. In the early evening of 17 April 1949, Easter Sunday, Mengele took a local train in the direction of the Brenner Pass. At Gries, the last stop before the Italian frontier, he got out. Under cover of darkness, and a safe distance away from the border-post, Mengele was led by a mountain guide, code-named 'Xaver', along an old smugglers' path into Italy. 'Xaver' was the first of the helpers hired by Mengele's old friend Sedlmeier. In his memoirs Mengele drew an idyllic picture of his secret border crossing; there was a crescent moon, and he had seen the first cowslips.

Mengele felt so confident that at the very first station beyond the border he stood and waited for the first train of the day. No police patrol made a check on him. He took the train to the picturesque little Tirolean town of Sterzing. In the Golden Cross inn a contact named 'Nino', who was waiting for Mengele, identified himself with the code-word 'Rosemarie' and handed him a forged South Tirol passport. Josef Mengele was now 'Helmut Gregor'. His decision to escape through South Tirol had been an easy one. He had friends who knew the area well. The Mengele farm-machine company had a branch in Merano. A few days later Sedlmeier also turned up in the Golden Cross, bringing family greetings from Günzburg and cash in the form of dollar bills for the long journey ahead. And he also had a surprise in his luggage: the 'research notes' from Auschwitz and photographic slides, which Mengele had taken in his laboratory. What became of these is uncertain. Armed with his new identity the Doctor of Death set off on the journey to his last jumping-off point in Europe: Genoa.

The South Tirol, a territorial bone of contention between Austria and Italy, had been occupied by German troops in 1943. The native inhabitants had been given their own personal identity papers. After the war, due to the continuing dispute over their nationality, they were classified as stateless by the International Red Cross. This gave Mengele his big chance. In Genoa he exchanged his South Tirolean passport for a refugee identity card issued by the Red Cross. Mengele's application for the document, with his fingerprint and photo, is still in the archives of the International Red Cross in Geneva. Mengele could travel wherever he wanted.

There was just one last obstacle to overcome: he had to get hold of an Italian exit visa. 'Kurt', Mengele's middleman in Genoa, knew a corrupt official. But the man was on holiday. So, off his own bat, Mengele tried the bribery trick with a man behind the desk at the visa office. But he had miscalculated: his attempt to grease that particular palm swiftly landed him in prison. There Mengele sank into an 'oppressive lethargy', as he wrote later. The game, it seemed, was up. But after three weeks in a cell, luck came to the mass murderer's aid. 'Kurt's' corrupt official came back from holiday and 'arranged' things. 'They suddenly discovered their mistake', Mengele later noted with glee. The police, he found, were now 'uncommonly friendly' and on 18 July 1949 'Helmut Gregor' embarked for Argentina. From the deck of the *North King* he watched the Italian coast slowly sink below the horizon. In his notebook he wrote the banal comment: 'Waves, nothing but waves.' Mengele regarded himself as an involuntary 'emigrant'. He was 'emigrating' without any feelings of guilt. Exactly four and a half years had passed since he had left Auschwitz.

Irene Mengele decided not to follow her husband. As her son Rolf told the American attorney and Mengele-hunter, Gerald Posner: 'My mother simply didn't want to go with him into the wilderness. She was strongly attached to Germany and Europe, the culture meant a lot to her, and she was very close to her parents. Besides, in 1948 she had met Alfons Hackenjos, who later became her second husband. But even so, it was a hard decision for her because she still felt something for Josef. With that decision she made a conscious effort to erase his image from her mind and put an end to her feelings for him.'

The *North King* berthed in Buenos Aires on 26 August 1949. The 'emigrant' from Europe expected to be met there. But his contact, whom he named as 'Rolf Nuckert' in his diary, did not appear and Mengele, alias Helmut Gregor, made his own way from the docks to the city. He took a room at the Palermo, a third-class hotel, where the toilet and wash-basin were at the end of the corridor. With this as his base, he set out to look for work.

In the early 1950s Argentina offered a refuge to virtually

anyone who had left Europe. Under the dictatorship of Juan Perón, SS thugs were just as welcome as their victims. Nazi criminals escaped there from their former homeland; Jewish survivors sought a new homeland to replace the old one that had been taken from them. Between 1945 and the fall of Perón in 1955, around 66,000 Germans and 14,000 Austrians emigrated to Argentina. Even before the war a large number of Jews fetched up in Argentina, one of the few countries willing to give them a safe haven. And many Germans had emigrated there in the nineteenth century. There were German clubs, German schools, German shops, German newspapers.

To the pragmatic President Perón the past history of these immigrants was of secondary importance. What chiefly mattered to him was the use they could be to his country. Thus scientists and technologists from the Third Reich were especially welcome. The *Caudillo* was fascinated by German military technology. German engineers developed the first Argentinian jet fighter and helped to build up the country's own motor industry. The dictator made no secret of his admiration for Nazi efficiency, which is why he established a special committee to handle the reception of Nazi refugees. It met in the presidential palace, the Casa Rosada, and was headed by a German-Argentinian named Horst Fuldner.

Using his false name, Mengele had no difficulty in obtaining an Argentinian identity card. But gaining admission to the smart clubs where wealthy Argentinians and German ex-Nazis met, took rather longer. A belief in Nazism alone was not enough; it was necessary to have money and, above all, influential friends. Mengele arrived in Buenos Aires almost penniless; the money which his father had asked Sedlmeier to hand over to him, had gone missing during his eventful stay in Genoa.

Mengele's first job was as a carpenter in a building firm. But gradually he gained access to the 'old comrades' in better social circles. Among his first acquaintances was the Dutch-born Willem Sassen, once a member of the SS, then the Nazis' contact in Buenos Aires, and finally PR man for the dictator of Paraguay, Alfredo Stroessner. Sassen introduced Mengele to Adolf Eichmann, the man who organised Hitler's 'Final Solution of the Jewish problem'. By now Mengele once more had his financial head above water, and his family was sending him money regularly from Günzburg. Eichmann, on the other hand, was almost destitute. The two men met from time to time at the ABC café in the city centre, but they never became friends. Mengele detested the sense of unspoken fear which hung around Eichmann. The 'Doctor of Death' looked upon the 'Bureaucrat of Murder' as a broken man.

Once Mengele had got his foot inside the door of the Old Comrades' club, one contact led to another. He got to know Hans Ulrich Rudel, Hitler's most highly decorated flying ace. And he made friends with the architect Frederico Haase, whose wife was the daughter of Stroessner's minister of finance. This is where Mengele's 'Paraguayan connection' can be traced to. From Argentina Mengele made frequent trips to Paraguay – as a representative of his father's agricultural machinery business. It was Rudel who tipped him off that Paraguay would be a lucrative market for the company's products.

Rudel, a fanatical Nazi until his death in 1982, served Perón's government in Argentina as adviser to the National Aeronautical Institute. With his connections and money he made sure that the 'comrades in exile' remained unmolested and free to sound off about the 'great days' of the past.

Many years after the Nazi barbarism had ended in Europe, there were numerous periodicals in South America which disseminated the National Socialist ideology. One of these was called *Der Weg* (The Way). In it there appeared in 1953 an article entitled 'Heredity as a biological process', and signed 'G. Helmut', a reversal of Mengele's alias, Helmut Gregor. Mengele's great career in scientific research had come to nothing. Yet he could not resist the temptation to publish, once more at least, a 'scientific article' about his very private realm of science – if only under a pseudonym and in an anti-Semitic smear-sheet.

Meanwhile Mengele's mentor and academic supervisor was advancing his own career in Germany once more. For just a few years Otmar von Verschuer had been obliged to set his sights lower. But in 1951 he was awarded a professorship at the University of Münster. True, he no longer wanted to hear about 'heredity' or 'eugenics'. Instead, he renamed his studies 'human genetics', and in this way hoped to make people forget their affinity with the 'racial hygiene' of National Socialism. 'Let us say nothing about that dreadful matter. It lies behind us', he wrote to a colleague. Euthanasia, human experiments – they were all water under the bridge. He made sure there would be no retrospective prying into the collaboration with his favourite assistant, the *Haupsturmführer* in Auschwitz: he got rid of his entire correspondence with Mengele. He also destroyed all the research material, such as the papers on the 'specific protein' project at the Kaiser Wilhelm Institute, for which Mengele had delivered blood direct from Auschwitz. The Nazi geneticist suppressed his past so thoroughly that he was able to accuse those reminding him of it of 'slander', 'intrigue' and 'smear campaigns'. He shifted all the blame on to the SS doctors.

Verschuer was never even questioned by a state prosecutor, let alone put on trial. Yet the evidence against the professor of genetics is overwhelming. For example, the famous researcher into twins wrote, on 4 October 1944, to Professor Bernhard de Rudder, head of the paediatric clinic at Frankfurt University hospital: 'We have obtained plasma substrates from over 200 subjects of different races, including pairs of twins and several extended families . . . The purpose of our various efforts is no longer merely to establish that hereditary influence plays a significant part in many infectious illnesses, but *how* it does so.' In another letter to de Rudder, dated 6 January 1945, Verschuer said he was pleased 'that now at last my [!] research into specific proteins has reached a critical stage'. Eleven days later the SS doctor, who had despatched the research materials from the death camp to Verschuer in his leafy Berlin suburb, disappeared from the scene of his hideous experiments.

'I cannot be happy about the fact that the man who sent my father to Auschwitz, who ordered him to go there and conduct those experiments, was never punished', says Rolf Mengele, who today lives under another name. 'In my view, those who sat behind desks during the war got off lightly. At the very least, Verschuer bears a moral responsibility.' Verschuer never accepted that responsibility. In fact, the medical profession in Germany never required him to do so – on the contrary: in 1952 he became President of the German Anthropological Society, and in 1954

Dean of the Faculty of Medicine at the University of Münster. After the war he trained an entire generation of geneticists.

While Verschuer was in Münster lecturing from his professorial chair, in Buenos Aires Mengele had opened a small carpentry workshop. There the man who had tortured children in Auschwitz manufactured wooden toys. From the profits he was able in 1954 to buy himself a Borgward 'Isabella' coupé. Even as a schoolboy he had been mad about cars, and in 1938 he boasted that he could do the journey from Günzburg to Frankfurt (about 180 miles) in three hours in his Opel.

Before long Mengele switched from toys to medicines – thus getting closer to his former 'trade'. Thanks to a generous donation from his father Karl in Günzburg, he became a partner in Fadrofarm, a pharmaceutical company producing medication for tuberculosis. Mengele's investment was a quarter of a million pesos. 'The man felt secure here in Argentina', remembers Heinz Trüppel, his partner in Fadrofarm, who found nothing unusual about his business colleague. But he did notice one thing: 'During the day he was always tired.' The Doctor of Death was unable to get a good night's sleep. Was this caused by nightmares of Auschwitz, or did the fear of exposure haunt him at night? He was an early riser and certainly always came to the office 'clean-shaven and with a nice-smelling scent' remembers the Fadrofarm secretary, Elsa Haverich.

Far removed from his bachelor existence, Irene, to whom he was still married, was all set to marry another man. She wanted a divorce and Mengele gave his immediate consent. His father had already sought out a new bride for his absent son. She was a close relative: Martha Mengele, the widow of Josef's brother Karl who had died at the age of thirty-nine. Martha was a 'captivatingly beautiful woman', as Mengele's son Rolf describes his aunt. Karl Mengele Senior was matchmaking because he wanted, through an arranged marriage, to keep the prosperous farm-machinery business entirely in family hands. Martha was not to marry an 'outsider'. That is why old Mengele, from whose financial contributions Josef benefited throughout his life, was pulling the strings as a marriage-broker in the background. The ground was to be prepared for the marriage between brother-in-law and sister-in-law in Switzerland – on a skiing holiday.

After months of preparation Mengele flew to Switzerland in March 1956. He and Martha met in the idyllic mountain resort of Engelberg. With them were Martha's son Karl-Heinz and Mengele's son Rolf. For Rolf, his father had only been Uncle Fritz, who had always written him letters from South America. Rolf liked 'Uncle Fritz'. 'He was a very interesting man; he told us stories about the war, at a time when no grown-ups spoke about the war. I liked him – as an uncle', Rolf remembers. The boy had been told that his father had been killed in Russia. Uncle Fritz told him tales of Russia and the heroic battle against the partisans. He never uttered a word about Auschwitz.

After the holiday in Switzerland Mengele took a tremendous gamble. He drove by car to Günzburg and crossed the German frontier officially, without being accosted. There were no police on his tail. No warrant was issued for his arrest on a charge of murder. He was so relaxed that from Günzburg he even made an excursion to Munich. There he was involved in a minor traffic accident, but his father dealt with this too. Some banknotes changed hands and the police conveniently forgot the matter. The next day Mengele left Europe, and not long afterwards Martha followed him. In the middle of October 1956 her furniture and possessions were packed into a container in the yard of the Mengele factory, and on 30 October Martha and her son Karl-Heinz emigrated to Argentina.

The former concentration camp doctor, now courting a new bride, did not intend to go to the registry office as 'Helmut Gregor'. Officially described as a 'manufacturer' he now also wanted officially to become Mengele again. At the German Embassy in Buenos Aires, on 9 November 1956, he applied for a passport in his real name. There were no charges against anyone of that name and Mengele had no problem in acquiring a German passport. Because his passport photo was the only picture of the war criminal that was 'of recent date', it was reproduced twenty-five years later on Mengele's 'wanted' posters.

Of course, when the camp doctor made his passport application, there was no question of his being brought to justice. The embassy staff did not even show any curiosity. 'I didn't know who Mengele was', claimed the then German ambassador Werner Junkers, as recently as 1985. German embassies in South America had no interest in hunting down Nazi war criminals, but took their lead from the Federal Republic's first minister of justice, Thomas Dehler, who said 'a thick line' had to be drawn under the Nazi period.

But by now the Auschwitz survivor Hermann Langbein was on Mengele's trail. As secretary-general of the International Auschwitz Committee Langbein corresponded with other Holocaust victims and probed into the whereabouts of war criminals. Mengele's divorce gave him the crucial clue that the concentration camp doctor was still alive. In his researches he had chanced upon the divorce documents lodged with the court in Germany, and from these he found out that Mengele was living in Buenos Aires. A call to international telephone enquiries gave him the exact address. Langbein reported Mengele to the authorities and continued with his own investigations. A visit to Günzburg made it clear to him that the Mengeles were guarding many secrets about their 'missing' son and were not about to reveal them to some stranger.

On 5 June 1959 a warrant for Mengele's arrest was issued in Germany for the first time. Bonn called for his extradition by Argentina. There Mengele had already been growing uneasy for some time. It is possible that someone had informed him about Langbein's enquiries in Günzburg. 'He was constantly receiving news from Germany', his business partner Heinz Trüppel is sure. His brief arrest by the Argentinian police in August 1958 had also unsettled him. Mengele was charged with having taken part in illegal abortions in Buenos Aires some years before. But a bribe of 500 dollars was enough to wipe the slate clean.

Nonetheless, Mengele's anxieties grew day by day. Trüppel once visited him at home. 'His nerves were all to pieces. At every little noise he looked round to see what it was.' By this time the Israelis also knew of Mengele's existence in Argentina. They wanted to get him back to Jerusalem along with Eichmann. But in May 1959 Mengele moved to Paraguay. His wife Martha, whom he had married in 1958, and his stepson Karl-Heinz, remained in Buenos Aires, where he visited them frequently. But Martha was not prepared to follow her husband to Paraguay. Life in the Argentinian capital, with its European influence, was something that Martha, accustomed to every comfort, could still accept. But its far less developed neighbour Paraguay seemed just too primitive for her. She chose to return to Europe, realising that with Josef Mengele a normal life was impossible.

> He fled from Buenos Aires after Eichmann was abducted. Someone had told him: 'They're looking for you', whereupon he folded his tent and slipped away to Paraguay.
>
> *Heinz Trüppel, Mengele's business partner in Buenos Aires*

Mengele knew Paraguay from his days as a travelling salesman for his father's farm-machinery business. And he also knew some 'old comrades' there. Soon after his arrival he applied for Paraguayan citizenship. In fact, he had no chance of getting it because the condition was five years' uninterrupted residence in the country. Mengele had scarcely been there five months. But two influential friends offered a helping hand. They were Alejandro von Eckstein, a captain in the army of the pro-Nazi dictator, Alfredo Stroessner, himself of German origin, and Werner Jung, who during the war had been leader of the Nazi Party in Paraguay.

Mengele was granted Paraguayan citizenship on 27 November 1959. His deed of citizenship was made out in the name of 'José Mengele'. Germany's request to Argentina for his extradition was now left high and dry. It was rejected in any case. The reasons given were that the application contained technical flaws, and that the crimes of which Mengele was accused were of a 'political character'.

Right from the start, the government of Israel worked on the assumption that South American dictators were unlikely to accede to any requests for extradition. The manhunt was entrusted to the bloodhounds of Mossad. On 11 May 1960 Mossad agents kidnapped Eichmann in Buenos Aires and spirited him back to Jerusalem. Hitler's executioners in South American exile were shocked. They feared that they would be next in line for the Israelis' attention. Mengele was in Paraguay, close to the Argentinian border, when he received news of Eichmann's abduction. In a place called Nueva Bavaria he had gone into hiding at the home of a pro-Nazi farmer, Alban Krug. 'I get the feeling that things are coming to a head and may call for drastic solutions', he noted with alarm. Eichmann's abduction finally drew the attention of the press to

Mengele as well. Detailed accounts of his crimes were published for the first time.

This media furore was an unpleasant experience for young Rolf Mengele, now a schoolboy: because of his surname he was frequently teased by his classmates. And Alfons Hackenjos, his stepfather, now felt that the time had come for him to reveal who Uncle Fritz really was.

> The political lie is triumphant and history is twisted and distorted.
>
> *Mengele, 1960*

Mengele, too, could read about his crimes in the newspapers. Friends brought articles from newspapers and magazines to him in his hideout on the farm. 'It's incredible what filthy smears those German picture-magazines are allowed to put out', he wrote indignantly in his diary. 'But behind it all there's just one thing: and that's the Old Testament hatred against anyone proud to be German, heroic and on a higher human plane.' Mengele's anti-Semitic attitude, his obsessive notion that the Jews must be destroyed, so that the Germans could rule the world – all that was still there. Fifteen years had gone by since Auschwitz.

Isser Harel, the head of Mossad, who was basking in the success of hunting down Eichmann, now wanted to bring in Mengele as well. Harel put the man who caught Eichmann, Zvi Aharoni, on to the Mengele case. 'When the Eichmann business came good and turned into a huge propaganda success for Harel, he thought to himself, we ought to do more of this', Aharoni remembers. 'For a whole year I did nothing but search for Mengele in South America.' But he was nowhere to be found.

> We searched in Montevideo, in Chile, in Paraguay. Finally, just when we had been put on his track by an SS man in Brazil, we were suddenly called off the case.
>
> *Zvi Aharoni, Mossad agent*

Five months after Eichmann's abduction Mengele left the country ruled by Alfredo Stroessner, the dictator who looked more like an operetta general. For although his Paraguayan friends were prepared to vouch for him when he applied for citizenship of their country, they certainly could not protect him from Mossad. Mengele was forced to stay in his rather insecure hideout on Krug's farm near the frontier. But even this became too risky. His 'old comrade', Rudel, helped him find a new home – this time in Brazil. 'For you the war's not over yet – be careful', were farmer Krug's parting words to him.

> We searched everywhere for Mengele, in Paraguay, in Brazil, in Argentina . . . He was very mobile, constantly crossing the frontier from one country to the other. We were always just behind him and every time we arrived in a place where he had been, he'd already given us the slip.
>
> *Isser Harel, former head of Mossad, who abducted Eichmann*

In 1964 Mengele had already been living in Brazil for four years, yet the Germans were still looking for him in Paraguay. The German ambassador Eckart Briest called upon the Stroessner regime finally to withdraw Paraguayan citizenship from Mengele. Soon afterwards, a message was daubed on the walls of the embassy building: 'Jewish embassy. Hands off Mengele. That's an order.' In late 1965 a new ambassador, Hubert Krier, arrived in Paraguay. Shortly before leaving Germany he had received instructions from the Foreign Ministry in Bonn to take no action on the Mengele affair. The reason given by the Permanent Secretary, Duckwitz, was that it had become clear that Germany's demand that Paraguay should extradite one of its own citizens to Germany was 'grotesque and absurd'. Not until 1979 did the Supreme Court in Asunción revoke Mengele's citizenship on the grounds that he had been living outside the country for more than two years.

While diplomats were closing their files on Mengele, and the State Prosecution Service was only half-heartedly pursuing him, the media began their hunt. He was extensively marketed as the 'Auschwitz Angel of Death'. Even Hollywood picked up on the murdering doctor. *The Boys from Brazil*, with Gregory Peck playing Mengele, was a box-office hit. Newspapers and magazines were full of sensational but inaccurate stories about the concentration-camp doctor. For example, in 1962 the South American papers reported that Mengele had been kidnapped by Israeli agents and was on a banana-boat bound for Haifa. When the ship berthed there the world's press was waiting on the quay. But neither Mengele nor the men from Mossad were on board. In fact Mengele was leading a tranquil rural life in Brazil. No secret service, no state prosecutor, no reporter could find a trace of him.

Rudel had placed Mengele under the protection of a fanatical Austrian Nazi, Wolfgang Gerhard. This man had left Europe in 1948 because he 'could no longer tolerate the oppressive occupation by the Allies'. Having served as a Hitler Youth leader in Graz, he remained a Nazi for the rest of his life. Being too young to have made a name for himself in the war, he jumped at the chance of playing the part of protector to one of the Third Reich's most notorious war criminals. Gerhard's scheme for providing secure accommodation for his charge was simple. He needed some people who, as he put it, preferred to have little to do with the 'dirty, tropical Brazilian environment, peopled by racially inferior semi-apes'; people who felt happier keeping their 'close-knit circle of friends' as small as possible, and who furthermore were short of money. Gerhard knew just such people: a married couple named Geza and Gitta Stammer, who had fled from Hungary to Brazil in 1948, when the Communists took over their country. The husband was a qualified engineer and worked as a surveyor. Because his wife did not feel comfortable in the huge and unfamiliar city of São Paulo, they intended to move 150 miles north to a farm near Nova Europa. During a social evening for the local Austro-Hungarian community Wolfgang Gerhard asked the Stammers if they would like to take on a Swiss farm manager with experience in stock-breeding. A manager did not seem absolutely necessary for their meagre 37 acres in Nova Europa. But Gerhard told them that the *soi-disant* Swiss, named 'Peter Hochbichler', would share in the purchase of the property. For the Stammers this was an attractive offer, especially as an extra pair of hands would fill the gap left by Geza Stammer, whose work as a surveyor kept him away all day.

So it was that Mengele, alias Peter Hochbichler, once again found refuge on a farm. Two years later he moved with the Stammers to a larger property, the 120-acre Santa Luzia estate in Serra Negra, 120 miles north-west of São Paulo. There they grew coffee and raised cattle. Geza Stammer went on working as a surveyor.

> He always had a great longing for Germany, and for his family and his son.
>
> He had read a lot and was very fond of classical music.
>
> *Gitta Stammer*

The forests and gently sloping hills were ideal surroundings for 'Peter Hochbichler'. He felt at ease in 'this utterly remote place. But it also has everything to provide hearth and home for a restless soul', he noted in his diary. But it was not only the beauty of the landscape that delighted him. Mengele had started an affair with Gitta Stammer. In his diary he wrote about the 'gorgeous' Gitta and dedicated love-poems to her. But Gitta's husband noticed none of this. He only came home at weekends. This relationship was no doubt one reason why Gitta did not send 'Peter Hochbichler' away when she saw his picture in a newspaper and discovered who he really was. For a while, not even the communist-hating Geza saw any reason why 'Don Pedro' should not go on staying with them. But he was soon to regret this. Mengele turned out to be an increasingly intolerable house-guest. In their remote farm, the Stammers were the only audience for his interminable lectures on racial and evolutionary theories, about the world economy or philosophy. Whenever the desire to pontificate came over him someone had to listen – even to his sermons on the morality of work, discipline or domestic frugality.

A further burden were his odd habits, prompted by anxiety. For when, on 1 June 1962, Mengele heard that Eichmann had been hanged, the terror of exposure, which he thought he had overcome long ago, assailed him once again. He would never be free from it. He became obsessed with security. Whenever he went for a walk he would take as many as fifteen dogs with him.

'Vicious animals', recalls Fernando Benati, who worked on the farm. 'At first they attacked me. Then they made friends with me.' On Mengele's orders Benati had to build a 20-foot-high wooden watch-tower. 'From there he would often observe the surrounding area through a telescope.'

For the fear-haunted Mengele Serra Negra became a green prison. 'I never once saw him laugh', Benati recalls. Intimations of death came to Mengele in his dreams: 'Sometimes I dream of a double-bladed guillotine', he wrote in his diary. Although only in his early fifties, the once promising young doctor turned increasingly into a moody hypochondriac, who kept a daily record of his state of health and continually suspected that he might have contracted some dreadful disease. The concentration camp doctor who infected children with deadly pathogens, now complained of migraines, ear-ache and sleep disturbance.

Geza Stammer had long since had enough of the tiresome whinger. And even Gitta, who was becoming more of a 'doormat' than the mistress of the domineering 'Don Pedro', no longer appreciated his company. But Mengele had never lived alone for any length of time in South America. He felt he needed the protective companionship of the Stammers. And he was willing to pay for it, which was why the Stammers needed him. Money continued to arrive from Günzburg. And so, when the Stammers moved into a new house near the town of Caeiras, in São Paulo state, Mengele went with them. The unwelcome guest had contributed half the purchase-price.

Yet the change of location brought no easing of tension. 'Mengele became more and more impossible', says Gitta Stammer. Wolfgang Gerhard, with whom Mengele had stayed in regular contact, first tried flattery to persuade the Stammers to keep their uninvited guest with them. They should feel honoured, he told them, to have 'such an important person' with them. Then he threatened them. Something might happen to their children if they did not continue to keep silent. But the Stammers never seriously considered taking the bull by the horns and handing Mengele over to the police. They were afraid that they themselves might be put on trial for harbouring the now internationally wanted war criminal.

In the end Gerhard realised he had to find some other 'carers' for Mengele. His choice fell on a fellow-Austrian, Wolfram Bossert, who had come to Brazil in 1952. Bossert had served as an NCO in the German Wehrmacht and spoke passionately of the 'injustice' that Germany had suffered. The German people should not bend their knee before the victors, he ranted. On the principle of equal justice for all, German war criminals should only be punished 'if the Russians, Yanks and French haul their own sinners up in front the judges'. That was the sort of thing Gerhard liked to hear. But there were other reasons why he thought Bossert would be ideal company for Mengele. Among his friends Bossert, a skilled metalworker, was known as 'brains' on account of his intellectual leanings. He was interested in literature, philosophy and politics, and the opportunity of having one-to-one discussions with a real 'academic' seemed to him very enticing. Gerhard's instinct was unerring: Bossert was an ideal pupil and recipient of Mengele's monologues. He and his wife Liselotte visited Mengele regularly and took him with them on their holidays.

When the Stammers moved to São Paulo in 1974, the moment had finally come for them and Mengele to part company. With the proceeds of selling their house near Caeiras, for which Mengele had paid half, they bought the ageing Auschwitz doctor a modest cottage with a gloomy bedroom, a shabby bathroom and a tiny kitchen. It was in a poor district of São Paulo, at 5555 rua Alvarenga. The Bosserts lived just a few miles away, and Mengele could count on their regular visits and support. But he was now living alone. Even his loyal protector Wolfgang Gerhard was no longer at his side. Gerhard had returned to Austria because both his wife and son were suffering from cancer. He left his Brazilian identity card no. 525951 with his protégé – a valuable farewell gift for a man wanted for war crimes. An exchange of photos was all that was needed and Josef Mengele became Wolfgang Gerhard.

Alone in his cottage the once fit and agile doctor went into a rapid physical decline. He did all he could to make his drab accommodation, with its cracked wooden floor and leaking roof, a bit more homely. He painted his bedroom dark green and laid a stone path in front of the house. Yet he was plagued by anxieties and bouts of depression. To make matters worse, his family in Günzburg now kept him on a tight financial rein. His father had died years ago. His brother Alois did not like him having a say, from such a distance, in company policy and family matters. The brother in Brazil had become a nuisance. Mengele noted bitterly that on his birthday he no longer received any good wishes from Günzburg. Even his son Rolf, now grown up, only wrote with extreme reluctance to his father. And when Rolf informed his father that he could not support him financially, Mengele replied drily: 'I can relieve you of any worry on my account, by keeping our relationship on the same basis as before. At all events there will still be no financial burden on you arising from it. And I'm sure you can manage one or two letters a year.' In 1977 Rolf came to Brazil on a two-week visit, but the meeting only confirmed the deep estrangement between father and son. Yet Rolf still felt under an obligation not to betray his father. 'I couldn't turn him in', he says. The two maintained their infrequent correspondence. But in his letters Mengele never mentioned the name 'Auschwitz'.

> Don't tell me that you, my only son, really believe the things that are written about me! On my mother's life – I swear I have never done any harm to anyone.
>
> *Josef Mengele to his son Rolf, 1977*
>
> I felt it was my fate to be the son of Josef Mengele, just as it is the fate of others to have an illness or physical handicap.
>
> *Rolf Mengele*

In his diary Mengele bemoaned his 'feeling of being abandoned, that hurts me deep in my heart'. Not even the work of brightening up his house offered much solace in his solitary existence. 'The cage is getting more comfortable all the time', he wrote to Wolfgang Gerhard in Austria, 'but it still remains just that – a cage'.

A little joy was brought into his life by his housemaid, Elza Gulpian de Oliveira, a small woman with sharp features and dyed blond hair, who was forty years younger then Mengele. He began an affair with her, took her to the cinema and to restaurants. She wrote him childish love-letters. 'I left little notes for him on his pillow. I wrote "good night" or "my beloved" on them', she remembers. Elza even thought of marrying him. But he knew that would not work. He just wanted to have her around. In the end, when she met a mulatto whom she wanted to marry, the aged Mengele hurried to Elza's mother and poured his heart out to her. 'He's a black man; he'll never make her happy. She deserves better than that', Elza remembers him saying. 'I can offer her a better life. I know I haven't much longer to live and I will leave my house to her.' Then, Elza tells us, he wept tears of despair. Even today, she can scarcely comprehend the fact that her elderly lover was a war criminal. 'I knew him as a completely different person. I can't see him any other way. I can't do it, even if I try.'

> He was a real friend. When I was unhappy he would say: 'Why are you sad? What's the trouble? You're so quiet!' When I was happy: 'My, my! You're so cheerful today, what's happened?' He was someone who took an interest in me, who cared about how my life was going.
>
> *Elza Oliveira, Mengele's housemaid and mistress in Brazil*

Mengele's last friends were the Bosserts. And it was with them that he spent his final days. They were holidaying together at Berioga Beach, 25 miles south of São Paulo. On 7 February 1979, while swimming, Mengele suffered a stroke. Bossert pulled him out of the water, but attempts to resuscitate him were in vain. The 'Angel of Death' was dead – thirty-four years after Auschwitz.

The Bosserts had Mengele's body buried under the name that was written on his identity card: Wolfgang Gerhard. The interment took place at the Embu cemetery, 12 miles west of São Paulo. Only the Bosserts accompanied the coffin. 'They didn't want it to be opened again', recalls the grave-digger, Zé Luzia. No-one wept as the coffin was lowered into the earth. After the ceremony Wolfram Bossert wrote to Sedlmeier in Günzburg: 'I believe we are of one mind in wanting to maintain the secrecy that has been preserved up to now. Not only to avoid any personal unpleasantness, but also to make the opposition continue wasting money and effort on what is already a thing of the past.'

In the years that followed the international hunt for the war criminal did indeed continue. The highest ever reward in criminal history up to that time was offered for his capture: a total of 10 million deutschmarks. By now around forty close friends and relatives knew what had become of Mengele – they were a group sworn to secrecy. No-one reported his death. Until the company secretary of the family firm gave the game away. For a long time both the German media and the state prosecution service had suspected that Hans Sedlmeier had information about Mengele. But he always pretended to know nothing. When a television reporter buttonholed Sedlmeier on the doorstep of his house in Günzburg, he tried to brush the man off: 'Three or four of you Johnnies come round here every day wanting to talk to me. I'm not talking to anyone.' But eventually he did talk.

It was on holiday in the autumn of 1984 that Sedlmeier and his wife got to know a professor from Giessen University. With his tongue loosened by drink Sedlmeier told the professor how he had transferred money to Mengele for all those years. The professor passed this information on to the police. But it was not until 31 May 1985 that the Sedlmeiers' house was searched. There the police found letters from Mengele and an address-book containing street names and telephone numbers in São Paulo. The Brazilian police swiftly descended on the Stammers and the Bosserts. Wolfram Bossert admitted that Mengele was buried in the Embu cemetery. On 6 June 1985 the body in grave number 321 was exhumed. The event was witnessed by 300 journalists. Now Mengele's son Rolf also went public: 'I have no doubt that the exhumed body is the mortal remains of my father, and I am certain that this will shortly be confirmed by forensic examination. I have remained silent up to now so as not to endanger the people my father was in contact with over the past thirty years.'

He thought he could demonstrate that Jews were different or abnormal. Be he couldn't provide any convincing proof. Most of his arguments were of a sociological, historical or political nature.

Rolf Mengele, after the meeting with his father in 1977

The mortal remains of the concentration-camp doctor consisted of a pile of bones, the skull, six teeth, a clump of hair, a rotted pair of trousers and a worm-eaten shirt. All this was exhaustively examined by eighteen leading forensic scientists from Brazil, Germany, Israel and the USA. On 21 June 1985, at the headquarters of the Brazilian federal police in São Paulo they announced their findings: the body from the Embu cemetery was 'with a probability bordering on certainty' that of Josef Mengele.

As far as world opinion was concerned, that was the end of the matter. But the senior investigating prosecutor at the district court in Frankfurt, Hans-Eberhard Klein, wanted to remove any lingering doubt. The prosecutor commissioned a genetic analysis by the British geneticist, Professor Alec Jeffreys of Leicester University. DNA molecules from a thigh-bone of the Embu corpse were compared with DNA molecules from the blood of Mengele's son Rolf and Rolf's mother, Irene. The comparison proved 'with a certainty greater than 99.99 per cent' that the body was Mengele's. His remains now lie stored in São Paulo's forensic institute: all that is left of an ambitious medical scientist who became a mass murderer, packed in two cardboard boxes.

> Mengele personally never beat us, he just carried out his experiments on us. But when I think that with a wave of his hand he snuffed out the lives of our whole family, our parents, our sister, all our relatives . . . There is so much blood clinging to his hands!
>
> *An Auschwitz twin*

INDEX

Page numbers in bold indicate main entries.